RIMBAUD: THE WORKS

To Patti Smith

with admiration

...ô saisons ô châteaux...

[signature]

4135-CARL

RIMBAUD: THE WORKS

A Season In Hell; Poems
& Prose; Illuminations

Translated from the French
with notes and commentary
by Dennis J. Carlile

Illustrations by Alexia Montibon

To order additional copies of this book, contact:
Xlibris Corporation
1-888-7-XLIBRIS
www.Xlibris.com
Orders@Xlibris.com

CONTENTS

This book is for
Arthur,
Alexia, Mafrivo,
Zig, and Brad
*

"The Drunken Boat"
is for Leo.
* *

"riverrun, past Eve and Adam's, from
swerve of shore to bend of bay . . . "
—Joyce: *Finnegans Wake*
* * *

"He embraced the darkness and the light."
—Miller: *The Time of the Assassins*

TRANSLATOR'S PREFACE

"I heard them say that dreams should stay in your head.
"Well I feel ashamed of the things that I've said.
"Put on these chains and you can live a free life.
"Well I'd rather bleed just to know why I died."

I.T.Z. Hanson: *This Time Around*

* * *

Although he walked away from the muse of poetry in his twentieth year, a few days short of his twenty-first birthday, Rimbaud possessed one of the most prodigious talents ever known. In five all-consuming years—rife with emotional instability, violence, drugs, and alcohol— he produced a vital body of work that resonates more than ever, more than a century later.

The order of works in this edition is not strictly chronological. Part One comprises *A Season in Hell,* a late work from the spring and summer of 1873. Many of the early poems are dated and they are presented, along with vers nouveaux in Part Two, more or less in se- quence. Some scholars believe that several of the *Illuminations* (Part Three) were composed in the year following *A Season in Hell.* All we really know is that in 1875 Rimbaud, finished with it, handed over the manuscript to Verlaine, who published it in 1886.

In translating the rhymed French poems into English verse, I have done my best to follow Rimbaud's originals line for line, and many times rhyme was simply impossible—so I have relied on assonance, alliteration, interior rhyme, and half-rhyme to carry the musical bur- den, especially in the longer works.

The testament of Arthur Rimbaud is contained in *A Season in Hell,* where his aims, concerns, and regrets are set forth in both prose and verse; the introduction by Delmore Schwartz presents an over- view of the poet's intentions. The verse poems, fragments, and pieces in prose illustrate the breadth of his vision. *Illuminations* (c. 1872–74) is the revelation, the vision's compendium; here he stretches the limits of poetic expression, forever changing the nature and uses of language. These translations attempt to convey something of his music and meaning.

DJC

PART ONE

A Season In Hell

Une Saison en Enfer

(1873)

INTRODUCTION

BY DELMORE SCHWARTZ

The numerous and various interpretations of Rimbaud are always very interesting and they have succeeded in making him a celebrated character in the history of poetry. It seems likely that his life as a poet would have sufficed for that purpose; but when to his life are added the many schools of doctrine, literary, political, and even religious, which have made much of Rimbaud, what we have, whether we want it or not, is a complex moment of Western culture, rather than merely an interesting life or interesting kind of poetry.

Rimbaud's life as a poet will always seem spectacular, and the surface of his writing tends to increase this kind of romantic attention. Its texture is violent and hallucinatory, or limpid, song-like, and full of mysterious comments and messages. It becomes natural then to use his text as a starting-point, and not as the readers' final interest and satisfaction.

It is worthwhile trying to reverse this process of the mind and attempting to see Rimbaud as the poet of a particular style and insight. It is true that "A Season in Hell" is not self-sufficient and self-explanatory to the qualified degree that most successful writing is, and we must look to external aids repeatedly in trying to understand what all the exciting and excited shouting is about. But in doing so, we can ask whether or not the aid we are using is bringing us closer to the text or taking us away from it, and by using this criterion we can be fairly sure that we are not finding in Rimbaud merely what we brought with us, or merely what we were looking for; but something else, which can only be known and enjoyed through our grasp of the formal working of the poet.

The literary form of "A Season in Hell" is that of the confession or the testament. So free a form is generally one to which an author turns when oppressed or even overwhelmed by his subject, as Rimbaud was. The form does not greatly modify or illuminate the subject, as, to cite an extreme, the sonnet form does. But it permits and invites the subject to have its way at all costs.

Rimbaud's subject is himself as a poet. His season in hell is the period of his existence when he was attempting to practice a new poetic method. However, to speak of himself as a poet, Rimbaud must speak of much else that has always been involved in the writing of poetry, but has not always required the direct attention of the author. He must discuss Christianity, the East, Science, France, morality and heredity, everything that has been engaged in his life. This is the result of the ambition of his new poetic method, which is to bring about a new art, a new system of vision, and a new way of life.

"A Season in Hell" was written when the effort to practice his method and to reveal all the mysteries of life and nature had been made and had ended in failure. Each of the nine chapters begins by rehearsing another aspect of his effort and his failure, but again and again the discussion is involved in extreme transitions to other aspects. The discussion shifts suddenly from childhood memories, to his longing to go to a tropical country, to his ambiguous feelings about Christianity, to his hatred of his *milieu* and his heredity, and his contempt for traditional ideals of poetry. The tone and the movement is continuously an exclamatory declamation in which leading symbols, ideas, and images revolve.

However, in the middle of the poem, in the two successive chapters, Deliriums I and II, the method of exclamatory declamation is replaced by different ways of viewing the subject. In the first of these, the poet and protagonist is seen from the outside, and yet with the utmost intimacy, by the person with whom he is living during his season in hell. If the personal connection is insisted upon, the foolish virgin whose monologue comprises the chapter is undoubtedly Verlaine. So far as the text goes, all one must recognize is the relationship of love; the protagonist is being seen from the outside by the one who is in love with him. It is worth noting the insight and sympathy Rimbaud was capable of, in thus presenting himself objectively, from the point of view of another person.

Deliriums II presents specific examples of the kind of verse

Rimbaud wrote, his alchemy of the word, when he was trying to unveil all the mysteries of life and nature. Here one ought to note that among his comments on this verse, he insists that the effort was folly and madness, just as his entire career was nothing less than an existence in hell. Later poets have studied the examples of verse, imitated the method, and ignored the fact that Rimbaud, having gone through it, judged it to be madness and believed that only when he had given it up did he know how to deal with beauty and art.

Why was Rimbaud seized by this immense ambition? The nature of the ambition is made quite clear: "I am going to unveil all the mysteries: mysteries of religion or of nature, death, birth, future, past, non-existence, cosmogony". The particular quality of the ambition undoubtedly had its source in Rimbaud as a unique individual, a prodigious and prodigal adolescent, the child of an unhappy marriage and a stern mother, greatly excited by the poetry of his time and perhaps also much moved by the provincial France of his boyhood, the Second Empire, the Franco-Prussian War, and the Paris Commune, for it was during the three years between 1870 and 1873 that most of his writing was done.

But a complete explanation is to be found only in a greater context. With the French Revolution and the Romantic Movement, the history of literature began to exhibit tendencies which reversed its customary aims, or at any rate the aims of the preceding centuries. In any period, an author may be critical of certain aspects of the community which supports him; but in general he accepts and depends upon its fundamental assumptions and values.

With the Romantic Movement, however, exactly the contrary began to be true. The aim of the author and the nature of his interests make him attempt to attack, deny, supplant, or run away from the dominant assumptions and values of the community. Blake's theology, Wordsworth's Nature, Coleridge's metaphysics, Shelley's Platonism, and Byron's Byronism are examples which by their very variety illustrate how continuous and how strong the tendency was. It continues and grows stronger until our own time; but the two instances most relevant to Rimbaud are Baudelaire and Flaubert.

For Rimbaud, Baudelaire was "the first visionary, the king of poets, a true God", and his predecessor in the effort to unveil all the mysteries. Not only did he give Rimbaud the basis of his style, but the explicit aspirations and obsessions of his verse, the concern with degradation and vice, the hatred of bourgeois culture, the interest in Christianity, rehearse the chief motives of Rimbaud's career:

> *Plonger au fond du goffre, Enfer ou Ciel, qu'importe?*
> *Au fond de l'Inconnu pour trouver du nouveau.*

Flaubert's writing had no direct influence upon Rimbaud, and this fact should give him independent value as a witness that the desire for the unknown and the new, for a new vision of life, was inspired by the whole character of society. In a letter he wrote when Rimbaud was a child, he stated with exactitude the relationship between the author and the society of his time:

> "I am turning to a kind of aesthetic mysticism. When there is no encouragement to be derived from one's fellows, when the exterior world is disgusting, enervating, corruptive, and brutalizing, honest and sensitive people are forced to seek somewhere within themselves a more suitable place to live. If society continues on its present path I believe we shall see the return of such mystics as have existed in all the dark ages of the world. The soul, unable to overflow, will be concentrated on itself. We shall see a return of world-sicknesses—beliefs in the Last Day, expectation of a Messiah, etc. But all this enthusiasm will be ignorant of its own nature, and, the age being what it is, what *will* be its basis? Some will seek it in the flesh, others in ancient religions, others in art; humanity, like the Jewish tribes in the desert, will adore all kind of idols. We were born a little too early: in twenty-five years the points of intersection of these quests will provide subjects for masters. Then prose (prose especially, the youngest form) will be able to play a magnificent humanitarian symphony. Books like the *Satyricon* and the *Golden Ass* will be written once more,

containing on the psychical plane all the lush excesses which those books have on the sensual". [Quoted by Francis Steegmuller, "Flaubert and Madame Bovary," pp. 327–328.]

Seen in this light, "A Season in Hell" is a record of the track which any poet must run when, for whatever reason, his attempt is to reject everything he has inherited (to be a poet, one might say, is to be an heir), and by himself and by his poetry attain to a new vision of life. When we say that this prose poem is a record, we must remember that it is rendered chiefly in terms of the emotions, and when we say *by himself and by his poetry,* we must recall the general character of the romantic poet. "A Season in Hell" presents the last extreme of Romanticism; but it is only last in the sense that no one can try to go further. It is by no means the last time that this kind of effort has been made or will be made. The symbolists, the dadaists, and the surrealists have repeated certain moments and multiplied the details of Rimbaud's effort, and in our own time, such authors as D.H. Lawrence and William Butler Yeats exemplify similar efforts, and in part the same condition of the spirit.

Probably such an effort is a permanent tendency of the poetic mind, one which is bound to recur whenever the community cannot satisfy or sustain the poet. Rimbaud's work represents the fate of that effort not with mere statement, but with the immediacy of first-hand experience.

(1939)

Delmore Schwartz (1913–1966) was called by John Berryman "the most underrated poet of the twentieth century." Among his major works are *In Dreams Begin Responsibilities* (1938) and *Summer Knowledge* (1959); *Last and Lost Poems*, edited by Robert Phillips, appeared in 1979.

"Who amongst us, in his ambitious moments, has not dreamt of a poetic prose which was simultaneously musical, but without rhyme or rhythm, supple enough and abrupt enough to lend itself to the motions of the soul, the meanderings of reverie, and to the jolts of consciousness?"

—Charles Baudelaire
1861 preface
Le Spleen de Paris

"And I went unto the angel, and said unto him, Give me the little book. And he said unto me, Take it, and eat it up; and it shall make thy belly bitter, but it shall be in thy mouth sweet as honey."

Revelation 10:9

"This is the voice of the prophet and the taskmaster, of the disciple and the initiate in one."

Henry Miller: *The Time of the Assassins*

A SEASON IN HELL

Une Saison en Enfer

Long past, if I remember well, my life was a party where all hearts were open, where all wines flowed.

One evening, I seated Beauty on my knees.—And I found her bitter.—And I reviled her.

I took arms against righteousness.

I took flight. O witches, misery, hatred, my treasure was entrusted to you!

I managed to clear my spirit of all human hope. To strangle every joy, I pounced on it like a savage beast, stealthily.

I called on firing squads in order to bite the butts of their guns while dying. I called for plagues in order to gag myself on blood, on sand. Disaster was my god. I wallowed in the gutter. I dried myself in the criminal breeze. And I played some fine tricks madly, passionately.

And springtime brought me the idiot's horrific laughter.

Now, suddenly finding myself at the point of producing my ultimate *croak!* I had a dream of searching for the key to the ancient feast, where I might recover my appetite.

Compassion is that key.—This insight is proof that I was dreaming!

"You're stuck being a hyena, etc." . . . protests the demon who'd crowned me in such lovely poppies. "Seize death with all your appetites, and your egotism and every deadly sin."

Ahh! I've had it up to here:—But, my dear Satan, I conjure you, an eye less angry! and while awaiting a few belated little acts of cowardice, you who love a lack of descriptive or instructive talent in a writer, for you I rip loose these few hideous pages out of my diary of the damned.

35-CARL

Bad Blood

I have the pale blue eyes of my Celtic ancestors, the narrow skull, and their clumsiness in a tussle. I find my wardrobe as barbaric as theirs. Only I don't butter my hair.

The Gauls were the most inept trappers and turf-burners of their day.

From them I get: Idolatry and love of sacrilege; oh! all the vices, anger, lust—magnificent lust—; above all, vanity and sloth.

I'm horrified by all trades. Masters and workers, peasants all of them, ignoble. The hand behind the pen's as good as the hand behind the plow.— What a century for hands!—I'll never have myself in hand. Next thing, you're deep into domestic servitude. The beggar's honesty breaks my heart. Criminals, like the castrated, nauseate. Myself, I'm intact, and it's all the same to me.

O Yet! who made my tongue so treacherous that it's guided and safeguarded my idleness up till now? Without using my body to make a living, and lazier than a toad, I've lived everywhere. There's not a family in Europe I don't know.—I mean families like my own, that owe everything to the Declaration of the Rights of Man.—I've known every son of good family.

*   *   *

If only I had forebears at some point in French history!

But no, nothing.

It's pretty clear to me that I've always been from a subordinate race. I have no concept of revolt. My people never roused themselves except for nipping booty: like wolves at the animal they haven't killed.

I recollect the History of France, first daughter of the Church. Servile, I must have made the voyage to the Holy Land; my head's full of roadways through Swabian plains, of Byzantine sights, of the ramparts of Jerusalem: veneration of Mary, tenderness for the Crucified One stirring within me amid a thousand profane enchantments. I sit, a leper, among thorns and broken pottery at the foot of a wall devoured

by the sun. A mercenary, later on, I must have camped under nightskies
of Germany.

Ah! there's more: I dance the Sabbat in a ruddy clearing, with old
women and children.

I can't remember any further back than this place on earth and
Christendom. I never tire of seeing myself in that past. But always
alone; without family. Even so, what language did I speak? I never see
myself among the counselors of Christ; nor in the councils of the
Lordly—representatives of Christ.

What was I in the last century? I don't find myself again until today.
No more vagabonds, no more vague wars. The subordinate race has
spread everywhere—we the people, it's called, rationality; nationality
and science.

Oh! Science! Everything's been made over. For your body and
soul—the last rites—here's medicine and philosophy—old wives' rem-
edies and popular songs rearranged. And the diversions of princes and
the games that they prohibited! Geography, cosmography, mechanics,
chemistry! . . .

Science! the latest aristocracy! Progress. The world marches on!
Why shouldn't it make a turn?

This is the vision of harmony. We're headed for the *Spirit.* That's
for sure, it's an oracle, I'm telling you. I understand it, and unable to
explain myself without heathen speech, I'd rather keep silent.

∗   ∗   ∗

The pagan blood rises again! The Spirit is close by; why doesn't Christ
come to my aid with nobility and freedom for my soul? Alas, the Gospel's
gone! The Gospel! The Gospel.

I wait on God with a greedy appetite. I am of low degree for all
eternity.

Here I am on the shores of Brittany. How the cities illuminate the
evening! My workday's done; I'm leaving Europe. The seafaring air will
burn my lungs; desert climes will tan me. Swimming, pounding the

grass, hunting, above all smoking; drinking liquor as heavy as boiling metal—just like those precious ancestors of mine around their fires.

I'll come back with iron limbs, dark-skinned, a savage eye. By my appearance, they'll judge me one of a powerful race. I'll have gold: I will be idle and brutish. The ladies nurse these fierce invalids, home from torrid zones. I'll mingle in political affairs. Saved.

Right now I'm out of it, I'm horrified by patriotism. Best thing's a deep drunken sleep on the beach.

*   *   *

There's no leaving.—Let's retrace the roads here, laden with my vice, the vice that—from the age of reason—put its roots for suffering down right by my side,—that climbs to the sky, beats me up, knocks me down, drags me around.

The ultimate innocence and the final timidity. It's all been said. I musn't carry my disgust and treachery into the world.

Let's go! The journey, the burden, the desert, the boredom and anger.

To whom do I hire myself? What beast should I adore? What holy image gets attacked? Whose heart shall I break? What illusion pursue?— In whose blood walking?

Sooner keep clear of righteousness.—The hard life, mere stupefication—lifting the coffin lid with a withering fist, to sit, to suffocate. And out of that, no more old age nor any dangers: terror isn't French.

Ah! I'm so deeply forsaken, I offer my zeal for perfection to any divine image.

Oh my renunciation, oh marvelous compassion mine! here below, for all that!

De profundis, Domine, what a jerk I am!

*   *   *

Still only a child, I admired the unruly convict on whom the prison
gates slam shut forever. I visited the inns and furnished rooms that he
was supposed to have made sacred by his stay. I saw *with his imagina-
tion* the blue sky and the countryside's blossoming labors; I sniffed out
his fatality in the cities. He had more strength than a saint, more
common sense than a traveler—and he, he alone! the witness to his
fame and reasoning.

On the road by winter nights, roofless, naked, breadless, a voice
would hobble my frost-bitten heart: "Strength or weakness: Go for
strength. You don't know where you're going or why. Enter anywhere,
answer to everything. They can no more kill you than a cadaver." In
the morning I had so forlorn a look, so dead a face, that for those I
met, *Maybe they didn't see me.*

In the cities the mud seemed to flash red and black, like a mirror
when a lamp passes from hand to hand in a neighboring room, like a
treasure in the woods. Good luck, I'd shout, and I'd watch a sea of
flames and smoke fill the sky; and left and right, all kinds of wealth
flaming like a billion thunderbolts.

Yet orgies and the intimacy of women were denied me. Not even
a chum. I saw myself before an enraged mob, facing the firing squad,
weeping out of misery that they couldn't understand, and forgiving
them!—Like Joan of Arc!—"Priests, professors, masters, you're mak-
ing a mistake to deliver me to justice. I've never belonged to these
people; I've never been a Christian; I'm one of a race that sings under
torture; I don't understand the law; I have no moral sense, I'm a brute:
You're making a mistake . . . "

Yes, I have my eyes shut tight against your light. I'm a beast, a
nigger. But I can be saved. You are phony niggers, you, maniacs, fero-
cious, greedy. Merchant, you're a nigger; Judge, you're a nigger; Gen-
eral, you're a nigger; Emperor, you itchy oldtimer, you're a nigger:
You've drunk the moonshine brewed in Satan's distillery.—These are a
people inspired by fever and cancer. Cripples and the elderly are so
very respectable, they just ask to be boiled.—The smartest thing's to

leave this continent, where madness prowls to provide hostages for these goons. I enter into the true kingdom of the children of Ham.

Do I know nature any more? Do I know myself?—*No more words.* I swallow the dead in my belly. Shouts, drums, dance, dance, dance! I can't even see the hour when, with white men landing, I tumble into nothingness.

Hunger, thirst, shouting, dance, dance, dance, dance!

*   *   *

The whites are landing! The big guns! We must submit to baptism, get dressed, go to work.

God's grace was pounded into my heart. Ah! I wasn't ready for it!

I've never done evil. My days will skip on by, I'll be spared repentance. I'll avoid the torments of a soul near dead to goodness, where the stark light flares like funeral tapers. The fate of the family son, a premature coffin draped in limpid tears. Doubtless, debauchery is bestial, vice is bestial; what's putrefied must be cast aside. But the clock cannot have gotten to the point of chiming only the hour of pure anguish. Will I be carried off like a child, to play in Paradise forgetful of every sorrow?

Quick! Are there other lives?—To sleep in riches is impossible. Riches have always been public property. Divine love alone grants the keys to knowledge. I see that nature's no more than a goodly spectacle. Good-bye to chimeras, ideals, and errors!

The intelligible song of angels rises from the savior's vessel: it's the love divine.—Two loves! I can die of earthly love, die from devotion. I've departed from souls whose pain will be amplified by my taking off! You choose me from among the castaways; those left behind, aren't they my friends?

Save them!

Reason is born in me. The world is good. I will bless life. I will love my brothers. These are no longer childish promises. Nor the hope of dodging old age and death. God makes me strong and I praise God.

*   *   *

Boredom's not my love any more. Rage, debauchery, madness,—I've known every outburst and breakdown,—every one of my burdens is laid aside. Let us apprize without vertigo the extent of my innocence.

I wouldn't be able to ask for the consolation of a beating with sticks. I don't believe I'm headed for a wedding with Jesus Christ as father-in-law.

I am not a prisoner to my intellect. I've said: God. I need freedom in salvation: how to pursue it? I've quit my frivolous ways. No more need for devotion or the love divine. No regrets for the century of sensitive hearts. Each has its reason, contempt and compassion. I reserve my place at the summit of that angelic ladder of common sense.

As for established happiness, domestic or not . . . no, not for me. I'm too wasted, too weak. Life thrives by labor, goes the old saying: My own life's not heavy enough; it soars and floats so high above the action, that precious point of the world's focus.

What an old maid I've become, to lack the courage for loving death.

If God would grant me celestial, ethereal calm, grant me prayer—like the old holy ones.—Saints, the bold ones! Hermits, unfashionable artists.

Non-stop farce? My innocence could make me weep. Life is the farce we're all forced to lead.

*   *   *

Enough! Here's the punishment.—*Forward, march!*

Ahh! My lungs are burning, my skull roars! Night rolls through my eyes by that sun! Heart . . . limbs . . .

Headed where? To combat? I'm so feeble. The others advance. Tools, weapons . . . time! . . .

Fire! Fire on me! Here! or I surrender.—Cowards!—I'll kill myself! I'll throw myself under the hooves of horses!

Ahh! . . .

—I'll get used to it.

That would be the French Way, the path of honor!

Night of Hell

I've gulped down a first-rate mouthful of poison.—Three times blessed be the impulse that came to me!—My guts are ablaze. The venom's violence contorts my limbs, deforms me, throws me to the ground. I'm dying of thirst, I choke, I can't even scream. It's hell, eternal pain! See how the flames rise again! How I burn! Go, demon!

I had glimpsed conversion to bliss and happiness, sanctuary. Can I describe the vision? the air of hell will not suffer hymns! There were millions of charming creatures, a soothing spiritual concert, power and peace, noble ambitions, I don't know what!

Noble ambitions!

And that's life yet again! So what if damnation is eternal! A man who'd mutilate himself is well enough damned, isn't he? I believe in hell, therefore I am in it. It's the upshot of catechism. I am the slave of my baptism. Parents, you have made my unmaking, and undone yourselves as well. Poor innocent! Hell cannot attack pagans.

—This is life yet again! Much later, the delights of damnation will truly deepen. A crime, quick! so I may tumble into nothingness, according to human law.

Shutup, oh shut up! . . . There's much of shame here, and reproach: Satan is saying the fire is vile, that my anger is shockingly stupid.—Enough! . . . Delusions whisper to me, magic, false perfumes, puerile music.—And to say that I possess the truth, that I perceive justice: I'm of sound and steady judgment, I'm ready for perfection . . . Pride.—My scalp dries up. Pity! Lord, I am afraid. I'm thirsty, so thirsty! Ah! childhood, the grass, the rain, the lake on the rocks, *the moonlight when the clocktower chimes twelve* . . . The devil's in the belfry at this very hour. Mary! Holy Virgin! . . . The horror of my stupidity.

Down there, aren't they honest souls who wish me well? . . . Come on . . . I have a pillow over my mouth, they can't hear me, they're phantoms. Besides, nobody ever thinks of anybody else. Let them keep their distance. I smell of burning, that's for sure.

Countless hallucinations. Truly, that's what I've always had. No more faith in history, forget any principles.

I'll keep quiet on that: Poets and visionaries are bound to be jealous. I'm a thousand times the richer, let's be as greedy as the sea.

Ah now! the clock of life's been stopped all this while. I'm no longer of this world.—Theology really means it, hell is certainly *down below*—and heaven on high.—Ecstasy, nightmare, sleep in a nest of flame.

What pranks in the vigilance of the countryside . . . Satan, Mister Scratch, he runs alongside the wild seed . . . Jesus walks on the purple brambles and they do not bend . . . Jesus walked on the angry waters. The lantern showed him to us standing pale, with long brown hair, on the flank of an emerald wave.

I shall unveil all the mysteries: mysteries of religion or nature; death, birth, future things, the past, cosmic origins, nothingness. I am the master of the phantasmagoria.

Listen! . . .

I have all the talents!—There's no one here and there's someone: I don't want to scatter my treasure.—Do you want negro songs, belly dancers from heaven? Do you want me to disappear, to plunge in search of the *ring*? That's what you want? I will create gold, create cures.

Believe in me, then; faith comforts, guides, and heals. Everybody, come—even the little children—that I may console you, that my heart may be spilled for you—the miraculous heart!—Poor men, laborers! I'm not asking for your prayers; your trust alone would make me happy.

And as for me: All this makes me so little regret the world. I'm lucky to be past all suffering. My life was nothing more than sweet madness, regrettably so.

Bah! let's make every imaginable face.

Decidedly, we're out of the world. Not a sound any more. My touch has vanished. Ah! my château, my Saxony, my wood of willows. Evenings, mornings, the days, the nights . . . I'm so tired!

I should have my own hell for anger, my own hell for pride— and the hell of caresses: a harmony of hells.

I die of lethargy. Here's the tomb, I go the way of worms, horror of horrors! Satan, you trickster, you try to dissolve me with your charms. Give it to me. Give it to me! a punch of the pitchfork, a nip of fire.

Ah! to come back to life! To cast an eye on our deformities. And that poison, that kiss a thousand times accurst! My weakness, the cruelty of the world! My God, pity me, hide me, I act so wickedly!—I am hidden and I am not.

Here's the fire that rises again with its damned.

Delirium I
The Foolish Virgin
The Infernal Bridegroom

Let's give a listen to a hell-mate's confession:

"O divine Bridegroom, my Lord, do not refuse the confession of the saddest of your handmaidens. I am lost. I am drunk. I am unclean. What a life!

"Forgive me, heavenly Lord, forgive me! Ah! forgive me! How many tears! And again how many tears later, I hope!

"Afterwards, I shall know the Heavenly Bridegroom! I was born submissive to Him.—The other one can beat me now!

"Right now, I'm at rock bottom, oh girlfriends! . . . no, not my girlfriends . . . Never such delirium, such torture . . . How besotted!

"Ah! I suffer, I scream. I really suffer. For all that, I get away with it, laden with contempt by the most contemptuous of hearts.

"Anyway, let me utter this secret, free to repeat it countless more times—just as gloomy, just as pointless!

"I am enslaved to the Infernal Bridegroom, the one who screwed the foolish virgins. He's that very demon. He's not a ghost, not a phantom. Yet I, bereft of all wisdom, damned and dead to the world— there's nothing left to kill! How to describe him to you! I can't even speak any more. I grieve, I weep, I am afraid. Cool me off, Lord, a little bit, if you will, if only you will!

"I am widowed . . . —I was a widow . . . —oh yes, I was very serious once upon a time, and I wasn't born to become a skeleton!— He was little more than a child . . . It was his mysterious delicacy that seduced me. I forgot all my human responsibilities to follow him. What a life! True life's gone missing. We are not in the world. I go where he goes, I have to. And often he rages at me, *me, poor soul.* The Demon! He is a demon, you know, he's not a man.

"He says: 'I don't love women. Love must be reinvented, that's plain to see. They desire nothing more than a secure position. Security in their grasp, heart and beauty are set aside: nothing remains but cool disdain, dished up daily in modern marriages. Or else I see women with signs of happiness, whom I could have made my fine playmates, devoured all at once by brutes as sensitive as a fencepost . . . '

"I listen to him turning infamy into glory, cruelty into charm. 'I'm from a distant race: my forefathers were Scandinavians; they pierced their sides, drank their own blood.—I'll cover my body with gashes, tattoo myself, I want to be as hideous as a Mongol: you'll see, I'll run howling in the streets. I want to go crazy with rage. Never show me jewels, I'd crawl convulsing on the carpet. My riches, I want them smeared all over with blood. I'll never go to work . . . ' Many a night, his demon would seize me, we tumbled rolling, I wrestled with him!— On several nights, drunk, he'd lie in wait for me in the streets or in houses to scare me to death.—'They'll really chop my head off; it'll be disgusting.' Oh! those days when he put on a criminal air!

"Sometimes he speaks in a kind of touching rigmarole of the death which brings repentance, of the malcontents who certainly exist, of troublesome labors, of departures that rend the heart. In the slums where we got drunk together, he used to weep for all those around us, misery's livestock. He'd lift up drunkards in the dark streets. He had a wayward mother's pity for little children.—He moved with all the grace of a little girl at catechism. He pretended to be enlightened about everything, business, art, medicine.—I followed him, I had to!

"I saw the whole scene with which, in his head, he surrounded himself: clothes, fabrics, furniture; I lent him weapons, another identity. I saw everything that touched him as he would have wanted it made in his image. When it seemed to me that he was melancholy, I followed him, I did, at a distance, in strange and complicated acts, good or bad: I was certain of never entering into his world. How many hours of the night have I kept watch at the side of his dear sleeping body, wondering why he wanted so much to escape reality. Never had a man such a wish. I recognized—without fearing for him—that he could be a serious danger in society.—Did he maybe have secrets for *changing life*? No, he's only searching, I would tell myself. All in all, his compassion is bewitched, and I am its prisoner. No other soul would have enough endurance—despair's endurance!—to put up with it, to be protected and loved by him. Besides, I couldn't picture him with another soul: I believe you can see your own Angel,—never the Angel of another. I lived in his soul, like a palace emptied of the sight of such lowly folk as myself, that's all. Ohgod! I depended so much on him. But what could he want with my tame and shameful existence? He was making me no better, if he wasn't walking me to death. Sadly vexed, I sometimes said to him: 'I understand you.' He would shrug his shoulders.

"Thus my heartache ceaselessly renewed itself, and finding myself more lost in my eyes—as in the eyes of all that might have fixed on me had I not been forever condemned to be forgotten by everybody!—I grew hungrier and hungrier for his favor. With his kisses and his loving embraces, it was really heaven, a somber heaven I entered, where I longed to be left—poor, deaf, dumb and blind. I already had the habit. I saw us as two good-natured children, at liberty to stroll through the Paradise of sorrow. We suited each other. Deeply moved, we used to work together. But, after a penetrating caress, he'd say: 'How queer it'll seem to you, when I'm no longer here, all you've gone through. When you no longer have my arms around your neck, nor my heart for a pillow, nor these lips on your eyelids. For I must go away, very far, one day. Anyway, I must be of help to others: it's my duty. Not that it's very appetizing . . . dear soul . . . ' Immediately I saw myself, with him gone, prey to vertigo, plunged into the fearfullest shadow: death. I made him promise not to leave me. He made it countless times, that lover's promise. It was just as futile as my telling him: 'I understand you.'

"Hey, I've never been jealous of him! I do believe he won't leave me. What would become of him? He has no understanding, he'll never get a job. He wants to live sleepwalking. Will his kindness and compassion alone give him the right to live in the real world? Momentarily, I forget the contempt into which I have fallen: he will strengthen me, we will travel, we'll hunt in the deserts, we'll sleep on the sidewalks of mysterious cities, without cares, without penalty. Or I'll wake up, and the laws and morals will all be changed—thanks to his magic powers— or the world, while remaining the same, will leave me to my desires, my joys, my nonchalances. Oh! the life of adventures that exist in children's books, since I have suffered so much, will you give me that by way of recompense? He cannot. I'm ignorant of his ideals. He's told me that he has regrets, has hopes: they can't mean anything for me. Does he talk to God? Perhaps I should address myself to God. I'm in the deepest abyss, and I can't pray any more.

"If he explained his sorrows to me, would I comprehend them any more than his jeering? He attacks me, passing hours in making me ashamed of everything that's touched me in the world, and he's indignant if I weep.

"—'You see that elegant young man? just entering that calm and beautiful house: his name's Johnson, Jackson, Tom, Dick, or whatsit? A woman has devoted her love to that sorry idiot: she's dead, she's certainly a saint in heaven right now. You will kill me in the same way he's killed this woman. That's our destiny, with our compassionate hearts . . . ' Alas! He had days where all the movers and shakers seemed to him the toys of grotesque delirium; he'd laugh frighteningly, a long time.—Then he'd revert in his manner to a young mother, an older sister. Were he less wild, we'd be saved! But his sweetness is deadly as well. I'm submissive to him. Ahh! I am crazy!

"One day perhaps, he'll miraculously disappear; but I need to know if he'll be heading back up to a heaven, so I can take a peek at my little buddy's assumption!"

What a queer set-up!

Delirium II
Alchemy of the Word

Now for me. The story of one of my lunacies.

For a long time I boasted of possessing every possible landscape, and I found ridiculous the celebrities of modern painting and poetry.

I loved idiotic paintings, decorated door panels, stage-sets, backdrops for acrobats, tavern-signs, popular posters; antiquated literature, church-Latin, badly written erotica, novels of our grandmothers, fairytales, little books for kids, old operas, inane refrains and natural rhythms.

I dreamt up crusades, untold voyages of discovery, republics with no history, hushed-up religious wars, revolutions in morality, races and continents swept away: I believed in every enchantment.

I invented the color of the vowels! *A* black, E White, I red, O blue, U green.—I regulated the shape and motion of each consonant, and with instinctive rhythm, I prided myself on inventing a poetic language accessible, one day or another, to all the senses. I reserved the rights of translation.

At first, it was a rehearsal. I wrote silences, nights, I notated the inexpressible. I set down vertigos.

*   *   *

Far from birds and flocks, and the village girls,
What did I drink? kneeling in that heather,
By the tender hazelwood encircled,
In the tepid green fog of afternoon?

What could I drink? in that young Lazy River,—
Elms voiceless, grass deflowered, an overcast sky!
—Drink from these yellow gourds, far from my cherished
Little hut? Some golden liquor that sweats me dry.

I seemed a cock-eyed signboard for an inn.

—A storm came chasing the sky. Night at hand,
Woodland water lost in virginal sands,
God's wind hurled icicles onto the ponds:

Weeping, I saw the gold—and could not drink.

*   *   *

At four in the morning, summer,
The slumber of love still endures.
Under the greenery's shade
Evening's festive scent evaporates.

Down there, in their vast lumberyard
Under the sun of Hesperides,
Carpenters are already hard
At work—in their rolled-up shirtsleeves.

Tranquil, in their mossgrown Wilderness
They dress the precious canopy
Where the city
Will daub false heavens.

O for these Workers! Charming men,
Subjects of a king from Babylon,
Venus! leave Lovers for a moment
Whose souls are crowned.

O Queen of the Shepherds,
Bring these craftsmen a little brandy
To put their muscles at ease
Before their noontide swim in the sea.

*   *   *

Old-fashioned poetry played a good part in my alchemy of the word.

I got into the habit of plain and simple hallucination: I quite frankly saw a mosque instead of a factory, a school of drummers made up of angels, carriages on the highways of heaven, a living room at the bottom of a lake, monsters, mysteries; one vaudeville title presented horrors before me.

I explained my magical sophistry with a verbal hallucination!

I ended up finding the disorder of my mind and spirit sacred. I was idle, prey to a heavy fever: I envied the happiness of stupid creatures—caterpillars, who represent the innocence of limbo, moles, the slumber of virginity.

My aspect grew bitter. I said farewell to the world in a species of romantic song:

Song of the Highest Tower

O let it come, O let it be,
The time we long for dreamily!

I've been patient through
To the end of memory.
Apprehension and pains
Flee to the skies.
And a thirsty disease
Darkens my veins.

O let it come, O let it be,
The time of love we share between.

Like the prairie
Delivered to oblivion,
Growing and flowering
With incense and weeds

To the sullen whine
Of nasty flies.

O let it come, O let it be,
The time of love twixt me and thee.

*   *   *

I loved deserts, burnt-out orchards, faded boutiques, luke-warm drinks.
I dragged myself through stinking alleyways and, with eyes closed, of-
fered myself to the sun, god of fire.

"General, if there's an old cannon left on your crumbling ramparts,
bombard us with dirt clods. Aim for the plateglass in splendid shops! into
the living rooms! Make the city eat its own dust. Turn the rain gutters to
rust. Fill the bedrooms with a blast of powdered rubies . . . "

Oh! the drunken fly in the privy at the tavern, amorous of herbal
grace, dissolved in a sunbeam.

Hunger

My appetite is not alone
A hankering for earth and stone.
I always eat my share
Of rocks, coal, iron, air.

Turn, my hungers. O hunger, feed
On meadows that have gone to seed.
Suck up the giddy venom
Of the morning-glory weed.

Eat pebbles till they crunch,
Cathedral stones for lunch;
The gravel from olden floods,
The grey valley's scattered crumbs.

*   *   *

Under the leaves, the wolf howls,
Spitting beautiful plumes
From his breakfasting on fowl:
Like him I am consumed.

The salads and the fruits
Are ready to be picked;
But the spider in the bush
Eats nothing but violets.

Let me sleep! let me seethe
At the altars of Solomon.
The bubbling overruns the blight
And blends with waters of Kedron.

At last, O bliss, O reason, I swiped from the sky the blue that's
really black, and I lived, a golden spark out of *nature's* lightshow.
From joy, I took on the most goofy and clueless expression pos-
sible:

*   *   *

Found it again!
What? eternity.
It's the sun mingled
into the sea.

My everlasting soul,
Keep faith, aspire—
Despite the night alone
And the day on fire.

So disengage
From human cravings,
From common ecstasies!
You fly accordingly . . .

—Hope, not a chance.
No more *oldtime religion.*
Knowledge and patience,
The torture is a given.

Tomorrows unremembered
In satiny embers,
Your fever
Is the needful deed.

It is retrieved!
—What?—Eternity:
The sun swimming wildly
in the˘ sea.

I became a fabulous opera: I saw that every being is fatally happy:
action isn't life, but a way of botching some kind of power, a gutlessness.
Morality is the brain's deficiency.

To every being, several *other* lives were due, it seemed to me. This
gentleman doesn't know what he's doing: he's an angel. That family is a
litter of dogs. Right in front of several men, I chatted aloud with a
moment from one of their other lives.—Thus, I was in love with a
pig.

Not one of the subtle reasonings of madness—madness to be con-
cealed—was ever forgotten by me: I could recite them all, I know the
system.

My health was menaced. And Terror came. I would fall asleep for
several days, and, rising, continue to dream the same sad dreams. I
was ripe for death, and along a dangerous way my weakness led me to
the confines of the world and to Cimmeria, land of shadow and
whirlwinds.

I had to travel, to distract the enchantments gathered in my brain. Over the sea, that I loved as if she'd wash me clean of stain, I saw the cross of consolation rise. I had been damned by the rainbow. Happiness was my fatality, my remorse, my worm: my life would be forever too immense to be devoted to strength and beauty.

O Happiness! its tooth, killing sweetly, warned me at cock-crow,—*ad matutinum*, at the *Christus venit*,—in the darkest cities:

> O seasons, O châteaux!
> What soul's without its flaws!

> I have studied the magical shapes
> Of the happiness no one escapes.

> O let it thrive each time
> The French cock chants his rhyme.

> Ahhh! How I long for nothing more:
> It's got me now, taken over!

> This charm's taken body and soul
> And scattered my endeavors whole.

> O seasons, O châteaux!

> The hour of its flight, alas!
> Will be death's hour come round at last.

> O seasons, O châteaux!

*   *   *

Well, that's done with. Today I know how to salute beauty.

Impossibility

Ah! that childhood life of mine! the highway in every weather, super-naturally sober, more carefree than the best of beggars, proud of having no country, no friends; what nonsense it was—And only now do I see it!

I had reason to despise those good old boys who never miss a chance to cop a feel, parasites of the health and cleanliness of our women, now that we've got so little in common with women.

I was reasonable in my disdain: because I'm escaping.

Escaping?

Let me explain.

Just yesterday, I was sighing: "Good God! aren't there enough of us damned down here!? Myself, I've spent plenty of time already in their company! I know them all. We recognize each other all the time; we disgust each other. Compassion's unknown to us. But we're polite; our dealings with society are really quite agreeable." Is that astonishing? Society! the world of sellers and simpletons!—We are not dishonored.—But the elect, how would they receive us? Now, there's a surly and joyous lot, the false elect, since we need audacity or humility to approach them. They are the only elect. They're not given to blessing!

Having recovered my two cents' worth of reason—it's quickly spent!—I see that all my uneasiness comes from not figuring out soon enough that we're in the West. The western swamps! Not that I believe that the light has faded, that form's debilitated, that progress went astray . . . Fine! here's my spirit, absolutely determined to take on every cruel development that mind and spirit have suffered since the end of the Orient . . . On this my spirit is definite!

. . . So much for my two cents' worth of reason!—The mindful spirit is in authority, it wants me living in the West. I'd have to suppress it to end up how I wanted.

To hell, says I, with laurels for martyrs, the sunbeams of art, the arrogance of inventors, the eagerness for plunder; I returned to the Orient and the first and everlasting wisdom.—A dream of gross indolence, it would seem!

However, I was hardly thinking of the pleasure of escaping from modern misery. The mongrel wisdom of the Koran wasn't what I had in mind.—But isn't there a genuine torture in this—that, ever since the declaration of knowledge, Christianity, man *deludes himself*, proves the obvious to himself, inflates himself with repetition of these proofs, and can live no otherwise? Subtle, silly torture: source of my spiritual vagrancy. Maybe Nature becomes bored! Babbitt was born with Christ.

Isn't it because we cultivate the fog!? We eat the fever with our watery vegetables. And drunkenness! and tobacco! and ignorance! and self-sacrifice!—Isn't all this far enough away from the thoughts, and the wisdom of the Orient, the primitive homeland? What need of a modern society, if such poisons are invented!

The Church-folk will say: "That's right. But you mean Eden. The history of Oriental people has nothing to do with you."—It's true; it is Eden that I meant! What's that purity of ancient ancestry got to do with my dream!?

Philosophers will say: The world is ageless. Humanity simply moves from place to place. You are in the West, but free to live in your Orient, as ancient as you need—and live well. Don't admit you're beaten. Philosophers, you belong to your Western Land.

My spirit, be on guard. No violent plans for salvation. Train yourself!—Ah! Science isn't quick enough for us!

—But I perceive that my spirit sleeps.

If it were wide awake always from this moment on, we'd reach the truth early and soon, where perhaps we'd be surrounded with its weeping angels! . . . If it had been awake up till now, I wouldn't have given in to my self-destructive instincts, in an epoch out of time and memory! . . . If it had always been awake, I'd be in full sail on the sea of wisdom! . . .

O purity! purity!

This moment of awakening gave me the vision of purity!—By the mindful spirit we go to God!

Tormenting misfortune!

Lightning Flash

Human labor! that's the explosion that illuminates my bottomless pit from time to time.

"Nothing is vanity: full speed ahead for science!" cries the modern Ecclesiastes, that is to say *Everybody*. And for all that, the cadavers of evil-doers and sluggards fall on the hearts of others . . . Ah! quick, hurry up; there, beyond the night, those future paybacks, eternal rewards . . . can we escape them?

—What can I do? I know what work is; and science is too slow. How prayer gallops and the light rumbles . . . I can see it all right. It's too simple, and it's too hot; you'll get along without me. I've got my duty; I'll do it proud in the way that many do, by setting it aside.

My life's used up. Come on! let's pretend and poke about, for pity's sake! And we'll exist for our own amusement, dreaming of monstrous loves and fantastical universes, complaining and quarreling with society's disguises: mountebank, beggar, artist, bandit—priest! On my bed in the hospital, the odor of incense intensely revisits me: guardian of sacred aromatics, confessor, martyr . . .

There, I've come to grips with my rotten childhood education. So what! . . . To go my twenty-odd years if others go their twenty-odd . . .

No! NO! Right now I rebel against death! Laboring looks too light for my arrogance: to betray me to the world would be a sentencing too short. At the last minute, I'd strike to the right, to the left . . .

Then!—O dear impoverished soul—eternity might not be wasted on us!

Morning

Didn't I *once* have a youth worthy of love, heroic, fabulous, putting my name to golden pages,—plenty of luck! By what crime, by what heresy have I deserved my current weakness? You who maintain that beasts heave sobs of heartache, that the sick despair, that the dead dream badly, try now to account for my downfall and my slumber. Me, I can no more explain myself than the beggar with his perpetual *Paters* and *Ave Marias*. I don't know how to speak any more!

However, today, I believe I have finished the telling of my hell. It was really Hell, the old hell, wherein the Son of Man flung open the gates.

Out of the same desert, in the same night, my tired eyes always awaken to the silvery star, always, although the Kings of life, the three magi, heart, soul, and mind do not stir. When do we get beyond the shores and the mountains, to salute the birth of the new labor, the new wisdom, the flight of tyrants and demons, the end of superstition, to adore—the first ones!—Christmas on earth?

The heavens are singing, populations are on the move! Slaves, let us not curse life.

Farewell

Autumn already!—Yet why regret an everlasting sun if we're engaged in
the divine light's discovery?—far away from folk who die with the seasons.

Autumn. Our boat rises through the motionless fog, turns toward
the port of misery, the big city of heaven smeared in fire and slime! Ah!
the rotten rags, the bread soaked in rain, drunkenness, the countless
loves that have crucified me! She'll never finish, ever, that Ghoul Queen
who rules millions of souls and bodies, all dead, *and all will be judged!*
I see myself again, skin eaten away by filth and plague, worms filling
my hair and armpits and even bigger worms in my heart—laid out
amid the ageless nameless, without feeling . . . I might have died there
. . . Fearful evocation! I loathe misery.

And I dread winter because it's the cozy season.

—Sometimes in the sky I see beaches without end covered with
white joyous nations. Just above me, a great golden vessel shakes out
her multicolored insignia in the morning breeze. I created all the festi-
vals, every triumph, all the drama. I tried to invent new flowers, new
stars, new flesh, new tongues. I believed I was acquiring supernatural
powers. Well then! I must bury my imagination and my memories! A
glorious career as artist and storyteller swept away!

I! who called myself magus or angel, dispensing with all morality, I
am rendered back to the soil with a duty for seeking and embracing
rough reality! A peasant!

Am I mistaken? Would compassion be the sister of death for me?
Anyway, I'll ask pardon for having fed myself on lies. Now let's go.
Yet no friendly hand! and where to turn for help?

*   *   *

Yes, the new-fashioned hour is tough enough.

For I can say that my victory is won: the grinding of teeth, the
whistling fire, the pestilential sighs grow less and less. All the noxious
memories are fading. My last regrets hightail it,—jealous of beggars,

brigands, death's friends, rear ends of every sort.—Damned souls, what if I avenged myself?

It is necessary to be absolutely modern.

Never a hymn: seize what's held. Arduous night! the crusted blood smokes on my face and I've nothing behind me except that hideous little tree! . . . Spiritual combat is just as brutal as the battle of men; but the vision of justice is the pleasure of God alone.

Meanwhile, here's the vigil. Receive every vigorous influx and every real tenderness. And at dawn, armed with ardent patience, we will march into splendid cities.

Why do I talk of helping hands! One fine advantage is that I can laugh at old lying loves, and put to shame these illusory couples,—I've seen women's hell back there;—and I'll be at liberty *to hold the truth in one soul and one body.*

April–August 1873

NOTES

I took arms against righteousness . . . *(Je me suis armé contre la justice . . .)*
Rimbaud's term *"la justice"* encompasses not only "justice" but the code of
    law (crime and punishment) and the whole moral structure behind it.
    Hence, "righteousness" in English, rather than "justice" or "the law."

O witches . . . *(Ô sorcières . . .)*
Steinmetz offers the view that the witches are personifications of the
    "misery" and "hatred" that follow immediately here.

And springtime brought me the idiot's horrific laughter.
April of 1873, when Rimbaud first returned home to Roche and began
    work on *Season in Hell*, originally titled "Livre Païen ou Livre
    Nègre" (Pagan Book or Negro Book).

**Now, suddenly finding myself at the point of producing my ultimate
    croak!**
A probable reference to the Brussels episode of July 10, 1873, when
    Verlaine shot Rimbaud during a drunken quarrel, wounding him
    in the left wrist. The wound became infected and Rimbaud was
    bedridden for several days in Brussels.

Bad Blood

" . . . my Celtic ancestors . . . " *(. . . mes ancêtres gaulois . . .)*
The 1903 edition of Cassell's New French Dictionary defines *"gaulois*
    (adjective): Gaulish, Gallic; (figuratively) old-fashioned." The 'old-
    fashioned' Gauls were of Celtic origin.

. . . trappers and turf-burners . . . *(. . . les ecorcheurs de bêtes, les
    brûleurs d'herbes . . .)*

Literally, "skinners of beasts, burners of grasses"—primitive activities
of a nomadic or 'uncivilized' folk.

... Declaration of the Rights of Man ...
An allusion to French Revolutionary ideals and the works of Thomas
Paine (1737–1809), American philosopher and patriot, author of
The Age of Reason and *The Rights of Man*. He published *Common
Sense* in 1776, followed by *Crisis* in 1777. In 1787, he went to En-
gland, where he published *The Rights of Man*. Paine then sailed for
France and was active in the French Revolution (1789). He was elected
Pas-de-Calais deputy to the National Convention and offended
Robespierre by voting to give asylum to Louis XVI in America. The
Declaration of the Rights of Man was the fundamental document of
the French Revolution and republican tradition; these basic rights
were freedom, property, security, and the right to resist oppression.

Swabian plains ... Byzantine sights
Swabia or Schwaben, an ancient land in southwest Germany, was a
route to the Middle East during the Crusades. Byzantium was the
old name for Constantinople, modern-day Istanbul, the capital of
the Eastern Roman Empire and then the Ottoman Empire. The
city is Europe's gateway to the Orient.

the Sabbat
A midnight assembly of witches and sorcerers in medieval and Renais-
sance times, purportedly on St. John's Eve, Walpurgis Night, or
Halloween, designed to celebrate and renew their 'satanic' rites.

... the vision of harmony. (... *la vision des nombres.*)
Literally, "the vision of numbers," but in French implying *variety and
harmony* in a mathematic (abstract) sense. The word "Spirit"
following seems to favor this reading.

The pagan blood rises again! (Le sang païen revient!)
"Pagan" is from the Latin *pagano,* for peasant, a tiller of the soil; peas-

ants, who lived out in the countryside, were among the last classes of people to convert to Christianity.

. . . laden with my vice (. . . *chargé de mon vice*)
Rimbaud never precisely defined what he meant by "vice." Certain commentators have associated the term with homosexuality or the relationship between Rimbaud and Verlaine, but this is an over-simplification.

In the *Lettres du voyant*, the poet names debauchery, drugs, poisons, crime, and sickness as methods to bring about "deregulation" or derangement "of all the senses. All shapes of love, suffering, madness."

Later on in "Bad Blood," however, he writes: "Doubtless, debauchery is bestial, vice is bestial," differentiating them; and at the beginning of the chapter he refers to " . . . idolatry and love of sacrilege; oh! all the vices, anger, lust . . . above all, vanity and sloth."

One might add excessive pride ("I have all the talents"), despair ("I was ripe for death"), and self-delusion ("what a jerk I am!") to his catalogue of vice. Whatever his *particular* 'vice'—pride, love of sacrilege, anger, lust, or self-delusion—Rimbaud keeps it to himself.

. . . keep clear of righteousness (. . . *se garder de la justice*)
Literally, "to guard oneself from justice/the law"—Rimbaud's sense of 'justice' involved all the restraints and penalties imposed by society as well as the official morality behind it all. This is the "righteousness" referred to at the very beginning: *"Je me suis armé contre la justice."*

lifting the coffin lid with a withering fist (*soulever le couvercle du cercueil*)
An echo of "this . . . tomb" *(ce tombeau)* in "Childhood V" (*Illuminations*).

. . . here below, for all that! (. . . *ici-bas, pourtant!*)
Still in hell, despite renunciation and compassion.

De profundis, Domine [Latin] "Out of the depths, O Lord"
The opening phrase of Psalm 130, in the King James version: "Out of
the depths have I cried unto Thee, O Lord."

Joan of Arc
French patriot and teen-aged martyr, Saint Joan (c. 1412–1431). In-
spired by heavenly voices, she led the armies of France to victory
during the Hundred Years War. Captured by the English in 1430,
she was put on trial for heresy and sorcery and burnt at the stake
in Rouen, faithful to her 'voices' to the last. She was canonized by
the Catholic Church in 1920.

. . . the children of Ham
Ham (*Black* in Old Hebrew) was the third son of Noah, mentioned in
Genesis 5:32 and 9:22. See Genesis 10:6–9 for "the sons of Ham;
Cush, and Mizraim, and Phut, and Canaan . . . And Cush begat
Nimrod: a mighty one . . . a mighty hunter . . . " After the Flood, the
children of Ham were believed to have populated the African conti-
nent.

"Livre Païen ou Livre Nègre" (Pagan Book or Negro Book/Book of Blacks)
was Rimbaud's original title for Season in Hell. According to Starkie,
this was "to indicate that his intention was to return to the days
before the advent of Christianity, before there had existed the
tragic dilemma of right and wrong." (Rimbaud: Part 2, Chapter X)

Night of Hell

The devil's in the belfry *(Le diable est au clocher)*
"The Devil In The Belfry" is the title of Edgar Allan Poe's mildly satirical
tale about the village of Vondervattimeitiss, where the town clock
strikes thirteen after a queer little gentleman takes up residence in the

belfry. Rimbaud may have known this story and his use of it here, in passing, heightens the irony of his remembered "innocence."

Satan, Mister Scratch . . . *(Satan, Ferdinand . . .)*
Ferdinand is a name for the devil in certain regions of France, much like the English folk equivalents, Mister Scratch, Old Scratch, Old Nick.

Jesus walked on the angry waters . . .
Matthew 14:22–32 and John 6:17–21

. . . to plunge in search of the *ring*
A reference to Germany's national epic, *The Ring of the Niebelungs*, wherein the Rhine-gold is stolen by the dwarf Alberich and forged into a ring of magic power that brings about the downfall of the gods. At the end of the tale (*Götterdämmerung*), the golden ring is returned to the depths of the Rhine. The entire story has been set to music by Richard Wagner (1813–1883) in four operas or music-dramas popularly known as *The Ring Cycle* (Der Ring des Nibelungen).

When the poet says he'll "create gold, create cures," he turns his back on the betrayal, greed, and cruelty that characterize misuse of the ring's power in this ancient epic. He would use his own powerful alchemy for enriching and healing the world.

Delirium I—The Foolish Virgin, The Infernal Bridegroom

The Foolish Virgin, with her mawkish sentimentality and self-proclaimed victimization, is a portrait of Verlaine, whose clinging, desperate affection eventually alienated Rimbaud. Some critics have read this chapter as a dialogue between Rimbaud and his soul, but given the tenor of the whole work, this is less convincing than the equation of Verlaine as Foolish Virgin and Rimbaud as Infernal Bridegroom. Perfectly attuning his voice to Verlaine's point of view, Rimbaud renders a portrait of himself as seen by his partner.

Enid Starkie calls this Delirium "a subtle picture of the relations of the two poets . . . It shows how much ascendance Rimbaud came finally to exercise over Verlaine by his stronger and more violent character, by his greater intelligence." (*Rimbaud*: Part 2, Chapter IV)

Jesus tells the original parable of the Foolish Virgins and the Wise Virgins in Matthew 25:1–13.

Delirium II—Alchemy of the Word

"The two *Délires* chapters are the relation of the two main causes of his downfall, love and art . . . In Délires II he criticizes his artistic follies and errors, the greatest cause of his fall." (Starkie: *Rimbaud*, Part 2, Chapter X)

Alchemy *(Alchimie)*
A 'magical' science, forerunner of modern chemistry, some would have it. According to others, a folly, misapprehended as a means of turning base metals into gold. "The Philosopher's Stone" was the quintessential ore for this transmutation; also known as "The Elixir of Life," this elusive substance was equated with the symbolic quest for spiritual perfection.

Medieval alchemists believed that all matter was made up of four opposing elements: water, fire, earth, and air; and that 'perfection' or 'gold' would be achieved by uniting them—effecting *change*.

To avoid charges of heresy, witchcraft, or sorcery, early alchemists cloaked their experiments in a language of ornate symbology. Rimbaud, familiar with Goethe's *Faust* and probably Baudelaire's *Alchimie de la doleur* ["The Alchemy of Sadness"] (*Fleurs du Mal*, 1861), utilized alchemical values in his sonnet "Vowels," to which he alludes in the fifth paragraph. In Jungian psychology, Alchemy is equated with the active imagination; Rimbaud's usage foreshadows this thought.

U green (U, vert)
Rimbaud here presents his alchemical vowels in standard alphabetical order; in the earlier sonnet *Voyelles*, he ends with O, the Greek omega, the end of all things.

. . . young Lazy River (. . . *jeune Oise*)
Perhaps only the name of a river, but also possibly derived from *oiseux/ oiseuse/oisif* meaning 'idle or indolent.'

["At four in the morning"] Hesperides
The Hesperides were the three daughters of Nyx (Night) and Erebus (Darkness) who had the gift of everlasting song. In their garden at the western end of the world grew the tree which produced the golden apples, which Gaia (Mother Earth) had given to Hera when she married Zeus; these symbolized fertility and love. The Hesperides, according to myth, sang a lullaby to the guardian of the golden apples—the dragon or serpent Ladon—every night, all night. Hesperus is also the name of the evening star (the planet Venus), which shines in the western sky. Venus the goddess reappears later in the poem.

. . . a king from Babylon
An allusion to Nebuchadnezar, the Chaldean King of Babylon from 605 to 562 B.C., who built the famous Hanging Gardens, and rebuilt and expanded the city walls. Hence, a princely architect or prince of builders.

["Hunger"] . . . the altars of Solomon . . . the waters of Kedron.
Solomon (10th Century B.C. King of Israel), who was noted for his
wisdom and his many wives, built the first Temple in Jerusalem (I
Kings 5:5 and 9:1). The Kedron brook flows between Jerusalem
and Mount Olivet and empties into the Dead Sea.

Thus, I was in love with a pig.
A harsh reference to *l'affaire Verlaine*.

Cimmeria, land of shadow and whirlwind
In Greek myth, Cimmeria, shrouded in mist and perpetual shadow, was
located at the western edge of the world. It was here, in Book XI of
the *Odyssey*, that Odysseus gained access to the spirits of the dead.

In Herodotus, the Cimmerians are a historical people who were driven
from their homeland north of the Black Sea by the Scythians (800–
700 B.C.). In the early 7th Century, the Cimmerians conquered
Phrygia, causing King Midas to kill himself by swallowing poison.
(Midas, in legend, was another who " . . . saw the gold—and could
not drink.") The Cimmerians were noted throughout the ancient
world for their ferocity and strength. Herodotus also mentions
their use of hemp as a sacrament in communal 'spirit sessions'
where, in a sealed sweat-lodge, cannabis would be thrown onto the
hot stones until the lodge filled with aromatic smoke and shamanistic
visions ensued. Thus, the "land of shadow and whirlwind" may
also allude to the poet's drug experiences.

. . . damned by the rainbow.
In Genesis 9:13–17, God sets His rainbow in the sky as a sign of His
promise to Noah that He will never again destroy the Earth with a
flood. Rimbaud perhaps considers the rainbow a symbol of 'all
revealed religion'—or a rainbow of sounds (poetry), as in *Vowels*,
the pursuit of which caused him such despair and 'damnation' (cf.
Revelation 10:1–6).

ad matutinum . . . Christus venit
Latin chant for Morningsong (Matins): "In the morning, Christ comes."
Sung on Sundays in Catholic and Anglican services.

["O Seasons O Châteaux"]
The seasons are the poet's experience, his life—the castles or *châteaux*
appear in the landscape as ordered points of reference or visions of
art, the poet's work, his poems.

The French cock *(le coq gaulois)*
The 'gallic' (old-fashioned, Gaulish) rooster or cock symbolizes masculin-
ity, virility, and resurrection, probably here meaning an erection.
"Happiness" above seems to be Rimbaud's code word for sexual
bliss.

This charm *(ce charme)*
The powerful incantation of desire and fulfillment; a magic spell uttered
aloud. ("Peace! the charm's wound up." Shakespeare, *Macbeth* I:3)

Today I know how to salute beauty. *(Je sais aujourd'hui saluer la beauté.)*
Ambiguity prevails in the verb *saluer*—is it a new beauty or vision "not
to be recorded in art, now rejected?" as Robert Greer Cohn says,
"Or is it the old beauty which, obviously, is dying hard and which
he greets as with a handkerchief-wave from the deck of that ship
which is about to leave from the shores of the present in 'Matin'? I
feel it is both."

Impossibility

Rimbaud here excoriates his youthful pride and arrogance, his anti-
social stance. The "damned souls here below" probably means the
literary crowd to which Verlaine introduced him. Their 'elite' sta-

tus was still below that of "the elect"—the aristocracy, the wealthy, the politicians, the "Church-folk."

. . . the mongrel wisdom of the Koran (. . . la sagesse bâtarde du Coran)

Organized religion or revealed religion (the faith of the Book) is Rimbaud's target here, but this particular phrase also serves, perhaps, as a veiled reference to the poet's father, Captain Frédéric Rimbaud, who had translated the Koran into French during a tour of duty in Algeria, where, after serving in action, he functioned as liaison for the Department of Arab Affairs, c. 1845–50.

Babbitt (M. Prudhomme)

A character in French literature from the pen of Henri Monnier (1857), M. Prudhomme was a smug and pompous mediocrity. "Babbitt"—a noun in English—comes from the character of George F. Babbitt in the novel by Sinclair Lewis (Babbitt, 1922): a professional or businessman who conforms unthinkingly to prevailing middle-class standards. This admittedly anachronistic term seems the closest American English equivalent to Rimbaud's "Monsieur Prudhomme," whose numbers, according to the poet, have increased with the advent of Christianity.

. . . we cultivate the fog (. . . nous cultirons la brume)

Imperfect vision, clouded insight, blindness: we wrap ourselves in obfuscation. We tend a garden of watery vegetables . . .

The Church-folk (Le gens d'Eglise)

Literally, "the people of the Church"—meaning either 'church-goers' or the hierarchy of organized religious orders—or both.

Lightning

Nothing is vanity; full speed ahead for science! cries the modern Ecclesiastes

"Vanity of vanities, saith the Preacher, vanity of vanities; all is vanity.
What profit hath a man of all his labour which he taketh under the
sun? One generation passeth away, and another generation cometh:
but the earth abideth for ever." (Ecclesiastes 1:2–4)

... it's too hot *(. . . il fait trop chaud)*
Still in hell, the temperature rises at the lightning flash.

To go my twenty-odd years *(Aller mes vingt ans)*
French for twenty can also mean 'many, or countless,' hence the
translation "twenty-odd"—an English phrase denoting 'twenty and
then some,' or 'twenty or so.' Rimbaud was not yet nineteen when
he wrote these lines, and had less than twenty more years left to his
life. In this era, twenty was the age at which one fulfilled one's
military duty (compare the ending of "Bad Blood"); see also
Illuminations "Jeunesse III: 20 ans."

Morning

... putting my name to golden pages *(. . . à écrire sur des feuilles
d'or)*
Another translation of this line could read 'autographing golden leaves.'
These opening lines echo *Illuminations* "Youth II" ("Jeunesse II"),
entitled "Sonnet."

Paters and *Ave Marias*
Roman Catholic prayers in Latin: "Our Fathers" and "Hail Marys,"
memorized by the faithful.

... wherein the Son of Man flung open the gates *(. . . celui dont le
fils de l'homme ouvrit les portes)*
The Harrowing of Hell, according to the Apostles' Creed in certain

Christian sects. Between his crucifixion and resurrection, Jesus Christ descended to Hell and opened the gates to free those souls that had been dead and buried before his coming.

Out of the same desert, in the same night
The three Wise Men, or Magi, are here evoked (Matthew 2), but in the manner of a reversal or parallel. The Three Kings are "heart, soul, and spirit," implying a humanistic trinity that dozes while "the silvery star" shines on above.

These Magi do not salute the advent of the Messiah (old superstition), but revere the new wisdom (the latest labor).

This three-part symbology may derive from Pascal's *Pensées*, according to Steinmetz, where Mankind is conceptualized as being made up of "body, spirit, and heart" ("le corps, l'esprit, le coeur"). Rimbaud's new nativity here bears comparison with the superhuman presences held up for adoration in *Illuminations*, particularly "Raison" and "Génie."

Farewell

A dimming of enthusiasm and energy from *Morning*'s high spirits. An "Adieu" to Satan for whom "these few hideous pages" were ripped loose from the poet's book.

Autumn already!
The fall ordinarily begins September 22; Rimbaud finished *Season in Hell* in August of 1873, so this is a prophecy or prognosis.

. . . the big city of heaven (. . . *la cité énorme au ciel*)
Perhaps an allusion to London, based on these lines from Verlaine's

Sonnet boiteux (1873), dedicated to Ernest Delahaye: "London smokes and howls . . . O the fire of heaven over this Biblical city!" ("Londres fume et crie . . . O le feu du ciel sur cette ville de la Bible!") Mixed into the metaphor is a glance at Dante's boat-ride with Charon to the city of Dis (*Inferno* Canto VIII). In Rimbaud's image, the "big city" is heaven, hell, and London all rolled into one.

that Ghoul Queen . . . *(cette goule reine . . .)*
Death, personified as a female vampire or Hecate, Queen of the Night, ruler of the souls of the dead, making her last appearance in Rimbaud's work.

. . . beaches . . . covered with white joyous nations
The sand of the beach as a metaphor for humankind, each grain an individual, is probably an allusion to God's promise in Genesis 22:17, " . . . I will multiply thy seed . . . as the sand which is upon the sea shore . . . " (The "nations" may also refer to clouds in the sky or the foam of waves crashing and washing on the beach, both visions in blue and white.) The "golden vessel" being the sun, the sky then becomes the sea becoming the sky becoming the sea. As William Blake concludes in his poem *Scoffers:*

> The atoms of Democritus
> And Newton's particles of light
> Are sands upon the Red Sea shore,
> Where Israel's tents do shine so bright.

A glorious career as artist . . . *(une belle gloire d'artiste . . .)*
According to Steinmetz, an ironic citation of the last words of Nero as he committed suicide: "*Quel artiste je fais périr!*" ("Qualis artifex pereo." "What an artist dies in me!").

My last regrets
The jealousy or envy for beggars, brigands, and death's friends (idleness,
    criminality, soldiers and suicides)—the "rear-ends" are retreating
    asses; also 'backward creatures' or 'the backward' (mentally
    deficient), 'the maladjusted.' Rimbaud threatens these phantoms
    with buggery or perhaps a kick in the pants.

. . . that hideous little tree *(. . . cet horrible arbrisseau)*
The tree of good and evil *(Illuminations: "Matinée d'ivresse")*
    from the Garden of Eden—or the tree of crucifixion, of
    martyrdom.

. . . these illusory couples *(. . . ces couples menteurs)*
Perhaps Verlaine and his wife Mathilde or maybe the 'queer couple' of
    Verlaine and Rimbaud *("drôle de ménage")*. "Women's hell" could
    refer to either case, or to any 'marriage' gone wrong, for Rimbaud
    had experienced all manner of illusion, lies, and hell "in one soul
    and one body."

" . . . But I will know the truth, possess it for my own, in *this* body,
    with *this* soul . . . " is Henry Miller's insightful rendering of
    the poem's last line. Further on in *The Time of the Assassins*,
    Miller notes, "His desire to possess the truth *in body and soul*
    is the longing for that nether Paradise which Blake called Beulah.
    It represents the state of grace of the fully conscious man who,
    by accepting his Hell unconditionally, discovers a Paradise of
    his own creation. This is resurrection *in the flesh*."

Op. Cit.

Arthur Rimbaud: *Oeuvres II (Une Saison en Enfer)*, ed. Jean-Luc
    Steinmetz; GF-Flammarion, 1989.

Enid Starkie: *Arthur Rimbaud.* New Directions, 1961.

The Oxford Companion to Classical Literature, ed. M.C. Howatson; Oxford University Press, 1989.

Derek Williams: *Romans and Barbarians.* St. Martin's Press, 1999

Henry Miller: *The Time of the Assassins.* New Directions, 1956.

PART TWO

Poems and Prose

The Orphans' New Year Gift

Les Étrennes des orphelins

December 1869

I

The room's full of shadows; one vaguely hears
The sad, soft whispering of two children.
Their heads are inclined, still heavy with dreams,
Under the long white wafting draperies . . .
—Outside, the birds are huddled close, frozen;
Their wings benumbed under the sky's grey tone,
And the New Year with her following of
Mists, trailing the folds of her snowy robe,
Smiling through tears and shivering, sings . . .

II

But these children, under the floating drape,
Talk low as one does in the dark of night.
They listen, pensive, as to distant sighs.
They often start at the morning chime's bright
Golden voice, striking, striking again its
Metallic refrain in its glassy dome.
—Then the room is icy . . . One sees clothes of
Mourning strewn by the bed, heaped on the floor:
The harsh winter wind lamenting at the
Doorsill breathes morosely through the dwelling.

One senses, at this, that something's amiss.
—Is there no mother, then, for these children,
No mom smiling brightly, gazing proudly?
So, did she forget, last night, looking in
Alone, to coax a flame from the ashes
And pile on the woolens and quilts before
Leaving them, calling to them: forgive me?
Didn't she know the morning would be cold . . .
Nor close the door against the wintry wind?
—A mother's dream is the cozy blanket,
A downy nest where children are tucked in
Like beautiful birds rocking in branches,
Sleeping their sweet sleep filled with white visions! . . .
—And here, a featherless nest, without warmth,
Where the children are chill, awake, afraid—
A nest the bitter wind must've frozen . . .

III

Your heart knows:—These children are motherless.
No mom at home! . . . —and the dad's far away! . . .
—An old servant, then, has been tending them.
The kids are alone in the icy house:
Orphans at four, in whose thoughts a smiling
Memory now rises by slow degrees . . .
Like a prayer that's told on a rosary:
—Ah! what a beautiful New Year's morning!
During the night each had dreamt on their own,
In a curious dream where they saw toys,
Trinkets dressed in gold, and sparkling jewels,
All whirling, dancing an echoing dance, then
Vanished behind the drapes, then back again!
And they're up in the morning, joyously
They rise, mouth watering, rubbing their eyes,
And with tousled heads, eyes shining as on

A holiday, with little bare feet, they
Skip across the floor to their parents' door
And with a gentle tap, walk right in! . . . And
Then the best of wishes . . . in their nightshirts,
Repeated kisses and romping allowed!

IV

Ah! those oft-repeated words are charming!
But how it's changed, their home of long ago:
A big fire used to crackle brightly in
The fireplace, the old room all aglow;
And the red reflections from the big hearth
Loved to caress the gleaming furniture . . .
—The wardrobe was keyless . . . no cabinet key!
They often glanced at its huge blackened door . . .
No keys! . . . that was odd . . . They often wondered
What mysteries slept in its wooden breast,
And thought they heard, from the gaping keyhole's
Depths, a far-off hum, vague murmurs of joy . . .
Their parents' room stands quite empty today:
No red reflection from under the door;
No more parents, nor hearth, nor missing keys:
So, no more kisses or sweet surprises!
Oh, their New Year's Day will be a sad one!
And thoughtfully, while they let a bitter
Tear fall silently from their big blue eyes,
They murmur: "When is mommy coming back?"

V

The little ones are sadly sleeping now:
To see them, you'd say they cry in their sleep,
Their eyes are so swollen, their breathing so hard!
All small children have such sensitive hearts!

—But the lulling angel comes, wipes their tears,
Brings a joyous dream to their heavy sleep,
So joyous a dream that, smiling, they seem
To murmur something with half-parted lips.
—They dream they are leaning on their plump arms
In that gentle waking pose, looking up
So their drowsy glance takes in the whole room . . .
They think they've been sleeping in a rosy
Paradise . . . bright hearth, gaily the fire sings . . .
Nature enraptured waking to sunbeams . . .
The earth, half-naked, happy to revive,
Shivers with joy under the sun's kisses! . . .
And in the old home all is warm and red:
No more black clothes scattered from floor to bed.
The wind under the door pipes down at last . . .
You could say that a fairy had just passed! . . .
—The children, full of joy, shout twice . . . There,
Near mother's bed in a lovely rosy
Sunbeam, there on the big rug, something gleams . . .
These are silver medallions, black and white,
Pearly trim with glittering jet facets:
Little frames in black and wreaths made of glass,
With three words etched in gold: "To Our Mother!"

Sensation

Sensation

March 1870

On blue summer evenings, down paths I'll go,
Pricked by the stubble, trampling the grass beds:
Dreaming, I'll feel the cool between my toes.
I'll let the breezes bathe my naked head.

I'll have nothing to say, no thoughts inside:
But infinite love in my soul unfurls
And, gypsy-like, I'll wander far and wide
In the world—as happy as with a girl.

Sun and Flesh

Soleil et chair

I

The Sun, the hearth of tenderness and life,
Sheds blazing love on the enraptured earth
And, when you've lain in the valley, you'll feel
How nubile the earth and brimming with blood;
How its immense breast, lifted by a soul,
Is made of love like God, flesh like woman
And, big with sap and sunbeams, how it holds
The vast swarming of every embryo!

And it all grows, it all rises!

O Venus, Goddess!
I miss the days of antiquity's youth,
Of lusty satyrs and animal fauns,
Gods who for love chewed the bark off trees and,
In the water lilies, kissed the blonde Nymph!
I miss those days when the juice of the world,
The river's flood, the saplings' rosy blood,
Put a universe in the veins of Pan!
When the soil throbbed, green, beneath his goat-feet;
Where, gently kissing fair Syrinx, his lips
Gave shape to love's great hymn under the sky;
When, standing on the plain, he heard all round
Him living Nature answer to his call,
When the speechless trees, cradling the songbird,
The earth cradling man, and the whole blue Sea
And every creature loved, loved in God!

I long for the time of great Cybele,

Hugely gorgeous, who, they say, drove a great
Brazen chariot through splendid cities!
Her two breasts poured forth in immensities
The streaming purity of endless life.
Man happily sucked at her blessed teat
Like a little babe, dandled on her knee.
—Because he was strong, Man was chaste and sweet.

Pitiful! Now he says: I know what's what,
And off he goes with eyes closed and ears shut.
So—no more gods! no more gods! Man is King,
Man is God! But then Love is the great Faith!
Oh, if only man still thrived at your breast,
Great Cybele, mother of gods and men!
If he'd not left immortal Astarte
Who, long ago, risen from the shining
Blue depths, flowering flesh in scented waves,
Showed her navel's rose in the snowy foam . . .
And, Goddess with huge dark eyes of conquest,
Made nightingales sing in woods, love in hearts!

II

I believe in you! In you! Divine mother,
Sea-borne Aphrodite!—Oh, the way is rough
Since the other God hitched us to his cross.
Flesh, Marble, Flower, Venus, I believe in you!
—Yes, man is ugly and sad under the vast sky,
Wearing clothes because he's no longer chaste,
Because he has defiled his proud godhead
And shrivelled, like an idol in the fire,
His Olympian body to soiled hire!
Yes, he even wants to live after death,
A pale skeleton, insulting primal beauty.
—And the Idol, whom you made a virgin,

Woman—in whom you made our clay divine
That Man might enlighten his needy soul
And slowly ascend in a love immense
From earthly prison to the beauty of day—
She no longer knows even the courtesan's way!
—What a fine joke! and society sniggers
At the sweet and sacred name of great Venus!

III

If only times gone by would pass again!
For Man's finished! Man has played all the roles!
Weary of smashing idols, he'll wake up
Right in broad daylight, free of all his Gods!
And since he's from heaven, he'll scan the skies.
Invincible eternal Thought, the all,
The Ideal—the god living in his flesh
Of clay—will rise, rise blazing in his brow.
When you see him search the whole horizon,
Despising old constraints, free from all fear,
You'll come to give him holy Redemption.
—Splendid, radiant, from the deep seas' bosom
You'll rise, beaming infinite Love with its
Infinite smile through the vast Universe.
The World, like an immense harp, will vibrate
In the quivering of an immense kiss!

The World thirsts for love: you come to quench it.

*   *   *

(Oh, Man raises his head free and proud!
And the instant ray of primal beauty
Makes the god pulse through his altar of flesh!
Filled with joy for now, pale from ills gone by,
Man wants to fathom it all—and to know!

Thought, jaded for so long, so long oppressed,
Will bolt from his brow. And she will know Why!
Let her spring free and Mankind will Believe!
—Why the mute azure and fathomless space?
And why the golden stars like swirling sand?
If you climbed forever what would you see?
Does a shepherd guide that immense flock of
Worlds on the move through the terrors of space?
Do all these worlds, held in the vast ether,
Quake at the sound of an eternal voice?
—And Man, can he see? can he say: I believe?
Is thought's language any more than a dream?
If man is born abruptly, and life so brief,
Where is he from? Does he sink in the deep Sea
Of germs, Fetuses, Embryos, to the
Bottom of that huge Crucible wherein
Mother Nature will revive him, alive,
To love in the rose, to grow in the wheat? . . .

We cannot know!—We're muffled in a cloak
Of ignorance and narrow fantasies!
Apes of men, tumbled from our mothers' wombs,
Our pale sense hides the infinite from us.
We try to see:—and Doubt's our punishment!
Doubt, a dismal bird, clips us with its wing
And the skyline fades in flight eternal! . . .

                    *   *   *

Great heaven opens! the mysteries are dead,
Faced with Man, his muscled arms crossed, standing
Amid rich nature's wide-open splendor!
He sings . . . and the woods sing and rivers murmur
A song full of joy rising to the daylight! . . .
That's Redemption! That is love! that is love! . . .)

IV

O splendor in the flesh! O splendor ideal!
O love's renewal, dawn triumphant where,
With Gods and Heroes humbled at their feet,
White-hipped Venus and little Eros, covered
In a snow of roses, caress while women
And flowers blossom at their lovely feet!
—O great Ariadne, heaving your sobs
On the shore there watching Theseus' flight,
Sails white in the sunlight across the waves,
O sweet virgin child, broken in a night,
Hush! Bacchus, in his golden chariot
Wrought with black vines, drawn through Phrygian fields
By lusty tigers and russet panthers,
Along blue rivers reddens dusky moss.
—Zeus the Bull cradles Europa's nude body
On his neck like a baby, her white arms flung
Round the God's brawny neck rippling in the wave . . .
He slowly turns his dreamy gaze upon her.
She lays her pale and florid cheek along
Zeus' brow; she closes her eyes; she dies
In a kiss divine, and the murmuring wave
Sets flowers of golden foam in her hair.
—Between the rose-bay and lotus gossip
The great Swan of dreams glides amorously,
Holding Leda in the whiteness of his wings.
—And while Venus, wildly lovely, strolls by,
Arching the splendid rondure of her back,
And proudly displays those large golden breasts,
Her snowy belly arrayed in Black moss,
—Hercules the Tamer, girding his huge frame
In a lionskin like haloed fame, strong,
His brow fierce and benign, strides to the skyline!

Vaguely illumined by the summer moon,
Standing naked, dreaming, pale and gleaming,
Splashed in heavy waves of her long blue hair
In the clearing dark with star-spangled moss,
The Dryad gazes at the silent sky . . .
—Timidly, white Selene floats her veil
Over beautiful Endymion's feet
And throws him a kiss along a moonbeam . . .
—The distant Spring weeps at length in ecstasy . . .
It's the nymph, one elbow on her vase, dreaming
Of the fine pale youth her wave swept on his way . . .
—A breeze of love has passed in the night and
In the sacred wood, in huge majestic
Frightful trees, erect, those dark Marbled Ones,
The Gods, in whose brow the Finch builds his nest,
—The Gods watch Man and the infinite World!

Ophelia

Ophélie

I

On billows calm and black where the stars are sleeping,
The white Ophelia floats like a giant lily,
Floats ever so slowly, resting in her long veils . . .
—One hears in far distant woods the cry of the kill.

For more than a thousand years mournful Ophelia,
White ghost, has passed over the long black river.
For more than a thousand years her gentle madness
Has murmured its romantic song to the evening breeze.

The wind kisses her breasts, unfolds the petals now
Of her wide veils cradled softly by the waters;
The shivering willows weep upon her shoulders,
And the reeds lean over her broad and dreamy brow.

The water lilies, wounded, sigh all around her.
She rouses now and then, in a sleeping alder,
Some nest from which a light flutter of wings escapes.
—A song full of mystery falls from golden stars.

II

O pale Ophelia beautiful so like the snow!
Yes, child, you died, carried off by a river's flow!
—It was the winds dwindling from Norway's high mountains
That spoke so low to you of bitterest freedom.

It was a breath of wind, twisting your long tresses,
That carried strange clamors to your dreaming spirit;

It was your heart, hearing the anthem of Nature
In the groaning of trees and the sighs in the night.

It was the voice of raging seas, immense rattling,
That shattered your childlike heart, too human, too sweet;
It was a pale handsome prince, one April morning,
A wretched madman, who sat mutely at your knees!

Heaven! Love! Freedom! What a dream, oh poor mad Fool!
You melted into him like snowfall in a fire;
Your visions of grandeur strangled your eloquence
—And grim Infinity terrified your blue eye!

III

And the Poet says that by the gleam of starlight
You come to search the night for the flowers you picked,
And that on the flood he saw, couched in her long veils,
The white Ophelia floating, like a great lily.

Dance of the Hanged Men

Bal des pendus

On the darkest gallows, the one-armed pal,
They dance, are dancing, the paladins,
The meager paladins of the devil,
Bony skeletons of Saladins.

Sir Beelzebub yanks them by the necktie,
His small black puppets grinning at the sky,
And slapping their heads with a backhand blow,
Makes them dance there, dance to an old Noël.

And the clashing puppets twine their lank arms,
Like black organ-pipes, their breasts pierced with light,
Where noble damosels once pressed their charms,
Longtime jostling in a love so blighted!

Hurrah! Blithe dancers, with no more bellies,
Caper about, the stages are so wide!
Hop! Whether battle or dance, never mind!
Raging Beelzebub scrapes on his fiddles!

Oh tough heels, never a worn-out sandal!
Almost all are stripped of their shirts of skin;
The rest, an awkward sight, but no scandal.
On the skulls, the snow sets a white chapeau.

The crow's a feather in those crack-brained caps,
A fleshy morsel wags at their meager chin:
One might say, they twirl in shadow combats,
Knights in cardboard armor, rattling, stiff.

Hurrah! At the bones' grand ball, winds whistle!
The black gibbet moans, an iron organ!
Wolves reply from the violet forest:
The sky's red as hell on the horizon.

Hey, shake those crafty funeral wailers
Who with clumsy broken fingers tell their
Rosary of love on pale vertebrae:
Hey, dead ones, this is no monastery!

Oh! Look, in the midst of the dance of death
A great mad skeleton leaps the red sky
In zealous transport, a horse rearing high:
And, feeling the rope still tight on his neck,

Clenches knuckles on his thighbone that cracks
With cries that parallel mocking laughter,
And back into his booth like a juggler,
Rebounds to the song of the bones that dance.

On the darkest gallows, the one-armed pal,
They dance, are dancing, the paladins,
The meager paladins of the devil,
Bony skeletons of Saladins.

The Blacksmith

Le Forgeron

Palace of the Tuileries, around August 10, 1792)
(Palais des Tuileries, vers le 10 Août 92)

Leaning on his mammoth hammer, laughing,
Monstrously tall and drunk, with a big face,
His mouth wide open as a bronze trombone,
And seizing that fat man in his wild-eyed gaze,
The Blacksmith spoke to Louis Sixteenth one day
When the People were there, coiled all around,
Rubbing their dirty sleeves on golden walls.
Now the good king, up on his gut, was pale,
As pale as a victim led to the gallows,
And meek as a dog he never struggled
Because that big-shouldered thug from the forge
Was telling him old saws and stuff so queer
That he's caught by the short hairs, plain and clear!

"Well, King, you'll recall we sang Tra la la
Driving our teams to another's furrow:
How the Priest in the sun told his prayers
On bright rosaries with pieces of gold.
The Lord passed on horseback, fanfares blaring,
And one with a noose, another a whip
Flogged us on.—Dazed as if cow-eyed, our eyes
Could weep no more; and on and on we went.
And when we'd made furrows in the landscape,
When we had left a bit of our own flesh
In this black soil . . . we got a little gift:
Someone set fire to our shacks in the night;
Our little ones like well-done cakes inside.

". . . Oh! I'm not complaining. Stupid story.
Just between us. Feel free to disagree.
But isn't it swell, in June, to see those
Big haywagons rolling into the barns,
To sniff the smell of sprouting things, of orchards
When it rains a little, of hayfields?
To see wheat, and more wheat, ears full of grain,
Thinking what a lot of bread is promised? . . .
Oh! how lively we'd fire up the forge and
Sing joyously hammering the anvil
If we knew we could take a little bit,
Being men, after all, of what God gives!
—But there you go! It's the same old story! . . .

"But now I know! I can't believe any more
When I've got two good hands, my head, my hammer,
That a man got up in cloak and dagger
Can come here and tell me: Boy, sow my land;
Or another can come, when there's a war,
And take my son away, out of my home.
—Now if I were a man and you were the king,
You'd tell me: I want it! . . . Look, it's stupid.
You think I love seeing your splendid barn,
Your gilded officers, your thousand bums,
Your goddam bastards parading like peacocks:
They've scented your nest with our girls' sweat
And little notes to put us in Bastilles,
And we'll say: Fine! let all the poor kneel down:
We'll gild your Louvre, giving our fat pennies!
And you'll get drunk and have a high old time,
—And these Nobles laugh, their butts on our heads.

"No. That garbage dates from our dads' old days!
Oh! the People's a whore no more. Three tries
And all of us pulverized your Bastille.

That beast sweated blood from every stone,
Disgusting, the Bastille while it stood
With its leprous walls that said it all
And still enclosed us in their shadow!
—Citizen! citizen! It was the dark past
Crumbling, gasping its last, when we took the keep!
And there was a kind of Love in our hearts.
We'd embraced our sons, hugged them to our chests.
And like horses, snorting through our nostrils,
We set out strong and proud, our hearts beating . . .
We marched under the sun, heads high—like this—
Into Paris! They met us dressed in rags.
At last! We felt like real Men! We were pale,
Sire, we were drunk with terrible hope:
And when we stood before the black towers
Waving our trumpets and our oak-boughs
With pikes in our hands, we held no hatred:
—We felt so strong, we wanted to go easy!

*   *   *

"Ever since that day we've all gone crazy!
The workers' mob has risen in the streets
And these outcasts, ever-swelling numbers
Of dark shadows, head for the rich man's door.
I run along to lay out informers;
I scour Paris, blackened, hammer shouldered,
Wild-eyed, sweeping fools from every corner—
And if you laugh in my face, I'll kill you!
—Well, you can count on this: it'll cost you
With your men in black who take our demands
And bat them to and fro like tennis balls
And, sly ones! whisper together: 'What dolts!'
To fake some laws, to put out bulletins
Full of cute pink decrees and sugar-pills,
To amuse themselves belittling others—

Then hold their noses when we pass too close,
—Our fine representatives who find us vile!—
To fear nothing, nothing but bayonets . . .
Fine! we've had enough of their snuff-box chat,
We've had enough here of these platter heads
And godly guts. Ah! so that's the dish that
You offer us, middle class, when we're fierce,
Already smashing scepters and croziers! . . ."

He takes him by the arm, rips the velvet
Curtains open and shows him in the square
Below, where it seethes, it seethes and rises,
The horrid mob that roars like an ocean,
Howling like a bitch, howling like the sea,
The mob with clubs and iron pikes, their drums,
Their loud clamoring from markets and slums,
Dark mass of rags spattered with blood-red caps:
The Man, through the open window, shows all
To the pale, sweating king whose knees buckle,
Made sick at the sight!
"That, Sire, is the Scum.
It slobbers at your walls, rises, bubbles:
—It's because they don't eat, Sire, they're beggars!
I'm a blacksmith: and my wife's down there; it's
Nuts! She thinks there's bread in the Tuileries!
—They won't let us in at the bakeries.
I've got three little ones. I'm scum.—I know
Old women who go weeping in their caps
Because their son or daughter's been taken:
They're scum!—One man had been in the Bastille,
Another was a convict: both honest
Citizens. Liberated, they're like dogs:
People spurn them! So they have something here
That hurts them, see! It's terrible, because
Feeling themselves broken, feeling accursed,
There they are now, howling under your nose!

Scum.—Those are the infamous girls down there
Because—you know, women are weak that way—
Milords of the court,—they're always willing—
You've spat on their souls like it was nothing!
Your beauties are down there today. They're scum.

*　　*　　*

"Oh! To all the wretches, those whose backs roast
Under the fierce sun, going on and on,
Feeling their heads burst at this laboring,
Hats off, middle class! Oh! these are the Men.
We're the Workers, Sire! Workers! All for the
Great new era where we'll seek to know,
When Man forges from dawn to dusk, hunter
Of great effects, hunter of great causes,
When, slowly victorious, he'll tame things
And mount them All as he would mount a horse!
Oh, splendid glare of the forges! No more
Evil, no more!—What's yet unknown, even
Though terrible, we'll know! Hammers in hands,
We'll sort what we know: then, Brothers, let's go!
Sometimes we have that great moving dream of
Living simply, ardently, to speak no
Evil, working under the worthy smile
Of a woman loved with a noble love:
And proudly you work all day, and answer
The call of duty like a clarion!
And you're so happy; and no one, above
All—Oh! no one can make you bend a knee!
You have a gun up on the mantlepiece . . .

*　　*　　*

"Oh! But the air's thick with smell of battle.
What'd I tell you? I'm one of the mob!

We've still got informers and greed-mongers
But we're free, we are! We're seized with terror
When we feel so great, oh! great! And just now
I spoke of calm duty, I spoke of home . . .
Just look at the sky!—It's too small for us,
We'd die of heat, we'd be down on our knees!
Just look at the sky!—I'll rejoin the crowd,
Sire, that great scary mob now rolling your
Old cannon over dirty cobblestones:
Ah yes! when we're dead, we will have washed them.
And if, against our cries, against our vengeance
The claws of the old bronzed kings call up their
Troops in full-dress uniform all over France—
Well, wouldn't you all, eh? Shit on those dogs!"

                    *   *   *

—He shouldered his hammer again.
The mob
Standing close to him is wonderstruck and
In the great courtyard and in apartments
Where Paris breathed with a kind of howling,
A shudder shook the vast population.
Then, although it made the pudgy king sweat,
The dread Blacksmith, with superbly huge and
Grimy hand, tossed a red cap on his head!

Tartuffe's Chastisement

Le Châtiment de Tartuffe

Poking, stoking his lovesick heart beneath
His chaste black robe, so happy, hand in glove,
One day as he went, horrifically sweet,
Yellow, drooling his faith from toothless gums,

One day as he went, "Let us pray,"—a Real
Hellion grabbed him by his blessed ear, then
Hurled abuse at him and began to peel
His chaste black robe right off his clammy skin.

Chastisement! . . . With his habit unbuttoned,
The long rosary of pardoned sins one
By one told in his heart, Saint Tartuffe paled! . . .

Then he confessed and prayed, like death he wailed!
Satisfied, the man walked off with his clothes . . .
—Pewh! Tartuffe stark naked from head to toe!

Set to Music

À la musique
Station Square, Charleville

On the square carved into measly grassplots,
Where the trees and flowers line up in lots,
Thursday evenings all the townfolk, wheezing
In the heat, flaunt their rival stupidities.

—Mid-garden, the military band is
Swinging its plumes to the *Waltz of the Fifes:*
—Around them, down front, parade the dandies;
Notaries dangle their graven trifles.

Stockholders in glasses note every blat:
Bloated big-deskers drag their wives so fat
That, like elephant-keepers by their side,
Their women walk with flounces billboard-wide.

The retired grocers' club, on green benches,
Poke the sand with gnarly canes, take a snort
From silver boxes, talk trade agreements
Very gravely, continuing: "In short! . . ."

The globes of his butt spread over the bench,
A town man, button-bright, with Flemish paunch,
Sucks his pipe full of shredded tobacco
Overflowing—black market, don't you know;—

Along the green turf hoodlums jeer and hoot;
And, all horny from when the trombones played,
Simply reeking of roses, raw recruits
Cuddle babies to woo the nursery maid . . .

—Like an unkempt student, I follow sweet
Young girlies under the green chestnut trees:
They know what I'm up to, and turn to me
Laughing, their eyes full of things indiscreet.

I don't say a word: I just keep staring
At their plump white necks, with stray locks twirled:
I follow, under blouse and frail array,
Past their shoulders, the divine dorsal curve.

Soon I've revealed the booty, the stocking . . .
—I re-imagine the flesh, burning with bliss.
They find me queer, they whisper mockery . . .
—And my rough desires fasten on their lips . . .

You Dead of '92

Morts de Quatre-vingt-douze

". . . Frenchman of '70, Conservatives, Liberals, remember your
forefathers in '92 . . . etc."—Paul de Cassagnac *The Nation*

You Dead of Ninety-two and Ninety-Three,
Calm and pale from the rough kiss of liberty,
Who've shattered underfoot the yoke that weighs
On the soul and brow of all humanity;

Exalted men, standing tall when storms rage,
You whose hearts jumped for love underneath rags,
O Soldiers whom Death, proud Lover, has sown
In all the old furrows to make them grow;

You whose blood washed every filthy greatness,
Dead of Italy, Valmy, and Fleurus,
O Christs by the million with soft dark eyes;

We let you sleep alongside the Republic,
We who cringe under kings like a cudgel,
—The Newspapermen rehash your history!

Venus Rising From the Waves

Vénus Anadyomène

From an old green zinc bathtub like a coffin
A woman's brunette head emerges, slow
And stupid, and heavily pomaded,
With its bald spots rather badly hidden.

Then the neck shows gross and grey, the broad flab
Shoulder blades, the squat back bunching bulges;
Then the rounding butt seems ready to soar,
The underskin blubber in leafy slabs.

The backbone blushes a little, the whole thing reeks,
Weirdly horrific; you notice especially
The oddities you'll need a jeweler's loupe to see . . .

Two engraved words on the ass: *Clara Venus;*
—And all of that flesh moves, thrusting its big rump,
Hideous beauty with a cankered anus.

First Evening

Première soirée

She was very nearly undressed now
And the big trees curiously
Beat their leaves against the window,
Closer and closer, knowingly.

Half-naked in my great big chair
She sat with hands clasped together.
Her tiny feet so fine, so fair
Shuddered on the floor in pleasure.

—I watched a little hopalong
Glint the color of a wax-light
Fluttering on her smile and on
Her breasts—On the roses, a fly.

—I kissed her delicate ankles.
She gave a laugh, sweet and brutal,
In a husky spill of clear trills,
A pretty laugh made of crystal.

Her quick little feet absconded
Underneath her slip: "Hey, stop it!"
—My first bold move permitted,
Her laugh pretends to punish it.

—I kissed her gently on the eyes,
Poor trembling things beneath my touch.
—She tossed her head back with a sigh
Of roguery: "Oh, you're too much! . . .

"Mister, we need to have a chat . . ."
—What was left I lay on her breast
In a kissing that made her laugh
The good laugh willing all the rest . . .

—She was very nearly undressed now
And the big trees curiously
Beat their leaves against the window,
Closer and closer, knowingly.

What Nina Said

Les Réparties de Nina

15 August 1870

HE: Your breast on my chest,
Hey? we could go,
Filling our nostrils with air,
Into the cool rays

Of lovely morning blue that bathes
You in the wine of day? . . .
When the whole shivering wood bleeds
Mute with love

From every branch, green droplets,
Bright buddings,
You sense in open things
The quivering flesh:

You'd plunge into the alfalfa
Your white peignoir,
Turning rosy in the azured air
Around your huge dark eyes,

Amorous for the countryside,
Scattering everywhere
Your playful laughter,
Like foaming champagne:

Laughing at me, roughly drunken,
Who'd catch you
Like this—by your lovely hair,
Oh!—who'd drink up

Your taste of raspberry, strawberry,
O flowery flesh!
Laughing at the quick wind kissing you
Like a thief,

At the wild rose pricking you
Pleasantly:
Laughing most of all, oh madcap,
At your lover! . . .

(Seventeen! You'll be so happy!
Oh! the grand meadows,
The great loving countryside!
—Come on, get closer! . . .)

Your breast on my chest,
Mingling our voices,
Slowly, we'd reach the ravine,
Then the tall woods! . . .

Then, like a lifeless little thing,
Heart swooning,
You'd let me carry you
With eyes half-closed . . .

I'd carry you quivering,
Along the pathway:
The bird would spin its andante:
By the Hazeltree . . .

I'll speak to you in your mouth;
I'll go on, pressing
Your body like a child at bedtime,
Drunk on the blood

That runs blue under your skin,
White with rosy tones:
And speak to you with a bold tongue . . .
There! . . . —so you know . . .

Our lofty woods'll smell of sap,
And the sun will
Shower gold-dust on their tall, green
And vermilion dream.

                    *   *   *

Evening? . . . We'll take the white
Road again, which
Meanders in every direction
Like a grazing flock . . .

The fine orchards of blue grass
And gnarly apple trees!
How their strong perfume can be
Scented a league away!

We'll get back to the village
Under a twilit sky;
And the smell of milking will fill
The evening air;

It will smell of the stable, full
Of warm manure,
Full of the slow rhythm of breathing
And broad backs

Turning white under whatever light;
And yonder,

A cow proudly crapping
At every step . . .

—Grandma's glasses
And her long nose
In her prayerbook; the pot of beer
Circled in pewter,

Foaming among the big pipes
Fearlessly fuming;
The scary big lips
Which, while puffing,

Snap up forkfuls of ham
So much, much more:
The fire brightening the bedsteads
And the cupboards.

The plump shiny buttocks
Of the fat baby
Who crawls about nuzzling cups
With his pale snout

Tickled by a growling muzzle
Soft and gentle,
Licking the chubby face
Of the little dear . . .

(Dark, haughty on the edge of her chair,
With a frightening profile,
An old woman keeps to her spinning
In front of the embers.)

What things we'll see, sweetie,
In these hovels

When the flames brightly illuminate
Those grimy windowpanes! . . .

—Then, little and nestled
Among the lilies
Dark and cool: the hidden window
Laughing over there . . .

You'll come, you'll come! I love you!
It'll be so fine!
You will come, won't you? even so . . .
SHE:—*And lose my job?*

The Runaways

Les Effarés

20 September 1870

Dark against the snow and fog,
At the big lit-up vent,
Their butts in a huddle,

Five urchins, kneeling—wretched!—
Watch the Baker making
Loaves of heavy blond bread.

They see the strong white arm knead
It and shove the raw dough
Into the oven's bright hole.

They hear the good bread baking,
The baker with a fat smile
Growling an old ditty.

They crouch there, not one budging,
At the red grating's breath
Just as warm as a breast.

When, shaped like buttery tarts
For some midnight party,
The bread is brought on out,

When, under the smoke-stained beams,
The fragrant crusts are singing
Along with the crickets,

When life breathes out from that warm hole,
Their souls are so enraptured
Under their ragged clothes,

They feel such lively bliss, those
Poor frostbitten Jesuses,
That they all gather close,

Gluing their pink little snouts
To the grating, mumbling
Such nonsense round about,

All foolish, at their prayers,
Hunkering toward that light
From heaven bright and fair,

So hard they split their pants,
And their shirt-tails flutter
In the winds of winter.

Romantic Fiction

Roman

29 September 1870

I

Nobody's ever serious at seventeen.
One fine evening,—screw the beer and the lemonade
And the rowdy cafés with lamplight glittering!
—You stroll beneath green lime trees on the promenade.

The lime trees smell nice in the lovely June evenings!
You close your eyelids, the air is so sweet at times,
The wind laden with noise—the town isn't far off—
Carries the scent of beer, the bouquet of the vines . . .

II

—There you can see, encircled by a frame of twigs,
The tiniest little patch of dark blue sky
Punctured by a mischievous little star, so white,
That melts away, dissolving in a trembling sigh . . .

A night in June! And seventeen!—It's all too much.
The champagne, like sap rising, making your head spin . . .
And you ramble on; you sense a kiss on your lips
That palpitates right there, like a little varmint . . .

III

The lovesick heart's a Crusoe tramping through novels,
—When, in the clarity of a streetlamp's glimmer,

A young miss full of dainty airs goes passing by
Under the shadow of her dad's ugly collar . . .

And because she considers you vastly naïve,
While she trots her little booties at quite a clip,
She turns away abruptly, so lively and quick . . .
Just then—as cavatinas die on your lips . . .

IV

You are in love. Leased out through the month of August.
You are in love.—Your sonnets only make Her laugh.
All your friends have taken off, you're a *real mess.*
—Then, one evening, SHE deigns to send her autograph . . . !

—That evening . . . you head back to the flashy cafés—
You ask for a glass of beer or some lemonade . . .
—Nobody's ever serious at seventeen,
Not when the lime trees are green on the promenade.

Evil

Le Mal

While the red spit of the machine-gunning
Whistles all day through the endless blue sky;
While scarlet and green, at their King's jeering,
Whole battalions crumble into that fire;

While an appalling madness pulverizes
Thousands of men into a smoking heap;
—Poor dead! in summer, in the grass, your delight,
O Nature! who made these men righteously! . . .

There is a God, who laughs at damask sheets
On altars, incense, and golden goblets,
Who, to lulling Hosannas, falls asleep,

And wakes right up when mothers in anguish,
Huddling and weeping in their black bonnets,
Offer him pennies tied in their hankies!

Angry Caesars

Rages de Césars

The pale Man strolls among flowering lawns,
Dressed in black, a cigar between his teeth:
The pale Man recalls blooming Tuileries
—Now and then his dull eye looks feverish.

Caesar's had his twenty-year drunken spree!
He told himself: "I'll snuff out Liberty
Like a candle, oh-so delicately!"
Liberty lives again! He feels worn out.

He's jailbound—Oh! what name is trembling on
His sealed lips? What's his relentless regret?
We'll never know. Great Caesar's eye is dead.

Perhaps he recalls his Pal in glasses . . .
—And watches, rising from his lit cigar,
A fine blue cloud, like nights at the Palace.

Dreaming Towards Winter

Rêvé pour l'hiver

(7 October 1870, on the train—"To . . . Her")

Winterbound, we'll go in a tiny tram all rosy,
It's got blue cushions.
We'll be cozy. A nest of wild kisses reposing
In each plush corner.

You'll close your eyes, not to see, through the glass,
The evening's grimacing shadows,
Those snarling monstrosities, populace
Of murky demons, murky wolves.

You'll feel a scratch on your cheek next . . .
A little kiss, like a crazy spider
Running all around your neck . . .

And bending your head, you'll tell me: "Catch it!"
—And we'll take our time at finding that beast
—Who travels quite a bit . . .

The Sleeper in the Valley

Le Dormeur du val

October 1870

In the hollow green where the river sings
Crazily catching silver tatters in
The grass; where the sun, from the proud mountain,
Shines: a little valley sparkles gleaming.

A young soldier, mouth agape, head bare, sleeps
With his nape awash in the cool blue cress.
Under clouds, he is sprawled on the grass,
Pale in his green bed where the light weeps.

His feet among the glads, he sleeps. Smiling
The smile of a sickly child, he's napping.
Nature, cradle him warmly: he is chill.

The sweetest smell won't tickle his nostril;
He sleeps in sunlight, hand on tranquil breast.
On the right side, two red holes in his chest.

At the Green Cabaret

(Five o'clock in the afternoon)
Au Cabaret-vert

20 September 1870

After a week, I had shredded my boots
On the stones of the road. I came on foot
To Charleroi.—At the Green Cabaret:
I ordered cold ham and bread right away.

Feeling good, I stretched out my legs under
The green table: while I gazed in wonder
At the bric-a-brac:—And the charming sight
When the waitress with big tits and blue eyes,

—One of those girls who aren't scared of a kiss!—
Smilingly brought me the bread and butter
And cooling ham on a painted platter,

Pink and white ham, fragrant with garlic bits!
And she filled my huge beer mug whose foaming
Was gilded in the sunshine's last gleaming.

The Sly One

La Maline

Charleroi, October 1870

In the dark dining room, relaxing where
It was fragrant with fruit-smells and varnish,
I scooped up a plate of some Belgian dish
Or other, sprawled in my enormous chair.

While I ate, I heard the clock,—snug and happy.
The kitchen door opened, with a breezy show,
—And the servant girl came in, for what I don't know,
With her blouse undone, her hair untidy.

And, wagging her little finger about
Her cheek, a velvet peach of pink and white,
Making a face, lips in a childish pout,

She cleared the plates for me, and standing close,
—Just like that—for a kiss, of course, quite low
Says: "Feel it: my cheek's caught a little *cold!*"

The Dazzling Victory at Saarebrück

L'Éclatante Victoire de Saarebrück

Won to shouts of Long Live the Emperor!
(Brilliantly colored Belgian print, on sale in Charleroi, 35 cents)

Spot on, in a blaze of blue and yellow
Glory, the Emperor jogs his gaudy
Hobbyhorse: so happy—vision rosy,
Fierce as Zeus and gentle as a daddy.

Below, the good Recruits who've been snoozing
Near the gilded drums and red-hot cannon
Rise up nicely. Pitt puts his vest back on
And, facing the Chief, is fame-struck, woozy.

Right, Mooney leans on the butt of his gun
And, feeling his neck-hairs bristle, shouts: "Long
Live the Emperor!"—His neighbor stays mum . . .

A plumed hat looms, like a black sun . . . —On the spot,
Red and blue, on his belly, blunt Bowles rears up
And—showing his ass—blurts: "Emperor of what?" . . .

The Cupboard

Le Buffet

Here's a huge carved cupboard; its old, dark oak
Has taken on the glow of elder folk.
It stands open, with fragrance as fine
In the shadows as a flood of old wine.

Jam-packed, it's a jumble of odds and ends,
Of yellowing scented linens, trinkets
From women or children, faded remnants
Of grandma's lace embroidered with griffins.

There you'll find the medallions, and snippets
Of blond or snowy hair, portraits, dried flowers
Whose fragrance blends with fruited fragrances.

O cupboard of old, so many stories
And tales ready to be told, and you moan
When your vast black doors open slowly.

My Gypsy Life (A Fantasy)

Ma Bohème (Fantaisie)

With fists in ragged pockets, off I went—
My topcoat too on its way to ideal.
I traveled under skies, muse, your vassal!
Oh! look now! what sumptuous loves I dreamt!

My only trousers were hugely holey.
—A dreamy Tom Thumb I, seeding rhymes there
Along my way:—I stayed at the Big Bear.
The stars above rustled softly for me,

And I heard them, sitting roadside
In the fine September twilight,
Felt dewdrops on my face like heady wine;

Where amid fantastic shadows I'd rhyme,
While plucking at the laces, like a harp,
On my battered shoes, one foot near my heart!

The Crows

Les Corbeaux

Lord, when the grasslands have grown cold,
When, in villages battered flat,
Tedious bells no longer toll . . .
Over nature there deflowered,
Let the sleek sweet body of crows
Swoop down out of wide open skies.

Outlandish army with harsh cries,
Chill winds are assailing your nests!
Disperse, along yellow rivers,
On roads toward old Calvarys,
Over the ditches and trenches,
All of you, scatter and rally!

By thousands, over fields of France,
Where the dead of yesterday sleep,
Wheel 'round, why don't you, in winter
So each passer-by remembers!
Be then the designated spokesman,
Our black bird of the funerals.

You, skyborne saints, high in the oak,
Tree-top lost in spellbound twilight:
Leave be the singing birds of May,
For those in depth of woods held tight
Under the grass of no escape,
Defeated, with no future day.

The Sitters

Les Assis

Swarthy knobbed and pocked, eyes ringed with green bags,
Swollen fingers on bony thighs like claws,
Their bald pates caked with a crusty vagueness
Like a leprous flowering on old walls;

In amorous fits they've grafted their weird
Bag of bones to the black skeletal husk
Of their chairs; their feet interlacing the
Rickety railings from daylight till dusk!

These geezers have always merged with their chairs,
Feeling the bright sun blotch their skin with nodes,
Or, eyes to windowpanes where the snows fade,
Shivering the sad shivering of toads.

And their Seats take a shine to them: breeched in
Brown, the straw gives in to their butts' indent;
The spirit of old sunlight glows wrapped up
In those braided strips of wheat fermenting.

The Sitters, knees to teeth, green pianists,
Drumming their ten fingers under their seats,
Hear each other's chopping sad barcaroles,
Their noggins rocking in amorous beats.

Oh! don't make them get up! That's a shipwreck . . .
They rise, like growling tomcats slapped about,
Slowly widening shoulders, mad as heck!
The whole swollen seat of their pants puffed out.

You can hear their bald heads bumping against
Dark walls, gnarled feet stamping, stamping always,

And their coat-buttons are tawny eyeballs
Staring into your eyes from deep hallways!

Then, they've an invisible killing hand:
On the way back, their gaze drips that black spite
Which floods the whipped bitch's suffering eye,
And you sweat, caught in that funnel of night.

Reseated, their fists plunged in filthy cuffs,
They muse on those who have made them get up,
And dawn till dusk, under their meager chins
Bunched wattles quiver as if they'd blow up.

When severe sleep has pulled their eyeshades low,
They dream, cradled in arms, of pregnant seats,
Of little true-love chairs with open legs
Bordering haughty desks on edge, in heat;

Flowers of ink spurt commas like pollen,
Like dragonflies buzzing rows of iris,
Lulling them, along the squat flowerpots
—And the prickly straw stiffens their penis.

Faun's Head

Tête de faune

Among the leaves, green jewelbox daubed in gold,
Among the restless foliage, blooming
With splendid flowers wherein kisses doze,
Vivid and rending the fine tapestry,

A startled faun, presenting both his eyes,
Nibbles on red blossoms with his white teeth.
As ruddy and sanguine as an old wine
His lips burst out laughing through boughs beneath.

And when he's taken flight—like a squirrel—
His laughter still quivers on every leaf,
And you can see, made fearful by a finch,
The Woodland's golden Kiss contemplative.

The Customs Men

Les Douaniers

Those who say: foo'cue, those who swear: By G—
Retired soldiers, sailors, Empire's debris,
Are nothing next to the Border Patrols
Who slash the frontier blue with hatchet blows.

Pipes clenched in teeth, blades in hand, stout, carefree,
When woods drool shadows like a bovine snout,
They go, with dogs on leash, to march about
Nightly in their terrible revelry!

They subject the fauness to modern laws.
They collar Fausts and Fra Diavolos.
"Hold it, old timers! Put the knapsacks down!"

When her majesty runs youngsters to ground,
The Customs Man grabs fleshy contraband!
Hell for the Delinquents frisked by his hand!

Evening Prayer

Oraison du soir (1871)

I live parked, like an angel in a barber's chair,
In my fist a fluted thick mug of beer,
My gullet and gut bend curving, pipe here
Clenched in teeth, veiled in puffs of impalpable air.

Like the dung in some old dovecot, simmering,
Countless Dreams within me gently smolder.
Soon enough my sad heart's like a sapling
Running bloody tears of young and sullen gold.

Then, when I've thoroughly damped down my Dreams,
I turn, after thirty or forty beers,
And address my prayers to a pressing need.

Easy as the Lord of cedar and of hyssops,
I piss to the dark skies, up high and oh-so far,
To the nodding assent of great heliotropes.

Parisian War Song

Chant de guerre parisien

Spring's here, it's clear to see, because,
From the heart of green Proprieties
The flight of Tears and Pickard holds
Wide open its resplendencies.

May! What bare-butt delirium!
Severs, Mutton, Bagnose, Assinair,
Listen to their rousing welcome
Now, as they sow the Springtime air!

They've got shako, swords, and tom-tom,
Not any old box of tampons,
And skiffs that've nev . . . nev . . . never
Cleft the lake of ruddy waters!

We're up to some rough and tumble
When they come rushing us in swarms,
Yellow boneheads crack and crumble
During those peculiar dawns:

Tears! Pickard! heroic Cupids,
Abductors of heliotropes;
They do Corots in gasoline:
See their buzzing fluttering tropes . . .

They're buddies with Biggus Trickus!
. . . And, bedded with gladiolas,
Mister Favor winks aqueducts
In a peppered snivelling fuss!

The Big City's pavement is hot
Despite your gasoline showers,
And, definitely, our what's what
Is the shakeup of your powers . . .

And the Farmboys, who are lounging
In the long squatting tedium,
Will listen for branches crashing
In the midst of red-hot mayhem.

My Loving Little Women

Mes Petites Amoureuses

An essence of teardrop
Washes cabbage-green skies:
Under the dripping, tenderly budding tree . . .
Your india rubbers

Whitened by peculiar moons
With goggle-eyed gaze,
Knock your knees together,
My ugly babes!

Those were the days we loved each other,
Blue ugly babe!
We used to eat hard-boiled eggs
And salad greens!

One evening, you anointed me poet,
Blonde ugly babe:
Get down here between my knees
So I can spank you.

I've puked in your pomaded hair,
Black ugly babe;
You'd interrupt my mandolin
Strum head-on.

Pwew! my dried saliva,
Red ugly babe,
Still pollutes the wrinkles
In your curving breast!

Oh my loving little women
How I hate you!
Plaster them with sorrowing zits,
Your ugly tits!

Trample my ancient crock
Of sentiment:
—Hop to it! Be my ballerinas
For a minute! . . .

Your shoulder blades turn awry,
O my loves!
A star for your limping loins
Turning your turns.

And yet it's for these lambchops
That I've rhymed!
I'd like to crack your hips
For the love they find!

Dull heap of burnt-out stars,
Pile up at the junctions!
You'll flare out in God, loaded
With vile compunction,

Under these peculiar moons
With goggle-eyed gaze,
Knock your knees together,
My ugly babes!

Squattings

Accroupissements

Very late, when he feels his gut sicken,
Brother Milo shifts his priestly belly
In the bedsheets, an eye on the skylight
Where the sun, shining like a scoured skillet,
Shoots him a migraine, dazzling his eyesight.

He toils and moils under his gray blanket
And gets out, with knees to his quaking gut,
Spooked like a geezer who's swallowed his snuff,
Because, with his fist gripping the white pot,
He's got to hoist his nightshirt on the spot.

Well, there he squats, chilly, his toes curled up,
Shivering in the bright sunshine plating
Yellow cake on the paper windowpanes;
The old boy's nose, where the lacquer lights up
Sniffs at sunbeams, like a carnal polyp.

*   *   *

The old boy seethes at the fire, arms twisted,
Big lip to his paunch: he feels his thighs glide
Into the fire, his scorched pants, his unlit pipe.
Something like a bird flutters deep inside
His tranquil belly like a pile of tripe!

All around, heaps of beat-up furniture
Sleep, greasy rags over dirty bellies;
Strange toads, footstools huddle in dark corners:
Cupboards have the open jaws of choirboys
Gaping in a sleep full of horrid hungers.

That sickening heat swells the narrow room.
The old boy's brain is crammed with odds and ends:
He hears the stubble sprout in his damp skin.
And then, in clownish loud belches of gloom,
He lets go, rattling his wobbly stool . . .

*   *   *

And in the evening, while drooling moonshine
Gleaming traces the contour of buttocks,
A detailed shadow squats, on a backdrop
Of rosy snow, like a hollyhock . . .
Fantastic, a nose tracks Venus through deep skies.

The Seekers of Lice

Les Chercheuses de poux

Just when the child's head, full of squirming red,
Implores the pallid swarm for shady dreams,
Two charming tall sisters approach his bed
With slender fingers, silver nails agleam.

The window open wide, they seat the child
Where the blue breeze bathes the flowery wild,
And through his thick hair where the red ooze drips
They walk their grim, beguiling fingertips.

He listens to their anxious breath singing,
Smelling of honeyed rose plants lingering,
Stopped sometimes by saliva-wet hisses
On the lip, or a desire for kisses.

He hears their dark lashes beat in fragrant
Silences; their sweet electric fingers
Crackling amid his woozy indolence,
Their queenly nails bring death to tiny lice.

How the wine of Languor in him rises,
Harmonica sighs, like to bring fevered sleep;
The child feels, under their slow caresses,
An endless, welling, dying desire to weep.

The Sisters of Mercy

Les Soeurs de charité

That bright-eyed youth of twenty, with brown, lovely skin,
A body made to be naked—he would've been
Idolized in Persia, with his copper halo,
Under the moon, a Genie incognito,

Impetuous with a deliciousness dark and
Virginal, prideful of his primitive insights,
Like those youthful seas, the tears of summer nights,
That turn themselves back into beds of diamonds;

That youth, who's out there facing this world's ugliness,
Shudders in his heart so far and widely vexed
And, drunk with deep and everlasting injury,
Harbors a desire for his sister of mercy.

But, Woman: O heap of feelings, delicious woe,
You can never be The Sister of Mercy: No,
Not the darkest look, nor sleepy slit's red shadow,
Nor fingering nimbly, nor glorious torso.

Blind unwaking beauty with your eyes open wide:
All of our coupling here is merely a query,
It's you, left holding your breasts, who cling to our side
And we rock you: delightful, serious Fury.

Your hates, your passive traits, your oversights
And the brutalities you endured long ago,
We get it all back—like Night, without spite,
Like an excess of blood, a monthly overflow.

When women transport him swiftly from fearfulness
To Love—the call to life, the anthem of action,—
Here come the green-eyed Muse and flaming Righteousness
To thrash him royally in their proud obsession.

Ah! forever thirsty for splendors and some calms,
Cast aside by those two ruthless Sisters, groaning
Tenderly for the knowledge of wide open arms,
He brings his bloodshot brow to Nature's flowering.

But alchemy's darkness and holy doctorates
Repel this wounded, somber sage of arrogance:
He senses grim solitude's relentless advance.
Then, as beautiful as ever, no grave distaste.

Just let him believe in vast finales, immense
Dreams or Journeys, traversing night's Reality
—And he will call you in his soul and stricken limbs,
O mystery of Death, oh sister of mercy!

The Righteous Man

L'Homme Juste

*   *   *

The Righteous Man sat up on his fat hams:
A sunbeam gilded his shoulder; I swam
In sweat: "So! You'd like to see gleaming red
Meteors? to stand and hear humming floods
Of milky ways and swarming asteroids?

"The farces of night are counting your hairs,
Righteous Man! Run for cover. Say your prayers,
Chewing your bedsheet in sweet atonement.
And if some vagrant knocks on your boneyard,
Say: Brother, just go away, I'm crippled!"

And the Righteous Man stood still, in the dread
Of pale blue lawns after the sun went dead:
"So you'd put your knee-pads up for sale, hey
Old Man? Blest pilgrim! Bard of Brittany!
Olive weeper, hand in glove with pity!

"Family whiskers and fist of the city,
Sweet Believer! Heart fallen in its cups,
Majesty, virtue, and love blindfolded,
Right Man!—dull and ugly as mongrel pups—
And I'm the one suffers, who revolted!

"And it makes my belly weep to laugh, jerk,
The famous hope of your pardon! I'm cursed
And you know it! I'm smashed, mad, and livid,
You name it! But now you go back to bed,
Right Man! I want nothing from you, you're brain-dead!

*   *   *

"You're Right, you are, Right Man! Isn't that plenty.
It's true that all your calm good intentions
Snivel mightily in the night, like whales—
That you stand off-limits, spouting laments
In a frightful, broken-down quacking wail.

"And you're the eye of God! You slug! When the
Frozen soles of Holy feet tread my neck,
You're a coward! O your wits swarm with nits!
Socrates and Jesus, holy and just, just puke.
Spare the Devil supreme these bloodshot nights."

*   *   *

"Ahh! let him go! Him, with necktie a noose
Of shame, always worrying my boredom,
As sweet as sugar on a rotten tooth . . .
—Like the bitch after a tiff with rough pooches
Licks her flank where a flap of gut hangs loose . . .

*   *   *

Forget progress and filthy charities . . .
—I despise all those paunchy chinese eyes,
The singalong: yum yum, like babes ready
To die, sweet idiots sing suddenly:
O Righteous Ones, we'll crap in your crock-pot guts!"

*   *   *

I have cried this to the earth, and the calm
White night filled the sky during my fever.
I looked up again: the phantom had flown,

Taking my lips' dreadful irony with him:
Night winds, visit the outcast. Speak to him!

Meanwhile, silently through blue colonnades,
As far as comets and the tangled hitch
Of the universe, huge motion unbroken,
Order, eternal watchman, rows through glowing skies
And from his fiery dragnet pays a line of stars.

First Communion

Les Premières Communions

July 1871

I

Stupid, really, these village churches where
Fifteen ugly brats, fouling the pillars,
Listen to the holy rolling babble
Of a freak in black with festering shoes:
But, there through the leaves, the sun awakens
The ancient colors of random stained glass.

The stone still smells of its maternal earth.
You can see heaps of these dirty flintstones
Out in the solemn rustling fields in rut,
Near the bending wheat, ochre paths, laden
With blazing bushes where the plums turn blue,
Black mulberries tangle and roses run.

Every century they dress up these barns
With a coat of blueing and curdled milk:
If mystic freakshows are worth a look-see,
Next to the Madonna or the stuffed Saint,
Flies reeking sweetly of pub and stables
Gorge themselves on wax on the sunlit floor.

The child is duty-bound to house and home,
Whose needs are plain, whose chores are drudgery.
They go, forgetting how their skin tingles
Where the Priest of Christ laid mighty fingers.
The Priest gets a shady trellis from which
He sends all those tanned mugs into the sun.

The first black suit, the best pastry all day,
Some color print beneath Napoleon
Or The Drummer Boy where the Josephs and
Marthas stick out their tongues in excessive
Love, joined on science day by two maps, these
Their sole sweet mementos of the great Day.

The girls always go to church, pleased enough
To hear themselves called sluts by the boys who
Strut their stuff after Mass or Evensong.
These boys are destined for garrison ways,
Sneering in the cafe at uptown folk,
New jackets, and yowling horrible songs.

Meanwhile, for the kids, the Priest picks out some
Pictures. In his garden, with vespers done,
When the air fills with far-off thrums of dance
He feels it, despite heavenly taboos,
His toes enraptured while his calves keep time
—Night comes, black pirate docked in golden skies.

II

Among the catechizers gathered there
From all over town, the Priest has noticed
That strange little sad-eyed girl with sallow brow.
Her parents look like humble caretakers.
"On the great Day, chosen above the rest,
God will snow blessings down upon this head."

III

The night before the great Day, she falls ill.
And like dismal murmurs during high Church,

The shivers come on first—the bed's untamed—
A superhuman chill refrains: "I die . . ."
Like stealing love from her stupid sisters
She counts, exhausted, with hands on her heart,
Angels, Jesuses, and gleaming Virgins:
Calmly then, her soul drinks up her captor.

Adonai! . . . —In the endings of Latin
Watered skies of green bathe scarlet Faces
And, streaked with purest blood from celestial
Breasts, great snowy linens cover the suns.

—For her virginities now and to come
She bites the coolness of Thy Remission;
Yet more than waterlilies, more than sweets,
Your pardon freezes, O Queen of Zion!

IV

The Virgin then is just the virgin of
The book: Mystic ardor breaks down sometimes . . .
And see, the poverty of images,
Boredom bronzed, vile colored prints, old woodcuts.

A vaguely shameless curiosity
Spooks her dream of the chaste kinds of blueness
Suddenly stripping away heavenly tunics,
The linen veiling Jesus' nakedness.

She's yearning, yearning, now, distressed soul,
Her face in the pillow pierced with dull sobs
Prolonging the last shocks of tenderness,
Drooling . . . —Shadows fill the houses and yards,

And she can bear it no longer. She stirs,
Arching her loins, and parts the blue curtain

With one hand letting some of the room's cool
Breeze under the sheet, her body on fire.

V

On waking—it's midnight—the window's white.
Beyond the moonlit curtain of blue sleep
Visions of Sunday's purity gripped her:
She had dreamt of red. Her nose was bleeding.

And feeling so chaste and weak, in order
To savor her love returning to God,
She thirsts for night, where the heart's exalted
And humbled, under the gaze of soft skies;

For night—impalpable Virgin Mother—
Bathes all young feelings in its grey stillness;
She thirsted for strong night, where the bleeding
Heart lets flow unwitnessed her mute revolt.

And playing the Victim and little bride
Her star has watched her with candle in hand,
Passing the yard where a shirt hangs drying,
White ghost, raising black ghosts on the rooftops.

VI

She spent her blessed night in the privy.
The candle guttered, a pale breeze flowing
Through holes in the roof where some wild purple
And blackish vine spilled over from next door.

The skylight made a heart of live brightness
In the yard where low skies plated windows

Ruddy gold; pavement stank of wash-water,
Brimstone shadows on dark walls crammed with sleep.

VII

Who'll speak for lethargy, this foul pity,
The hatred she'll feel, O dirty madmen
Whose divine work still deforms whole worlds, when
Leprosy eats that sweet body at last?

VIII

Repressing her tangled hysteria
She sees, through the sorrows that come of joy,
The love dream of a million white Marys
In light of the morning after, sadly:

"Don't you know I've done you to death? I took
Your mouth, your heart, everything, all you have.
It's made me sick: Oh! lay me down among
The Dead who've steeped in the waters of night.

"I was really young; Christ tainted my breath.
He stuffed me to the gullet with loathing!
And then you kissed my hair as thick as wool
And I let you . . . Ah! there, it's good for you,

"Men! who so little dream that beneath her
Conscience debased with fears, the most loving
Woman is more than whored and more than sad,
And all our zest for You is heresy!

"So my first Communion is now done for.
Your kiss, I will never know: For my heart
And my flesh in your flesh's embrace will
Tingle with the putrid kiss of Jesus!"

IX

Then the rotten soul and the dismal soul
Will feel your curses as they drip on down.
They will lie with your inviolate Hate
Having lost, for death, all righteous passions.

Christ! Oh Christ, eternal thief of energies,
God who for two thousand years now has granted
Your pallor to the brows of anguished women,
Thrown or nailed to the ground by shame and headache.

Parisian Orgy *or* Paris Repopulated

L'Orgie parisienne ou *Paris se repeuple*

May 1871

O cowards! there she is! Mob the stations!
The sun's hot breath swept the boulevards clean,
One evening, of thronging barbarians.
Look, the holy City, in the sunset!

Come! we'll stay ahead of the ebbing fires,
Here the quays, here the boulevards, here the
Houses against the radiant light blue
That had, one evening, blushing bombs for stars!

Hide the dead mansions in boarded-up holes.
The ghastly twilight refreshes your eyes.
Here come the troupe of hip-wriggling red-heads:
Go mad! you'll be as loony as you're wild-eyed!

Bloody bandage-eating bitches in heat,
The golden houses cry out to you. Steal!
Eat! See the joyous night of darkest spasms
Down in the street. O desolate drinkers,

Drink up! When the light comes, madly intense,
To probe the gushing splendors at your sides,
Won't you be drooling in your cups, wordless,
Motionless, eyes lost in blank distances?

Drink, to the Queen of torrential buttocks!
Hear the skirmish of stupid heart-rending
Hiccups! Hear them leap through fiery nights, the
Panting idiots, geezers, puppets, dupes!

O hearts of garbage, terrifying mouths,
Work harder, you mouths of stinking grossness!
Wine for those lowlife slugs at these tables . . .
Your bellies melt with shame, O conquerors!

Open your nose to this gorgeous nausea!
Drench the ropes on your necks with strong poison!
With his crossed hands draped on your childish napes,
The Poet tells you: "O cowards, go mad!"

Because you probe the belly of Woman
You fear another convulsion from her
That cries out, smothering your vile nuzzling
At her breast, with an ugly compression.

Syphilitics, loons, kings, ventriloquists,
Puppets, what are you to Paris the whore?
Your souls or bodies, your poisons and rags?
She will shake you off, snarling poxy dogs!

And when you're down on your bellies, whining,
Demanding your money back, dazed and spent,
The big-breasted red harlot of battles
Remote from your stupor swings a hard fist.

When your feet danced so fiercely in anger,
Paris! when you took so many knifings,
Laid out flat, retaining in your bright eyes
A bit of the shine from tawny springtime,

O city in pain, O half-dead city,
Both head and breasts aiming for the Future,
Its billion gates open to your pallor,
City whom the gloomy Past could bless:

Body remagnetized for immense pain,
You drink up horrid life again! you feel
The flux of pale worms rising in your veins
And your pure love prowled by icy fingers.

And it's harmless. The worms, the livid worms
Will no more stop the breath of your Progress
Than Stryx could snuff the Caryatids' eye
From whose blue degree fell starry tears of gold.

Though it's dreadful to see you overcast
Like this again; though never a city
Was a more putrid sore on Nature's green,
The Poet tells you: "What Splendid Beauty!"

Disorder consecrates your poetry
Supreme; those huge moiling forces aid you;
Your work boils and death growls, chosen City!
Hoard the shrill of dull trumpets in your heart.

The Poet will take the sobs of Ill-fame,
Hate from Convicts, the clamor of the Damned,
And his rays of love will scourge the Women.
His verses lash out: There! take that! bandits!

—All society restored:—the orgies
Weep their old last gasp in the old brothels:
And gaslights in a sinister frenzy
Flare up reddening walls to lurid skies!

The Tortured Heart

Le Coeur supplice

May 1871

My sad heart's drooling at the poop,
My heart drenched in tobacco-spit:
They spit on it in streams of soup,
My sad heart's drooling at the poop:
Under the jeering of the troop
Who burst out laughing at it,
My sad heart's drooling at the poop,
My heart drenched in tobacco-spit:

Fishy-phallic and soldier-blue
Their dirty jokes debauch it!
The sternpost scrawled with frescoes too,
Fishy-phallic and soldier-blue.
Abracadabra-like billows
O take my heart and wash it!
Fishy-phallic and soldier-blue
Their dirty jokes debauch it!

When they have spent their wad of quid,
O stolen heart, what's to do?
They'll belch like the Hiccupping Kid
When they have spent their wad of quid,
My queasy gut will flop and flip
If my weeping heart's abused:
When they have spent their wad of quid,
O stolen heart, what's to do?

The Clownish Heart

Le Coeur du Pitre

June 1871

My sad heart slobbers at the poop,
My heart full of tobacco-spit:
They spurt their juice in jets of soup,
My sad heart slobbers at the poop:
Under the jeering of the troop
While they burst out laughing at it,
My sad heart slobbers at the poop,
My heart full of tobacco-spit.

Fishy-phallic and soldier-blue
Their abuses have debauched it!
Vesperal frescoes daubed there too,
Fishy-phallic and soldier-blue.
Abracadabra-like billows
O take my heart and wash it!
Fishy-phallic and soldier-blue
Their abuses have debauched it!

When they have used up all their quid,
O looted heart, how to behave?
There'll be drunken refrains with it
When they have used up all their quid:
My queasy gut will churn with it
If my sorrowing heart's depraved:
When they have used up all their quid,
O looted heart, how to behave?

The Stolen Heart

Le Coeur volé

October 1871 (Verlaine's copy)

My sad heart slavers at the poop,
Heart slathered in tobacco-spit:
They spew their juice in spurts of soup,
My sad heart slobbers at the poop,
Under the jeering of the troop
While they burst out laughing at it,
My sad heart's drooling at the poop,
My heart swamped in tobacco-spit.

Fishy-phallic and soldier-blue
Their dirty jokes debauch it!
The rudder's marked with frescoes too,
Fishy-phallic and soldier-blue.
Abracadabra-like billows
O take my heart and wash it!
Fishy-phallic and soldier-blue
Their dirty jokes debauch it!

When they have spent their wad of quid,
O stolen heart, how will I act?
They'll belch their booze in Bacchic fits
When they've exhausted all their quid:
My queasy gut will churn with it,
I, if my heart is leveled flat:
When they have spent their wad of quid,
O stolen heart, how will I act?

Poets at Seven Years Old

Les Poètes de Sept Ans

26 May 1871

And, shutting the lesson book, the Mother
Left satisfied, so proud, without seeing
In the blue eyes under the knotted brow
The soul of her child possessed with loathing.

———

All day he sweated obedient, so
Bright; yet certain gloomy traits he displayed
Foreshadowed some bitter hypocrisies.
Passing darkened hallways hung with moldy
Tapestries, he'd stick out his tongue, both fists
At his crotch, and in his clenched eyes saw spots.
A door opened on evening: by lamplight
You'd see him, gagging, hanging over the
Stairs up high, engulfed in the skylight's glow.
Above all in summer, stupefied, beat,
He'd hide in the coolness of the privy:
At peace with his thoughts, sniffing deeply.

———

And when, in the little garden out back,
In winter, moonlit, washed of daily smells,
Stretched out under a wall, buried in clay
And scrunching his dazzled eyes for visions,
He'd listen to the blighted shrub-trees creak.
Compassion! His only pals were puny,
Bare-faced kids who, fading eyes down their cheeks,

Hiding thin yellow fingers black with mud
Under old clothes that stank of runny shit,
Communed with the sweetness of idiots!

———————

And if, having caught him at these unclean
Compassions, his mother was horrified;
His tender feelings overthrew her surprise.
It was good. She had the blue gaze—that lies!

———————

At seven, he made up novels of life
In the wilderness, where joyous Freedom shines,
Forest, sun, shore, savannah! He took to
Picture-magazines where, blushing, he'd stare at
Fun-loving Spanish and Italian girls.
And when she came, dressed in calico, the
Brown-eyed crazy eight-year-old—the daughter
Of workers next door—the little bully,
She cornered him, jumped him, tossing her hair,
And pinned beneath, he bit her in the ass
Because she never wore any panties.
—And black and blue from her fists and heels, he
Savored the taste of her skin in his room.

———————

He dreaded glum December Sundays when,
Hair slicked, at mahogany bench, he read
A Bible thick with cabbage-green pages;
Dreams oppressed him every night in his bed.
He didn't love God; but the men he'd see
In the tawny dusk, dirty, in workshirts,

Heading home, where criers, to three drumrolls,
Make the crowds laugh and groan at their decrees.
—He dreamt of the amorous prairie, where
Luminous billows, wholesome fragrance and
Golden pubic fluff calmly stir, take flight!

————

And since he really relished somber stuff,
When closed up in his barren, shuttered room,
High and blue, stricken with humidity,
He'd read his novel, endlessly plotted,
Heavy with ochre skies and forests drowned,
Flowers of flesh in starry woods unfurled,
Vertigo, wreckage, mayhem and pity!—
Meanwhile, neighborhood noise ran on below
—Alone, and lying on raw linen sheets
While violently envisioning sails.

Poor People in Church

Les Pauvres à l'église

Corralled between oak pews in corners of the church,
Warmed by the stink of their breath, with every eye
On the choir-loft dripping with gilt, the chorus
Of twenty jawbones yowling pious hymns on high;

Sniffing hot wax like the smell of bread in the air,
As happy and humble as a pack of whipped dogs,
The Poor offer up to the Lord and Master, God,
All of their stubborn and ridiculous prayers.

For the women, smooth-worn benches are a blessing
After the six black days where God makes them suffer!
Bundled in outlandish capes, they nurse their offspring,
The kind of kids who cry like they're ready to die.

Their slovenly tits hang out, these munchers of soup,
With a prayer in their eyes, but not really a prayer,
Gawking at the mischievous parade of a group
Of young hussies showing off their battered hats there.

Outside, the cold and hunger, (plus) the men on booze.
All right. There's an hour to go: and then the nameless blues!
—Meanwhile, all around, whimpers, whispers, and sniffling
From a collection of dewlapped ancient ladies.

There they are, the spooky ones and epileptics
That you avoided yesterday at the crossroads;
And, poking their noses into oldtime hymnals,
Those are the blind, led by a dog through the courtyards.

And all of them, drooling a dull beggarly faith,
Recite their endless complainings to Jesus

Far from the lean, mean and potbellied wicked,
Who dreams on high, in livid yellow stained-glass,

Far from the odors of meat and moldy fabric,
The prostrate, sullen farce of gestures repulsive;
—And as prayers bloom into choice exfoliations
And the tone of the mysteries gains urgency,

Then, down from the naves where the sun fades, insipid
Silken wrinkles, green smiles, those Ladies from better
Neighborhoods—oh Jesus!—those with cirrhosis
Dip long yellow fingers in the holy water.

The Hands of Joan-Marie

Les Mains de Jeanne-Marie

Joan-Marie has got strong hands,
Dark hands that summer has tanned,
Hands as pallid as dead hands
—Are these Ms. Juana's hands?

Do they take their mocha tone
From voluptuary pools?
Have they been drenched in the moons
Of serenity's lagoons?

Have they drunk barbaric skies,
Calm on knees of pleasing charm?
Have they rolled cigars
Or cut a deal in diamonds?

Have they flung golden flowers
At the fiery feet of Madonnas?
It's the dark blood of belladonnas
That glints and sleeps in their palms.

Hands chasing twin-winged flies
Which buzz in the bluish
Dawns toward the nectars?
Hands decanting venom?

Oh! what Dream has held them
In hysterical outstretched yawns?
An amazing dream of Asias,
of Khenghavars or of Zions?

—These hands haven't sold oranges,
Nor burnished the feet of godlings:
These hands haven't washed the swaddling
Of hulking babies with no eyes.

These aren't the hands of cousins
Nor working girls with fat faces
That burn in the tar-drunk sun
By woods near stinking factories.

These are benders of backbones,
Hands that do no harm nor worse,
More fatal than machinery,
Much stronger than any horse!

As restless as a furnace
And shaking off all their chill,
Their flesh sings national anthems
And never piteous old hymns!

They'd wring your necks, O wicked
Women, they'd crush your hands,
Contessas, infamous hands
Replete with white and red.

At the glint of those loving hands
The heads of the sheepish all turn!
On every savory knuckle
Bright sunlight makes a ruby burn!

A mob of blemishes there
Browns them like yesterday's tits;
The backs of these Hands is where
Each proud Rebel plants a kiss!

They've turned pale, it's marvelous,
In broadest daylight charged with love,
Above the bronze of machine guns
Through a Paris in rebellion!

Ah! yet sometimes, at your fists,
O sacred Hands, where our lips,
Never sobered, are trembling,
Screams a chain of shining links!

A strange Tremor possesses
Our beings when, Angel-Hands,
Sometimes to whiten your tan,
Your fingers are made to bleed.

Vowels

Voyelles [and fragment]

A black, E White, I red, U green, O blue: vowels,
I will someday spread the word of your hidden birth.
A, black velvet corset of glittering flies
Buzzing around cruel fungoid stink, engulfing

Shadows; *E*, vaporous and tented innocence,
Proud glaciers' lances, white kings, quivering bouquets;
I, purple, blood-spat, beautiful lips that laugh
In anger or the repentance of raptures;

U, cycles, viridian seas' divine vibration,
Peace of beasts in pastoral scenes, peace of wrinkles
Printed by alchemy on study's broad brow;

O, Clarion supreme, full of weird stridency,
Silences passed over by Worlds and Angels:
—O the Omega, violet ray from Those Eyes!

*   *   *

(Pink wept the Star at the heart of your hearing,
Infinity tossed whitely from neck to hips;
The Sea's dropt rosy dew on your breasts' ruby tips
And Man, blood so black, right at your sovereign side.)

Some Words to the Poet Concerning Flowers

Ce qu'on dit au Poète à propos de fleurs
To Mr. Theodore de Banville

I

Ever thus, toward the azure dusk
Where the topaz ocean quivers,
Lilies, those blissful enemas,
Will operate in your evening!

In our age of powdered palm-starch
When every Plant is put to work,
Lilies will drink the disgusting
Blueness from your punctual Prose!

The lily of Mister de K.
The Sonnet of 1830.
The Lily given to Minstrels
With amaranth and marigold!

Lilies! Lilies! None to be seen!
Yet these white blooms, like the sleeves of
Sinful women walking softly,
Always tremble in your Verses!

Always, my Dear, when you take a bath,
Your Shirt with its yellow armpits
Blowses out in the morning breeze
Above the vile forget-me-nots!

Love is letting only Lilacs
Through your customs—oh, to and fro!
And the Violets of the Wood,
The sugared spittle of black Nymphs! . . .

II

O Poets, we can see you've got
The Roses, the full-blown Roses,
Red on laurel stems, inflated
In your thousands of eight-beat lines!

Although *Banville's* roses will snow,
Whirling in a bloody blizzard,
Blacking the wild eye of strangers
Who read him unreceptively.

In your forest and your meadow
—Oh you're such calm photographers!—
The Flora's about as diverse
As the stoppers atop carafes!

Always the French vegetation,
Surly, tubercular, absurd,
Where the bellies of basset hounds
Placidly navigate the dusk;

Always the rosy prints, holy
Pictures for girls at communions,
After some dreadful sketches of
Sunflowers or the Lotus blue!

Your Ode to the Asoka fits
The Rhyme in bordello windows;
And clumsy, brilliant butterflies
Defecate over the Daisy.

Ancient greenery, old striping!
O vegetable muffin-cupcakes!
Fantastic blooms in olden Rooms!
—For may-bugs, not for rattlesnakes

These vegetable baby dolls weep,
Doodles in margins by Grandville,
And they have sucked up their colors
From wayward stars in pointed caps!

Yes! your salivating panpipes
Make such a valuable glucose!
—Fried eggs piled up inside old hats,
Lilies, Asokas, Lilacs, Roses! . . .

III

O white Hunter, running barefoot
Across the Pastures of panic,
Couldn't you, shouldn't you know your
Botany just a little bit?

I'm afraid you'd only exchange
Red crickets for the Spanish Fly,
The Rio gold for Rhenish blue—
Briefly, Floridas for Norways:

But, my Dear—it's true now—no more
Will Art indulge itself in the
Amazing Eucalyptus of
Your python-long hexameters.

There! . . . Even though our Guiana
Mahogany might serve only
For monkeys to swing from in the
Dull delirium of creepers.

—In short, is there any Flower,
Lily, Rosemary, alive or
Dead, worth a turd from a sea-bird?
Worth a candle's only tear-drop?

—And I mean every word I say!
You, down there, sitting just the same
In a bamboo hut—with shutters
Closed, brown Persian rugs for curtains—

You'd botch flowerings worthy of
Extravagant lazy Rivers! . . .
Poet!—these are reasons no less
Arrogant than ridiculous! . . .

IV

Speak, not of springtime pampas, dark
With appalling revolutions,
But of tobacco and cotton!
Tell us of exotic harvests!

Tell us, white face tanned by Phoebus,
How many dollars Havanaise
Pedro Velasquez puts away;
Feculate the Sorrento Sea

Where the Swans migrate by thousands;
May your Stanzas be commercials
For the felling of mangrove trees
In search of hydroids and fungi!

Your quatrains plunge into bloody
Thickets, returning to offer
Humanity so many things:
White sugar, cough-drops, and rubbers!

Interpret for us the blonding
Of snowy Peaks near the Tropics,
Is it insects laying their eggs
Or some microscopic lichen!

O Hunter, we insist you find
A few perfumed rosy madders
Which Nature will bring to bloom
In baggy pants—for all the Troops!

Find, at the edge of sleeping Woods
The Flowers that resemble snouts,
Drooling a golden brilliantine
On the somber pelts of Buffalo!

In wild meadows where silvery
Peachfuzz shivers in the Blue, find
Flower-cups full of Eggs afire,
Simmering in their essences!

Find some downy Thistles that'll
Have ten asses with eyes enflamed
Working hard to spin the tangles!
Find Flowers to use for chairs!

Yes! at the core of black fissures
Find Flowers—nearly precious stones!—
Those with tonsils, gem-like nodules
Next to their hard blond ovaries.

Serve us—you can do it, you Clown—
On a splendid crimson platter,
Syrupy Lily stew that'll
Corrode our nickel-plated spoons.

V

Someone talks about the Great Love,
Absolved like a Thief in the night:
But neither Renan nor Murr the cat
Have seen the immense Blue Thyrsi!

You, quickening our torpors with
Perfume-induced hysteria:
Lift our spirits toward candors
More outspoken than the Marys . . .

Merchant! Colonist! Medium!
Your Poetry spills forth, rosy
Or white, like a sodium ray,
Like an effusive rubber-tree!

Out of your black Stanzas,—Juggler!
Refractive reds, greens, and whites
Let loose the weirdest of flowers
And electrical butterflies!

Look! it's the Century of hell!
And the lines of telegraph poles—
Lyres of iron song—will adorn
Your magnificent shoulder blades!

Above all, give us a version
In rhyme of the potato blight!
—And for the composition of
Poetry full of mystery,

Stuff meant to be read from Podunk
To Patagonia—go buy
Some Volumes by Mister Figtree
—Illustrated!—in Bookstores now!

The Drunken Boat

Le Bateau Ivre

As I descended Rivers undisturbed
I sensed the haulers no longer steered me:
Howling Redskins took them captive, nailing
Them naked like targets to painted poles.

I was carefree of all or any crew,
Freighting Flemish wheat or English cotton.
When that racket with my haulers had done,
The Rivers led me wherever I wished.

Through the rippling fury of the tides,
Last winter, emptier than childhood's mind,
I ran! And Peninsulas let slip
Have not brought down more triumphant hubbub.

The tempest has blessed my sea-borne wakings.
Lighter than a cork I danced on the waves,
Those rolling beds of the eternal dead,
Ten nights, no thought for dull-eyed harbor lights!

Sweeter than sour apples' flesh to kids,
Green waters pervaded my hull of pine,
Washed clean the dregs of vomit and blue wine,
And swept away my rudder and anchor.

Since then, I've been bathing in the milky
Way, in the star-steeped Poem of the Sea,
Ravenous green azures; where sometimes a drowned
Man drifting by, rapt, pale and pensive, goes down.

Where, tinting all at once the blue, the slow
Delirious rhythms of the day's rosy glow,

Stronger than alcohol, vaster than poetry,
Ferment the freckled red bitterness of love!

I know the heavens cracked by lightning, surfs,
Waterspouts and currents: I know the night,
And the Dawn exalted like doves in flight;
I've seen sometimes what men have thought they saw!

I've seen the low sun, smeared with mystic awe,
Lit with violet congealing fingers,
The rolling waves, like actors in old plays,
Their shuttered shivering so far away!

I've dreamt the night green to the dazzling snows,
Kissing to the sea's eyes climbing and slow,
Unheard-of juices' flow, blue and yellow
The waking of singing phosphorescence!

For months I've followed hysterical herds
Of surf surging and crashing on the reefs,
Without dreaming Marys' luminous feet
Could force back the panting Ocean's muzzle!

I've jostled incredible Floridas,
You know, mingling flowers with panthers' eyes
On the skins of men! Rainbows stretched like reins
To the seas' limits, gleaming droves of grey!

I've seen enormous bogs fermenting, snares
Where in the reeds a Leviathan rots!
Waterfalls crashing in the midst of calms,
And horizons tumbling into chaos!

Glaciers, silver suns, pearly waves, fiery skies!
Hideous wrecks in the depths of dark harbors

Where giant serpents devoured by insects
Drop with black perfumes out of twisted trees!

I'd show these Eldorados to children,
Blue seas, these golden fish, those fish who sing.
—Flowering foams have cradled my driftings;
Ineffable winds gave me timely wings.

Sometimes the sea, wearied martyr of poles
And zones, whose sobs had me gently rolling,
Raised her yellow cupped shady blooms to me
And I rested, like a woman kneeling . . .

All but an island, I sideswiped quarrels
And the turds of clamoring blond-eyed birds,
And I sailed, while through my fragile rigging
The drowned fell back, descending into sleep!

Now I, in the ringlets of back bays lost,
A boat in the birdless air, storm-tossed,
The Monitors and the schooners of Hanse
Wouldn't salvage my water-sloshed carcass;

Free and fuming, decked with violet fogs,
I who pierced the blushing sky like a wall,
Bearing solar fungus and azure snot,
The exquisite jam of all good poets,

Who ran, spattered with electric lunettes,
Planking warped, black seahorses in escort,
While the hammering heat of these Julys
Beat fiery funnels out of sea-blue skies;

I, who trembled fifty leagues off, hearing
Behemoths in rut, gross Maelstroms moaning,

Eternal spinner of motionless blues,
I miss the Europe of ancient ramparts!

I've seen atolls full of stars! and islands
Whose fevered skies are open to drifters:
—Exiled in these deepless nights do you sleep,
Countless golden birds, O future Vigors?—

Too true, too many tears! Dawns of heartbreak.
Each moon is cruel, and every sun bitter:
I'm swollen with harsh love's drunken torpor.
O let my keel burst! Let me go to sea!

If there's a water in Europe for me
It's the cool, dark pond at balmy twilight
Where a child squats full of sadness, launching
A frail boat like a butterfly in May.

Bathed in your languors, O waves, no longer
Can I clear the wake of cotton freighters,
Nor pass through blazoned flags and banners' pride,
Nor pull beneath prison hulks' dismal eyes.

NOTES

The Orphans' New Year Gift

The poet had just turned fifteen at the time he wrote this lengthy verse, his first major poem. He touches upon his own situation, the father being "far away" and the mother (emotionally) "dead." The "New Year Gift" is a funerary plaque that the children discover on the first morning of the new year.

Sensation

This is one of three poems submitted to Theodore de Banville in a letter of 24 May 1870—the other two being *Ophélie* and Credo in unam (*Sun and Flesh*). In these two quatrains, the poet sets forth certain essential themes and images that recur throughout his work.

Sun and Flesh

Rimbaud's original title was *Credo in unam,* meant to set forth a new poetic "credo" devoted to beauty as traditionally represented by the goddess Venus. The numerous mythological references are part and parcel of the Parnassian school of poetry to which the young Rimbaud aspired, a classical, elevated style of versifying laden with mythic and floral metaphor.

I. Sun and Flesh
. . . le clair syrinx ("the fair Syrinx")
The nymph Syrinx, pursued by an enamored Pan, was changed into a reed in order to escape him. Pan fashioned her "body" into a panpipe of seven reeds thus called the syrinx, whereon he played his love songs.

... *le grande Cybèle* ("great Cybele")
The great mother-goddess of the ancient world, Cybele was primarily a
goddess of fertility, but also of wild nature. She was believed to
cure (and send) disease and to protect her people in wartime. She
was often paired with her young male consort, Attis. Worship of
Cybele was one of the chief "mystery" religions of the Roman
Empire.

Astarté ("Astarte")
Also known as Ishtar, Astarte was a goddess of the sky among Semitic
peoples. Rimbaud here confuses her with Venus rising from the
sea, an image lifted from Alfred de Musset's poem *Rolla ("Où
Vénus Astarte, fille de l'onde amère* ... " / Where Venus Astarte,
daughter of the bitter waves ...). Later, in his Lettres due voyant,
Rimbaud sarcastically dismissed Musset and *Rolla* in particular.

IV. Sun and Flesh
... *Kallipyge la blanche* ("White-hipped Venus")
The word Kallipyge or Callipyge is from the Greek, meaning "beauti-
ful buttocks." The "Vénus callipyge" was the name of a statue of
the goddess discovered in Rome.

... *Ariadné* ... *Thésée* ... ("Ariadne ... Theseus ... ")
In Greek myth, Ariadne was the daughter of Minos and Pasiphae, king
and queen of Crete. When Theseus, prince of Athens, arrived in
Crete, she fell in love with him and gave him the thread by which he
found his way out of the labyrinth after killing the Minotaur. He then
fled, taking her with him; but he abandoned her on the island of
Naxos, where the god Dionysus (Bacchus) found her, married her,
and made her immortal.

Lysios ... ("Bacchus ... ")
Lysios (comforter) is another name for Dionysus, denoting his aspect
as a giver of joy and soother of cares. Dionysus, the god of wine

and ecstasy is often represented as an androgynous youth, with
luxuriant hair, with grapes or a wine-cup in his hand—or holding
the *thyrsos,* a rod with bunched ivy leaves and a pine cone at the
top.

... *le champs Phyrygiens* ("Phrygian fields")
Phrygia was a territory in the west of Asia Minor (modern-day Tur-
key). According to legend, after wandering in Egypt and Syria,
Dionysus visited Cybele at her shrine in Phrygia.

Zeus, Taureau ... (**Zeus the Bull** ... ")
Zeus, the supreme god, fell in love with Europa, daughter of the king
of Tyre. In order to woo her, he took the form of a bull that swam
to the seashore where she was playing, and seemed so mild that
she climbed upon his back. He then swam away with her to Crete
where she bore him a son, King Minos. In Rimbaud's version of
the myth, she dies at sea, overcome by the "kiss divine."

... *le grand Cygne rêveur* ... *Léda* ("The great Swan of dreams ... Leda")
The Swan is Zeus in yet another guise. Leda was the wife of Tyndareus,
king of Sparta, and the mother of Clytemnestra, Helen of Troy,
and the twins Castor and Pollux. She was loved by Zeus, who
approached her in the form of a swan. Stories vary as to which of
the children were fathered by Zeus.

Cypris ("Venus")
Cypris or "The Cyprian" was another name for Venus in ancient times.
Her sanctuaries on the island of Cyprus, at Paphos and Amathus,
were especially renowned. According to one version of the myth,
she was born from the seafoam at Paphos.

Héraclés, le Dompteur ("Hercules the Tamer")
Hercules was a legendary mortal famous for his feats of strength and

his prowess in the hunt. He killed his first lion at age eighteen and
wore the skin as a trophy.

La Dryade ("The Dryad")
Dryads were the nymphs of trees, especially oak trees, nymphs being
the young and beautiful female personifications of various natural
objects. Naiads were the nymphs of springs, lakes, and rivers,
while oreads were those of the mountains.

Séléné ... Endymion ("Selene ... Endymion")
In Greek myth, Selene was the moon goddess, sometimes identified
with Artemis. Endymion was a beautiful youth, a hunter famed for
his eternal sleep on Mount Latmus, and beloved of Selene, who
cast the spell of eternal sleep upon him so she could embrace him
unobserved.

les bois sacrés ("the sacred wood")

The famous oracle at Dodona was the most ancient in all Greece. It
was dedicated to Zeus, and the oracles were delivered from the
tops of oak and other trees, the rustling of the wind in the branches
being interpreted by the priests. Also, brazen vessels and plates
were suspended from the branches, and these, clanging together
when the wind blew, made various sounds that were likewise inter-
preted.

... les sombres Marbres ("those dark Marbled Ones")
The statues of abandoned gods.

Ophelia

Inspired by Shakespeare's *Hamlet* (Act 4 scene 7) where the mad Ophelia
drowns herself in the river following her father's death at Hamlet's

hands, this poem was the first work Rimbaud presented to his teacher Izambard. A few images are lifted from poems by Theodore de Banville.

Dance of the Hanged Men

A sarcastic "danse macabre," this poem derives from the *Ballad of the Hanged Men* by François Villon (1431–1462?), the outlaw poet of 15th century France.

Saladins ("Saladins")
Saladin (1138–1193), sultan of Egypt and Syria, was the famous adversary of Richard Lionheart, Philip-Augustus, and Frederick Barbarossa during the Third Crusade. The image is one of infidels hanging from crosses or gallows ("the one-armed pal").

Messire Belzebuth ("Sir Beelzebub")
The devil's right-hand man is presented as a knight and a puppet-master.

The Blacksmith

According to Steinmetz (*Rimbaud: Poésies*, pp. 232–33), this poem was inspired by a famous 19th century engraving from *The History of the French Revolution* by Auguste Thiers, showing Louis XVI in conversation with the butcher Legendre, and wearing the red cap of the revolutionaries. Rimbaud changes the butcher into a black-smith for the purpose of greater contrast and mythic resonance (the blacksmith is huge, a Titan facing the "Olympian" ruler). Louis XVI here also symbolized Napoleon III, who was emperor of France when the poem was composed.

Tartuffe's Chastisement

Tartuffe is the hypocritical title character in Moliere's play—a dishon-
est "holy man" who cheats and lies and attempts to destroy his
gullible benefactor. Rimbaud apparently equates this character with
certain priests he knew from school in Charleville. Echoes of this
sonnet appear in other works, notably *A Heart Beneath a Cassock*
and *Squattings*.

Set to Music

This is Rimbaud's satirical picture of a holiday concert at the band-
stand in Charleville. He observes others from the sidelines, even-
tually entering the picture in the seventh stanza, where he's follow-
ing a group of giggling schoolgirls.

You Dead of '92

An ironic salute to the men who died at the end of the first French
Revolution, Rimbaud's sonnet concludes with a reminder of how
the media trivialize the raw stuff of history.

Paul de Cassagnac . . . Messieurs de Cassagnac (" . . . The Newspaper-
men")
In an article in *Le Pays*, 16 July 1870, Paul de Cassagnac, a conserva-
tive journalist, defended the Franco-Prussian War, invoking the
courage of those who had given their lives to liberate France. But
the causes of the war were not the same. Rimbaud, a liberal
(républicain) who despised the royalist conservatives (Bonapartistes),

condemns the false patriotism of Cassagnac and his father Adolphe, another journalist who wrote for *Le Pays*.

Venus Rising From the Waves

Here is the paradox of grossness made gorgeous. In Latin, *Clara Venus* means "Bright" (or "Radiant") Venus—a prayer or invocation to the goddess.

First Evening

This was first published under the title *Trois Baisers* ("Three Kisses") in La Charge, a satirical pamphlet issued in Paris, 13 August 1870.

What Nina Said

The poet is taking an imaginary walk with his perhaps equally imaginary girlfriend. He wants to wander all day in the woods, but she has other plans.

The Runaways

The French title, *Les Effarés,* has also been translated as "The Intimidated," "The Transfixed," and "Kids In A Daze." Effaré basically means "bewildered, scared or frightened," and the kids in the poem seem to be hungry and homeless; hence "Runaways."

Romantic Fiction

In this "Novel" (a tale of romance), the poet serves up dreams of
youthful passions. In Part III, he compares his lonely heart to
Robinson Crusoe, stranded on his desert island.

Evil

Anti-war, anti-religion, anti-sentimental, this sonnet expresses the waste
of wartime slaughter (not what nature intended, the poet seems to
say). God sleeps during Mass, awakened by the weeping of the
mothers of the slain.

Angry Caesars

"The pale man" is Napoleon III, exiled, under arrest after the Franco-
Prussian War. The "Pal in glasses" is his minister of state who
persuaded him to go to war.

Dreaming Toward Winter

How much of this poem is based on actual events is entirely unknow-
able—except that it was written on a train journey, on 7 October
1870, and is dedicated to a mysterious girl or woman who caught
the poet's fancy.

The Sleeper in the Valley

This sonnet, among the most famous of Rimbaud's poems, first appeared in print in 1888 in Lamerre's *Anthologies des Poètes français du XIXe siecle.*

At the Green Cabaret

The "Green Inn" became a recurring symbol of peaceful repose and relaxed happiness in Rimbaud's work (see "Comedy of Thirst" and *Illuminations).* During this period in his life, he had run away from home and walked for days, sleeping in the open, headed nowhere and everywhere, living the life of a vagabond.

The Sly One

Another snapshot of tranquility from his life on the road. In chapter 1 of *Somebody Else,* Charles Nicholl notes: "Scholars have confirmed the existence of this truck stop (actually La Maison Verte), and even the name of the pneumatic waitress, a Flemish girl called Mia."

The Dazzling Victory at Saarebrück

Based on a patriotic print seen in a shop window, this sonnet presents the emperor and his troops as a clownish gaggle of poseurs.

The Cupboard

Rimbaud here stuffs a world of lifetimes into an ancient wardrobe (like
the mysterious cabinet in Part IV of *The Orphans' New Year Gift*).

Ma Bohème / My Gypsy Life

Rimbaud's "Fantasia" bears little resemblance to *Scènes de la vie bohème*
(1852), the romantic novel of Henri Murger that became the basis
of Puccini's opera *La Bohème* (1896). Instead, Rimbaud's 'bohe-
mian' existence is that of a vagabond obsessively wandering, a life
in which the world's ordinary realities become charged with magi-
cal resonance.

Mon paletot aussi devenait idéal ("My topcoat too on its way to ideal")
His coat is so full of holes, it's a mere sketch, the *idea* of an overcoat.

ton féal ("your vassal")
Your devoted servant or slave; *féal* is Old French, out of the Latin
"fidelis" (faithful). The word is often found in the songs of the
medieval troubadours in a romantic or passionate sense.

Mon auberge était à la Grande Ourse ("I stayed at the Big Bear")
Sleeping under the stars; literally, "my inn was at [the sign of] the Great
Bear [Ursa Major, the Big Dipper]."

The Crows

Verlaine, when he published it in *Les Poètes maudits,* called this poem "a
patriotic thing, but finely patriotic," ("chose patriotique, mais

patriotique bien"). The "dead of yesterday" are not only the victims of the recent Franco-Prussian War, but the dead of any and all wars.

The Sitters

When he returned to Charleville after his early Paris adventures and refused to go back to school, Rimbaud haunted the municipal library and made the librarians search out arcane and exotic texts for him. These old men found him annoying and no doubt thought he was a hooligan or worse. There was no love lost between them, as this poem attests.

Fauns' Head

A woodland fantasia, probably dating from days and nights spent in the forest outside of town, or on the road; Rimbaud here combines the mythic world with a "modern" sensibility—a sort of "now you see it, now you don't."

The Customs Men

macache ("foo'cue")
A French transliteration of an extremely negative epithet in Arabic (meaning roughly "drop dead" or "f—k you"), brought back to France by troops who'd served in North Africa.

Cré Nom ("By G—")
In French, a common abbreviation used as a swear word, shortened from *sacré nom*, "holy name" (of God).

les Fausts et les Diavolos ("Fausts and Fra Diavolos")
Nocturnal travelers up to no good. In the *Faust-Book* (1587) and
   Marlowe's Dr. Faustus (1593), the magician meets the devil in
   the woods at midnight; the devil Mephastophilis appears in
   the guise of a monk. Fra Diavolo (Brother Devil) was the alias
   of the notorious Italian rebel Pozza, subject of Scribe and
   Auber's popular comic opera of the same name (1830); see
   also the Laurel and Hardy film *The Devil's Brother* (1933) based
   on the operetta. Arthur Rimbaud's childhood friend Delahaye
   remarked that this sonnet was based on his and Rimbaud's
   adventures smuggling tobacco across the Belgian border at age
   16—a couple of kids playing at Faust and Fra Diavolo, outwit-
   ting the law.

sa sérénité ("her majesty")
Literally "his/her serene highness," a satirical jibe at the customs offi-
   cials' inflated sense of self-importance and suavity.

appas contrôlés ("fleshy contraband")
The phrase literally means 'charms' or 'enticements' *(appas)* in the
   physical sense (breasts, butt, basket, etc.) that are officially
   examined or tax-stamped (contrôlés): "contraband charms," as
   one translation has it. While searching for illicit goods, the
   customs men grope any cute young thing who falls into their
   hands.

Evening Prayer

. . . *une Gambier* ("pipe here")
Gambier was a popular brand of clay pipe favored by Rimbaud.

. . . *le Seigneur du cedre et des hysopes* ("the Lord of cedar and of
   hyssops")

A paraphrase out of the Bible—or in Biblical style—indicating the "Lord of great things and small." Hyssop is a healing herb mentioned several times in the Bible.

... *grands héliotropes* ("great heliotropes")
The heliotrope is a plant that turns toward the sun. The poet's golden arc of piss causes the heliotropes to nod in his direction.

Parisian War Song

This is another wartime satire based on the poet's experiences in Paris during the days of the Commune. The names of the various generals, communards, traitors, and patriots have been Anglicized.

My Loving Little Women

Rimbaud here mocks the standard love poems of the era in language at once slangy and derisive. The "mandolin strum" in stanza five is probably a euphemism for masturbation.

Squattings

The mention of Venus at the very end of this poem elevates the tone to absurd heights. Rimbaud returns to the paradoxical aesthetic first voiced in "Venus Rising From the Waves," turning flab and excrement into things of beauty.

The Seekers of Lice

This poem is based on the poet's stay with Izambard's "aunts," the sisters Gindre, after his week in jail in Paris where he was arrested for vagrancy. The lice were apparently a "memento" of his prison days.

The Sisters of Mercy

In a letter to Paul Demeny, Rimbaud tells how he always needed a woman or an idea *"ne trouveront pas la Soeur de charité."* The underlining of the phrase suggests that the poem was written concurrently with the letter or shortly before, in April of 1871. Rimbaud identifies with the Genie-like youth.

un Génie ("a Genie")
The first appearance of this Oriental spirit in Rimbaud's work.

jeunes mers . . . lits de diamants ("youthful seas . . . beds of diamonds")
An incestuous pun occurs in the French: *"jeunes mères, lits, diamants"* (young mothers, beds, little lovers).

The Righteous Man

The text of this poem is incomplete. According to Steinmetz, four stanzas probably preceded the 55 lines that survive. The manuscript, in Rimbaud's hand, is found in the notebooks of Verlaine, who dated the poem "July 1871" and describes it as containing 70 or 80 lines. (Rimbaud *Poésies,* ed. Steinmetz; Flammarion 1989, pp. 258–9.)

This poem has often been cited as Rimbaud's harshest critique of religion, Paul Schmidt going so far as to translate *"Le Juste"* as "The Savior." However, Yves Reboul in "À propos de L'Homme Juste," cited by Steinmetz, has shown that Rimbaud is here satirizing Victor Hugo, the grand old man of French letters, for his 'neutral' stance during the 1871 revolution. The "Bard of Brittany" sat out the fall of the Empire and the rise of the Commune from a self-imposed exile on the island of Guernesey. Between April and May, the period of the commune, Hugo published three poems appealing for reconciliation between Versailles and the Communists. He refused to meet with a party of exiled Communards in May ("vagrants") and advocated prayers of forgiveness and peace ("kneepads up for sale . . . Olive weeper . . . Sweet Believer").

The order of the last four stanzas is in question. Wallace Fowlie places the eighth stanza at the very beginning of his translation. The order followed by Schmidt seems to make the most sense and I have used it here.

First Communion

Like "Poets at Seven Years Old," this is a poem of childhood visions and crisis. In this, a young girl's sexual awakening coincides with her first communion. The priest here—"a freak in black with festering shoes"—is related to the obsessive seminarian Leonard in "A Heart Beneath A Cassock."

Parisian Orgy

This phantasmagoria reflects the looting, burning, and mob violence
that filled Paris during the days and nights of the commune (March
18–May 18, 1871).

. . . les Stryx . . . des Cariatides ("Stryx . . . the Caryatids")
The Stryx, in ancient superstition, were a kind of demon or vampire
that wandered the night looking for victims. Caryatids are statues
of women that were used as pillars or columns in classical archi-
tecture. *Cariatides* was also the name of a collection of poems by
Theodore de Banville published in 1842. Rimbaud, an early ad-
mirer of Banville's poetry, surely knew this book and his image
here probably conflates the architectural and the poetic "caryatid"
into an image of blind destruction.

The Tortured Heart

Also known as *The Clownish Heart* and *The Stolen Heart.* There are three
different manuscripts of this poem, one sent to Georges Izambard (18
May 1871), another to Paul Demeny (10 June), and the third sent to Paul
Verlaine in August. Each version has a different title and varies slightly in
the internal details. I have therefore translated each version on its own
terms. While a runaway in Paris, during the chaos of the Commune
following the Franco-Prussian War, Rimbaud either witnessed or was the
object of a gang-rape by a troop of soldiers or national guardsmen. He
sent a copy of this poem to his tutor Georges Izambard, who, uncompre-
hending, thought it was a nonsense parody.

Poets at Seven Years Old

As Steinmetz has noted, this poem "constitutes an astonishing 'know thyself' from Rimbaud. The plural of the title intends to generalize an experience that is nonetheless profoundly individual and recalls the period when the Rimbaud family lived at 73 Rue Bourbon in a lower-class neighborhood of Charleville." The poem traces his relationship with his mother, his compassionate outbursts, his discovery of books and magazines, and the awakening of his sexuality. The world of his "novel, endlessly plotted" recalls the one traversed by *The Drunken Boat.*

Poor People in Church

The poet gives free rein to his anti-clerical feelings in this poem, another portrait of stultifying small town existence where everybody appears grotesque.

The Hands of Joan-Marie

Dating from February 1872, this poem, according to Steinmetz, was inspired by Théophile Gautier's 1852 poem *Études des mains* ("Studies of Hands"). Rimbaud asks rhetorically what kind of hands Joan-Marie might have, observing how different they are, the one from the other. From the seventh stanza on, it becomes apparent that these are the strong hands of a heroine of the commune, "Above the bronze of machine guns . . . "

—Sont-ce des mains de Juana? ("—Are these Ms. Juana's hands?")
The feminine form of Juan, Spanish for "John" as in Joan and Jeanne.

Rimbaud's meaning is unclear. Is she (Juana) a female adventurer like Don Juan, a magician, or a crossdresser? Or, as Claude Jeancolas has opined in *Le Dictionnaire Rimbaud,* does Juana refer to a feminized Janus, the two-faced Roman god of doorways? (Two different faces on one head and torso compared to two different hands on one female body, each facing opposite or appearing to the eye as opposites.)

Khengavars ("Khenghavars")
An imaginary country or people invented by Rimbaud.

. . . une chaine aux claires anneaux ("a chain of shining links")
Handcuffs or shackles.

Vowels

This sonnet is probably the most discussed work of the poet—there are sexual, mystical, scholarly, and alchemical interpretations of all kinds. Robert Faurisson, is his essay *"A-t-on lu Rimbaud" (Bizarre* no. 21–22, 1961) has suggested that the poem is a description of the female body during coitus. Some critics have mentioned that hashish may have been an influence on the composition. One interpretation takes into account the varying shapes of the letters as a key to their descriptions. (See p. xxviii of Bernard's introduction to Collected Poems; Penguin, 1962.)

I have appended the fragment *"L'étoile a pleuré rose au coeur de tes oreilles"* (Pink wept the star at the heart of your hearing) immediately following Vowels because of its apparent continuation of the poet's world-view color scheme.

Some Words to the Poet Concerning Flowers

This botanical extravaganza is a send-up of the Parnassian school of
poetry to which the 15-year-old Rimbaud had aspired. He sent
three early poems *(Sensation, Ophelia,* and *Credo in unam)* to Banville
on the selection committee of Parnasse Contemporain, the
movement's periodical. (Banville, chief among the Parnassians along
with Leconte de Lisle and François Coppée, is not much read any
more, but his brief commedia dell'arte pastiche *Charming Léandre*
held the stage in various revivals through the mid-20th century.)

Rimbaud submitted this poem a little over a year later, with a letter
asking Banville if he remembered the earlier submission. "The
same idiot is sending you the above verses, signed Alcide Bava
[Hercules the Drooler].—I beg your pardon . . .

"I am eighteen.—I'll always love the verses of Banville.

"Last year I was only seventeen.

"Have I made any progress?"

Rimbaud was actually sixteen when he penned the letter, and his
Parnassian ambitions were a thing of the past.

I *Les Lys, ces clystères d'extases!* ("Lilies, those blissful enemas")
Parnassian poetry is full of images of exotic flowers and precious stones.
Rimbaud mocks the inevitable lily again in the Album "Zutique."
The shape of the lily recalls the nozzle of an enema pump *(clystère).*

Proses religieuses ("punctual Prose")
The term "religious" also connotes regularity or punctuality in French
as it does in English. Steinmetz interprets this line to mean

"Latin hymns composed in rhymed lines," but the image is also satirizing a poetry that is little more than prose with metrical regularity conferred upon it.

Monsieur de Kerdrel ("**Mister de K.**")
Audren de Kerdrel was the foremost conservative politician of the day. He wanted to reclaim the old royal fleur-de-lis as a political symbol. "Mister Decay" seems an apt translation for this elder statesman of a moribund social order.

. . . le sonnet de mil huit cent trente ("**The sonnet of 1830**")
The year 1830 was a turbulent one in French history. The insurrection of that year led to the suspension of the free press, the dissolution of the legislature, and changes in the election laws. There were three days of bloody street fighting in Paris.

Under the guise of a political jibe, Rimbaud probably hides a harsh critique of Banville, who took pride in his (poetic) lineage from the literary revolution of 1839, when Romanticism was at its height. In his poem "Romantic Dawn" (1866), Banville waxed nostalgic: "Eighteen Thirty! Dawn / That still dazzles me, / Promise of destiny, / Smiling morning!" There were many that year who saw no more smiling mornings.

l'oeillet et l'amarante ("**amaranth and marigold**")
Garlands awarded to laureates of the *Jeux floraux de Toulouse,* a poetic competition of the Romantic era aimed at reviving the poetic competitions of the Middle Ages—hence the "minstrels" in the line preceding.

les myosotis immondes ("**the vile forget-me-nots**")
The myosotis or forget-me-not is not a particularly "vile" flower until one observes that the properly botanical name ("myositis") is derived from the ancient Greek for "rat's ear."

(It might be noted here that when Rimbaud graduated from the college de Charleville at age 15, he won first prize in Rhetoric and in Greek and Latin and French grammar, Latin verse and Greek verse, and second prize in Recitation . . . No prizes in Math; fourth prize in Geography. The Greek origin of *myosotis* would not have escaped him.)

Lilas . . . Violettes ("Lilacs . . . Violets")
Standard images or emblems of passion found in Romantic love poetry; Banville had strewn them freely in his *Cariatides* ("The Caryatids").

II . . . *de mille octaves enflées* (" . . . inflated/ In your thousands of eight-beat lines")
The octave, in French and English, is a musical term. It also designates an eight-line stanza in a poem or, as here, the octosyllable or eight-beat line that Rimbaud himself uses in this parody.

. . . *paisible photographes . . . bouchons de carafes* ("calm photographers . . . stoppers atop carafes")
Banville himself coined this rhyme—*photographes / bouchons de carafes*—in *Odes funambulesques*. In his paraphrase, Rimbaud mocks the "still-life photography" of Parnassian verse that reduces the variety of flora into the same old shapes.

Lotos, Hélianthes ("Sunflowers or the Lotus")
Exotic flowers that the Parnassians often cited in their poems.

L'Ode Açoka (" . . . **Ode to the Asoka**")
The Asoka is one of a number of sacred trees venerated by the Hindus.
Catulle Mendes (with Banville, an editor of *Parnasse contemporain*)
wrote a poem in praise of this tree.

fenêtre de lorette ("**bordello windows**")
A "lorette" was an attractive young call-girl during the Second Em-
pire, so named after the Parisian neighborhood, Notre-Dame
de Lorette, where they lived. The "Rhyme" in the window prob-
ably refers to the establishment's prices and/or business hours,
posted for passers-by to see.

croquignoles ("**muffin-cupcakes**")
Steinmetz defines these as *"petites pâtisseries sèches"*—little dry pastries.

Grandville ("**Grandville**")
The celebrated 19th century French illustrator (1803–1847) who pub-
lished, among other things, a collection entitled *Fleurs animées* ("Ani-
mated Flowers") followed by one called *Les Étoiles* ("The Stars");
these were "high-toned" comic-strip art wherein planets, stars,
and flowers were "humanized." Rimbaud (in a letter to Izambard
25 August 1870) called Grandville's drawings the "most idiotic"
thing he'd ever seen.

le Pâtis panique ("**the Pastures of panic**")
Another reference to the Parnassian universe peopled by elemental
divinities like the god Pan (Steinmetz).

un seul pleur de chandelle ("**a candle's only tear-drop**")
The candle is here evoked because the stuff of which is it made is
provided by a "utilitarian" animal, the whale . . . sperm, amber-
gris, tallow, et al.

Toi . . . là-bas ("You, down there")
Rimbaud is here perhaps addressing himself. *"Oises extravagantes,"* the
"Extravagant lazy Rivers," recall Rimbaud's nature poem entitled
Larme / Teardrop, which resurfaces in *A Season in Hell* as an ex-
ample of his "botched" early poetry ("Delirium II: Alchemy of the
Word").

Phébus ("Phoebus")
The sun, one of the aspects of Apollo as the god of light; Phoebus
meaning "bright" in the cognomen *Phoebus Apollo.*

Pedro Velasquez, Habana ("Havanaise / Pedro Velasquez")
An imaginary character whose wealth probably comes from the cigar
trade. Here again, the plants (tobacco) are "put to work."

Incaque la mer de Sorrente ("Feculate the Sorrento Sea")
The term "incaque" is an ironically elegant term for the spreading or
dumping of excrement. I have coined a Latinate verb out of "fecal/
feculent/feculence" to approximate Rimbaud's Latin-derived
"incaque." The image is the inappropriate spreading of fertilizer—
on the sea instead of a field. Sorrento is a town on the coast of
Italy about 20 miles south of Naples; Banville sang the praises of
the sea at Sorrento in his *Odes funambulesques.*

. . . réclames / Pour l'abatis des mangliers ("commercials / For the
felling of mangrove trees")
Rimbaud opines that Banville should aspire to advertising jingles or
commercials for the exploitation of nature. The mangrove was
harvested for use in dyeing and tanning. The hydroid *(hydres)* is a
small tubular freshwater polyp likewise used in textiles. *Lames* re-
fer to the gills on the underside of mushroom caps.

garances perfumées ("perfumed rosy madders")
The rose madder or madder root was used in the dye for the bright red
baggy trousers of the French infantry.

... fleurs, pareille à des mufles ("Flowers that resemble snouts")
For the next four stanzas, Rimbaud invents a few new flowers as an
example of what Banville might attempt to "serve up."

le grand Amour ("the Great Love")
"Greater love hath no man than this, that a man lay down his life for
his friends." Jesus is here quoted in the gospel of John (16:13).
Christ was crucified between two thieves, the one who asked blessing
being absolved of his sins.

Renan ... le chat Murr ... les Thyrses ("Renan ... Murr the cat ...
Thyrsi")
Ernest Renan (1823–1892), French philologist and historian, was noted
(and notorious) for his realistic, rationalistic *Vie de Jésus (Life of
Jesus)*, 1863. "Murr the cat" is a fantastical feline in the epony-
mous tale by E.T.A. Hoffmann, German composer, author, and
illustrator whose tales were the basis of Delibes' *Coppélia*,
Offenbach's *Tales of Hoffmann*, and Tchaikovsky's *Nutcracker*.

Rimbaud seems to be saying that the ways of realism and rationalism
(including Hoffmann's urbanized "mechanical" magic) stifle spiri-
tual vision—or turn a blind eye to it—as symbolized by the wand
of Dionysus, a rod wreathed in ivy and topped with a pine cone,
emblem of his Dionysian revels. The "perfume-induced hysteria"
in the next stanza might compare to the frenzy of the Bacchae (the
god's wild female devotees). Rimbaud calls on Banville to "lift our
spirits" beyond Christian devotion with his odes to nature's floral
aroma.

le mal des pommes de terre ("the potato blight")
In the last two comedic stanzas, Banville is told what he should *really* do
to raise the quality of his verse.

Tréquier ... Paramaribo ("Podunk ... Patagonia")
Tréquier was the tiny Breton village where Renan was born; Paramaribo

was the capital and port of Dutch Guyana in South America—two places at opposite ends of the earth, hence "Podunk" (after the name of a village in Massachusetts—a noun in English for any small, unimportant, and isolated town) and "Patagonia" (a barren region in the south of Argentina and Chile, between the Andes and the Atlantic Ocean).

Monsieur Figuier ("Mister Figtree")
A literal translation of the name of Louis Figuier, a tireless popularizer and vulgarizer of knowledge, whose *Histoire des Plantes* was published in 1865 by Hachette and prominently displayed in their bookshops.

The Drunken Boat / *Le Bateau Ivre*

Rimbaud composed this poem between the first exchange of letters with Paul Verlaine, August to September 1871. It is the longest single poem in his entire output and full of "astonishing verbal virtuosity," as Enid Starkie has noted. "Rimbaud wrote *Le Bateau Ivre* without ever having seen the sea. (. . .) It is . . . an anthology of separate lines of astonishing evocative magic which lingers in the mind, like isolated jewels . . . " (Starkie: *Rimbaud* Part One, Chapter XI).

Starkie lists Figuier's *Ocean World* and *The Sea* by Michelet as primary sources of this poem (both of which were highly popular with young people of the era, profusely illustrated in the case of *Ocean World*).

Other works that sparked his imagination were Jules Verne's *20,000 Leagues Under the Sea*, Victor Hugo's *Toilers of the Sea*, Poe's *Narrative of A. Gordon Pym*, and *A Descent Into the Maelstrom*; but primary among these is *Le Voyage* of Charles Baudelaire, from whence Rimbaud launches his own mad voyage, the ship devoid of human activity, "all its crew massacred save the poet alone . . . " (Starkie).

"Each little island sighted by the watch at night
Becomes an Eldorado, is in his belief
The Promised Land; Imagination soars; despite
The fact that every dawn reveals a barren reef."

Baudelaire: *Le Voyage* (excerpt)
transl. Edna St. Vincent Millay

When that racket with my haulers had done *(Quand avec mes haleurs ont fini ces tapages)*
The howling of the Redskins ceases when all the crew are dead.

vaster than poetry *(plus vastes que nos lyres)*
Literally "vaster than our lyres," meaning "poetic art."

hysterical herds/Of surf *(vacheries/Hystériques, la houle)*
An image derived from Poe's *Descent Into the Maelstrom,* wherein he compares the sound of the rising storm to a buffalo stampede.

"This vision of the buffaloes . . . brings to Rimbaud's mind the thought of Camargue, where the fighting bulls are bred. In the Camargue, on an island at the mouth of the Rhone, is the little town of Les Saintes-Maries-de-la-Mer, where, according to tradition, the three Maries— Marie Jacobé, Marie-Salomé, Marie-Madeline—with their black servant Sara, Lazarus, and Saint Maximin landed after being buffeted by the waves and suffering a fate similar to that of Rimbaud's *bateau ivre* . . . The feast of Trois Maries—25 May—is celebrated by an important bull-fight . . . " (Starkie: Rimbaud Part I Ch. XI).

Leviathan
A sea monster mentioned in the Bible; *Job,* chapter 41, is devoted to a description of leviathan. (Cf. Chapter 40; 15–24: behemoth, a land monster.)

Eldorados *(dorades)*
From Spanish for "the gilded one." A legendary kingdom and king of the Amazon (according to 16th Century explorers of the new America). The king was oiled and powdered in gold-dust in a yearly ritual so that, as the legend has it, he was permanently and literally gilded. His city, Manoa, was enormously wealthy and fabulous, supposedly hidden far up in the mountains. Thus "Eldorados" are any rich, strange land.

Monitors
The name of a modernistic armored-plated warship of the American Civil War (1860-1865); The *Monitor* consisted of a flat iron-clad deck close to the waterline with a revolving steel turret midships that was armed with two cannons which fired alternately.

Hanse
During the Middle Ages, the Hanseatic League was a commercial association between certain cities in Germany and Western Europe; its purpose was to protect local shipping against pirates from the Baltic Sea. War ships and rescue vessels will not help to save the drunken boat.

Behemoths . . . Maelstroms *(Béhémots . . . Maelstroms)*
Behemoth is a gigantic land-monster described in the *Book of Job* (Chapter 40; 15-24). The word "Maelstrom" is from Old Danish ("Grinding Stream") and denotes a powerful, violent whirlpool capable of sucking objects into its vortex.

Too true, too many tears! *(Mais, vrai, j'ai trop pleuré!)*
Literally "But, true, I've wept too much!" As Starkie succinctly puts it: " . . . the poem ends unconsciously prophetic of the poet's destiny, showing the vanity of all his dreams. (. . .) He knew that his wild journey was over and he must content himself with everyday reality."

VERS NOUVEAUX

LATER POEMS

1872–1874

Memory

Mémoire

I

Bright water; like the brine of childish tears,
the whiteness of women's bodies against the sun;
silken mobs of pure lilies of banners
under walls that a virgin girl defended once.

Angel's play;—No . . . the swift gold current sways
her arms, dark and dull, above all cool, through the grass.
She sinks under the blue Sky's canopy,
calling for curtained shade from hill and overpass.

II

Hey, the wet sheen extends its limpid swirls!
The stream fills ready beds with endless, pallid gold;
the faded green dresses of little girls
make for willows, out of which birds dart free and bold.

More pure than a doubloon, a fierce blonde eye
the marsh marigold—wedded faith of thine, O Spouse!—
at noon, from its dim glass, is jealous now
of the Sphere so pink and dear in the hot grey sky.

III

Madame holds herself so tall in the field
near the blizzard of toiling chaff; her parasol
in hand; blooms trod upon; so proud and all.
In the flowering greenery the children read

their book of red morocco! Alas, HE,
like countless white angels parting ways on the road,
heads far beyond the mountain! SHE, wholly
frigid, in black, runs! chasing the man on the go!

IV

Longing for stout young arms in the pure grass!
Gold of an April moon at the sacred bed's core!
Joy in abandoned boatyards, a prey for
August evenings that seed all this rottenness!

Let her weep now under the walls! A breath
in the poplar trees above is the only breeze.
Next, the glassy sheet, opaque, sourceless, grey:
One old man, in his boat becalmed, dredging away.

V

Out-of-reach toy in this dull water's eye,
O motionless boat! oh! arms too short! Nor
flowers: not the yellow yelling nearby;
nor the blue, so nice with ash-grey waters.

Ah! the willow dust shaken off a wing!
The roses in the reeds devoured a long time
ago! My boat, ever fixed, anchored fast
in that deep, rimless eye of water—in what slime?

What Do We Care . . .

Qu'est ce pour nous . . .

What do we care, my heart, for streaming sheets
Of blood, hot coals, and countless murders, the long screams
Of rage, every weeping hell upsetting
All order; the North wind still scouring the debris

With every vengeance? Nothing! . . . All the same,
We crave it! Industrialists, princes, senates,
Perish! power, law, history, go down!
We lay claim to it. The blood! blood! the golden flame!

All-out for war, for vengeance, for terror,
My Soul! Let us writhe in its Bite: Ahh! pass away,
Republics of this world! We've had enough
Of nations, colonists, regiments, emperors!

Who better to stir the furious fire
In whirlwinds than we and our imagined brothers?
It's our turn! Fictional friends: let's have fun.
We'll never have to work, O billowing fire!

Europe, Asia, America, vanish.
Our avenging march has occupied them all, whole
Cities, entire countrysides!—We'll be crushed!
Volcanoes will blow! and the Ocean frozen cold . . .

Oh! my friends!—My heart, they're brothers, for sure:
Dark strangers, what if we started! Come on! let's go!
O disaster! I feel myself quake, the old earth,
More and more yours, on me! The earth dissolves.

It's nothing! I'm here! I'm still here.

Michael and Christine

Michel et Christine

So what the hell if the sun leaves these shores!
Bright flood, let flow! Here's darkness on the roads.
Among the willow trees, in honored yards
Of old, the storm unleashes its downpour.

O hundred lambs, blond troops of idyll days,
Flee the waterways and barren heather!
Plains, deserts, prairie, and horizons are
Dressing themselves in the storm's red array!

Black dog, brown shepherd whose cloak is windblown,
Flee the high lightning in the nick of time;
Blond flock, drowning here in shadow and brimstone,
Seek better shelter in a lower clime.

Yet I, Lord! how my Spirit flies away,
Chasing after icy red skies beneath
Celestial clouds that race above to leap
A hundred long Solognes like a railway.

See, thousands of wolves, thousands of wild seeds
Which, in this religious afternoon storm,
Are swept along with loving twining weeds
To flood old Europe like hundreds of hordes!

Afterwards, the moonlight! Across the land
Red warriors have turned to face black skies
On their pale chargers, slowly riding by!
The pebblestones ring under that proud band!

—And will I see the yellowed woods and bright glens,
O France,—the blue-eyed Bride and blushing man,
At their precious feet, the white Paschal lamb?
—Michael and Christine—and Christ!—the Idyll ends.

Teardrop

Larme

May 1872

Far from birds and herds and village girls
I'd drink, squatting out in the heather
Surrounded by tender young hazel trees
In an afternoon fog of tepid green.

What could I drink from that youthful Oise?
Elms voiceless, grass deflowered, grey skies.
What did I pull from the gourd on the vine?
Some pale golden liquor to sweat me dry.

Just so, I'd have been a battered tavern sign.
Then the cloudburst changed the sky till evening.
This made for dark vistas, lakes and pilings,
Colonnades under the blue night, railway stations.

Woodland waters got lost in virgin sands.
The wind from heaven flung ice to the ponds . . .
Now then! like a fisher of gold or shells,
To say that a drink wouldn't suit me well!

The Black Currant River

La Rivière de Cassis

The Black Currant River flows invisibly
Through hidden valleys:
The voice of a hundred crows alongside,
Angel voices true and kind:
Along with tall commotion in the pines
When several winds dive.

It all, with revolting mysteries, flows
From lands of long ago,
From castles visited, from lofty sites:
On these banks you can hear
The long-dead passions of wandering knights:
Yet the wind blows fresh and clear!

Let the hiker peer through these ancient gates:
He'll walk on more bravely.
Forest soldiers whom the Lord designates,
Dear crows, lovely ravens!
Chase away the crafty rube who raises
Bumpers with an old stump.

Comedy of Thirst

Comédie de la Soif

May 1872

1. *The Parents*

We are your Grandparents,
The Grown-ups!
Covered in the chilly sweats
Of the moon and greenery.
Our dry wines, they were hearty!
Sunlit without illusion
What's a man to do? drink up.

ME:—Death in barbarous rivers.

We are your Grandparents
In the fields.
The water is willow-deep:
See it flowing in the moat
Round the anchored castle keep.
Let's go down to our cellars
After cider and milk.

ME:—Heading for where the cows drink.

We are your Grandparents:
Here, take it,
The liquor in our cabinets;
The Tea, the Coffee, so rare,
Simmering in the samovars.
—Look at the pictures, the flowers.

We're back from the cemetery.

ME:—Ahh! Drinking up all the urns!

2. *The Spirit*

Everlasting Ondines,
Divide the water clean.
Sister of azure, Venus,
Arouse the spotless billows.

Wandering Jews from Norway,
Tell me about snow.
Beloved ancient exiles,
Tell me of the sea.

ME:—Nope, no more of these pure drinks,
These flowers in glasses of water.
Neither legends nor shapes
Quench my thirst!

Singer of songs, it's your god-daughter,
She's my thirst and craze,
Mouthless hydra, my secret sharer,
Who preys and desolates.

3. *Friends*

Come! Wines head for the beach
And billows by the millions!
See the savage Bitters
Rolling down from high mountains!

Wise pilgrims, let us reach
The green-pillared Absinthe . . .

ME:—No more of these landscapes.
Friends, what is drunkenness?

I'd as soon, rather, should,
Putrefy in the pond
Under the creamy scum
Near the floating driftwood.

4. *The Poor Man Dreams*

Maybe a Night awaits me
Where I can drink in peace
In some old-fashioned Town,
And die the more content:
Seeing that I'm patient!

If my ills were put on hold,
If I ever get some gold,
Will I choose to go North
Or to the Land of the Vine? . . .
—Ah! Dreaming's a waste of time

Since it's pure disaster!
And if again I'd be
The olden traveler,
The green inn will never
Open its doors to me.

5. *Conclusion*

The pigeons fluttering on the prairie,
The game that sees in the dark, pursued,
The water-animals, the beast enslaved,
The last butterflies . . . they're thirsty too.

But to melt where that wandering cloud melts,
—Oh! lifted up by that cool refreshment!
To die among those humid violets
Whose golden mornings command these forests?

Lovely Thoughts for Morning

Bonne Pensée du matin

May 1872

At four in the morning, summer,
The slumber of love still endures.
Under the dawn's green shade
Evening's festive scent evaporates.

Yonder in that vast lumber-yard
Towards the sun of Hesperides,
Carpenters already at work
Are toiling in rolled-up shirtsleeves.

Tranquil in their mossy Deserts,
They prepare the rich canopies
Where the city's wealthy laugh
Beneath imitation skies.

Ah! for these charming workers, these men
Who serve the King of Babylon,
Venus! leave Lovers a moment,
Those with haloed souls.

O Queen of the Shepherds,
Bring these craftsmen a little brandy
To put their muscles at ease
Before their noontide swim in the sea.

In Praise of Patience

Fêtes de la patience

1. Banners of May *(Bannières de mai)*

From luminous branches of lime trees
The cries of the hunt fade and die.
Yet among the currant-bushes
Spirited songs take wing and fly.
Here the vines are all entangled
So that our blood laughs in our veins.
The sky's as cute as an angel.
Azure and wave sharing the same.
I'm off! If a sunbeam wounds me,
I'll swoon on the moss, succumbing.

It's too easy, being patient,
Being bored. Fie on my complaints.
I want spectacular summer
To lash me to its lucky car.
O Nature, so much in your sway
—Less alone, less worthless!—I die.
The same way Shepherds, strange to say,
More or less the world over, die.

———

I want the seasons to use me.
I offer you my self, Nature;
And my hunger and all my thirst.
If you please, feed and water me.
Nothing at all can delude me.
Laughing at parents, at the sun
Alike, but I don't want to laugh at all.
And be free by that misfortune.

2. Song of the Highest Tower
(Chanson de la plus haute tour)

Idle youth
All enthralled,
With delicate nicety
I wasted my life.
Ah, let the time come
When hearts beat as one!

I told myself: let up,
And go into hiding:
Forget the promise
Of the highest joys.
Let nothing keep you
From dignified retreat.

I've been patient
To the end of memory.
My fears and pains
Flee to the skies,
And a thirsty disease
Darkens my veins:

Like the prairie
Delivered to oblivion,
Growing and flowering
With incense and weeds
To the sullen whine
Of a hundred nasty flies.

Ah, the countless bereavements
Of the impoverished soul
That's got only the image
Of the Lady Madonna!

Is there anybody who prays
To the Virgin Mary these days?

Idle youth
All enthralled,
With delicate nicety
I wasted my life.
Ah, let the time come
When hearts beat as one!

3. Eternity *(L'Éternité)*

Found it again.
What?—Eternity.
It's the sea going
Into the sun.

Vigilant soul,
Whisper the avowal
Of the night so void
And the day on fire.

So disengage
From human craving,
From common ecstasies
And fly accordingly.

For from you alone,
Embers of satin,
Breathes out the Task
Without it being said: At last.

Hope, not a chance,
No *oldtime religion.*
Knowledge with patience,
The torture is a given.

It is retrieved.
What?—Eternity.
It's the sea on the run
With the sun.

4. Golden Age *(Age d'or)*

Some one of those voices,
—It's always angelic—
Is talking about me,
Severely and self-righteously.

Those thousand questions
That ramble on and on
Bring nothing in the end
But rapture and madness;

Remember this bit
So gay, so easy:
It's only a wave, a flowering,
And it's your family!

Then it sings: Ohhh
So gay, so easy,
Visible to the naked eye
—And I sing along with it—

Remember this bit
So gay, so easy:
It's only a wave, a flowering,
And it's your family! . . . et cetera . . .

And another voice
—How angelic!—

Is talking about me
Severely and self-righteously;

And instantly begins to sing,
Like sisters of the wind,
In a German accent,
But fiery and full.

The world is cruel;
This astonishes you!
Live and let dark misery
Be consigned to flames.

Oh! lovely castle!
How luminous your life!
What Age are you from,
Natural princedom
Of our big brother? et cetera . . .

I too sing, I do:
Many many sisters: Voices
Not for every audience!
Surround me then
With modest glory . . . et cetera . . .

Young Marrieds

Jeune ménage

The room's wide open to the turquoise sky;
Not an inch of space: stacked boxes and trunks!
The outer wall is flush with birthwort vine
Where the chops of chattering goblins buzz.

These are actually plots of genies,
This expenditure and vain disorder!
There's the African fairy furnishing
Blackberries and the cobwebs in corners.

Snooping in cupboards, a few malcontent
Godmothers in lappets of light sit glum
And do not budge! The couple is absent
For no good reason, so nothing gets done.

The groom has always got the daily breeze
To cheat on him while he's away from home.
Even water sprites with malicious ease
Flow all around the garret as they roam.

At night, oh love! the honeymoon yet
Will gather up their smiles and fill the sky
With a thousand copper coronets.
They must face a knavish rat by and by

—If no pale will o' the wisp has arrived
Like a rifle-shot, when vespers is through,
—O Specters of Bethlehem, sanctified
And white, be sure you charm their windows' blue.

Brussels

Bruxelles

July, Regent's Boulevard

Beds of deathless flowers reach up to
The pleasing palace of Jupiter.
—I know that it's *You,* in these places, who
Mixes in your near Sahara-Blue!

Then, as the sunlit rose and pine
And vine have closed in on their prey,
A little widow's cage!
... What fine
Feathered flocks! O ee ah, ee-i-yay! ...

—Placid mansions, ancient passions!
Cottage of the Madwoman's lovelorn woe.
Back of rosetree bottoms, the shadowy
Balcony of Juliet, very low.

—Miss Juliet reminds me of Miss Harriet—
A charming stop on the railway there
In the heart of a mountain like an orchard's depths
Where countless blue devils dance in the air.

The green bench where the pale Irish girl
Sings to her guitar how paradise rages.
Then from the Guyana bar and grill
The chattering of kids and from those cages.

The ducal window makes my thoughts run
To poisonous slugs and boxwood shrubs
That sleep here under the sun,

And then,
It's gorgeous! too fine! Let's guard our tongues.

—Boulevard without motion or commerce,
Mute, every dramatic and comic urge,
Infinite shows that gather and merge,
I know you and admire you in silence.

*   *   *

Est-elle almée?
Is she a dancing girl? . . . In the early blue hours
Will she self-destruct like those withering flowers . . .
In front of that splendid sweeping view where you sense
The city's flourishing breath, its whisper immense!

It's gorgeous! too fine! Yet it's just got to be there—
For the Fisher Wife and for the Wild Pirate's air,
And, too, the last of the maskers who yet believe
In festivals by night on the purest of seas.

Feasts of Hunger

Fêtes de la faim

I'm famished, Anne, Anne,
Take your ass on the lam.

If I have any *taste,* I own
It's not for much but earth and stone.
Dinn! ding! dinn! ding! Let's eat our share
Of rocks and coal, iron and air.

Turn, my hungers: Graze on fields
Of husky seed!
Suck up the merry venom
Of twining weeds.

Eat
The pebbles poor men crush,
Ancient stones from churches
The gravel, sons of floods,
Bread embedded in grey gulches!

My hungers, they're tips of dark air;
The bell-man azure.
It's my stomach pulling me there.
It's a disaster.

Over the earth, leaves sprout afresh!
I go for leafy fruited flesh.
And at the furrow's breast I pick
Sweet lettuce and the violet.

I'm famished, Anne, Anne!
Ride your ass, on the lam.

The Wolf Howls

Le Loup criait

Under the leaves the wolf howls,
Spitting up lovely plumes
From his breakfasting on fowl:
Just like that, I'm consumed.

The salads and the fruits
Are waiting to be picked;
But spiders in the bush
Eat only violets.

How I sleep! How I seethe
On the altars of Solomon.
The bubbling overruns the blight
And blends into the Kedron.

Hear How It Bays

Entends comme brame

Hear how it bays
near the acacias
in April, the viridian
shoot of the pea!

In its misty purity,
towards the moon! you'll see
the heads of the old-time
saints wagging restlessly . . .

Far from the bright haystacks
Of the capes, from lovely rooftops
Those dear Old Codgers desire
That cunning elixir . . .

Gold neither of haloes
nor stars! that's
the fog breathed off
by this nocturnal show.

Nevertheless, they remain,
—Germany, Sicily—
in that sad and paling
haze, precisely!

O Seasons, O Châteaux

Ô Seasons, Ô Châteaux

O seasons, O châteaus!
What soul's without its flaws?

O seasons, O châteaus.

I have studied the magical shapes
Of the Happiness no one escapes.

O let it thrive each time
Your French cock chants his rhyme.

But! I'll no more seek and strive,
It's taken charge of my life.

This Charm's taken body and soul,
And scattered all I have to show!

What sense will my words come to know?
It sets them flying, lets them go!

O seasons, O châteaus!

O Seasons, O Citadels

O seasons, O citadels
Where's the soul without faults?

O seasons, O castles,

The studious magic I've made
From the Blissfulness none evade.

O raise it lively, when you hear
Each time the cocky Chanticleer.

Why! there's nothing more that I crave,
It's in charge, I'm a lifetime slave.

This Charm! it took body and soul,
And cast away my strivings whole.

My words well understood, who knows?
It sets them flying, off they go!

O seasons, O châteaus!

[And if mishap drags me away,
Disfavor names my certain fate.

My book at this disdain, alas!
More than ready to breathe its last!

—O Seasons, O Palaces!
Where is the soul without flaws?]

Ô Saisons, Ô Châteaux

Ô saisons, ô chateaux
Quelle âme est sans défauts?

Ô saisons, ô chateaux,

J'ai fait la magique étude
Du Bonheur, que nul n'élude.

Ô vive lui, chaque fois
Que chante son coq gaulois.

Mais! je n'aurai plus d'envie,
Il s'est chargé de ma vie.

Ce Charme! il prit âme et corps,
Et dispersa tous efforts.

Que comprendre à ma parole?
Il faut qu'elle fuie et vole!

Ô saisons, ô chateaux!

[Et, si le malheur m'entraine,
Sa disgrâce m'est certaine.

Il faut que son dédain, las!
Me livre au plus prompt trépas!

—Ô Saisons, ô Chateaux!
Quelle âme est sans défauts?]

Shame

Honte

As long as the blade hasn't
Sliced into that brain-flesh—
That white-green-fatty packet,
Never a fume that's fresh—

(Better yet! HE should clip
His nose, and ears and lips,
His paunch! And say a farewell
To his legs! Oh miracle!)

Really, I know for a fact
Since that blade held to his head
Since the rocks hitting his back
Since his guts burnt flaming red

Haven't done the deed, the killjoy
Kid, the feckless beast, must never
For a minute cease his ever-
Lasting treachery's cheating ploys,

Like a Rocky Mountain polecat
Stinking up all around its path!
So that, O my God! when he dies
Some kind of a prayer might rise!

NOTES

Memory

According to most sources, this poem dates from Rimbaud's return to Charleville in 1872. Memory is a river, the "bright water" carrying poet and reader through the landscape of the poem.

I . . . *quelque pucelle* **("a virgin girl")**
A reference to some kind of virginal heroine—a maiden—such as Joan of Arc, who was also knows as *La Pucelle* ("The Maid").

II . . . *ta foi conjugale, ô l'Épouse!* **("wedded faith of thine, O Spouse!")**
As in *Michael and Christine*, the term "spouse" has been capitalized for emphasis, perhaps symbolizing France or the land, the planet. The "wedded faith" may signify the marriage of earth and sky (producing offspring in the plants and flowers). The marigold, a round yellow flower growing in the marsh, is jealous of the sun above, glowing pink through the overcast haze.

III *Madame* **("Madame")**
Undoubtedly an allusion to Madame Rimbaud, the poet's mother, keeping an eye on the field hands while the air is filled with a blizzard of threads and filaments ("chaff") from the work of harvesting.

III *Hélas, Lui* **("Alas, HE")**
The emphasized HE is most likely referring to the poet's father, who was "far beyond the mountain," having deserted the family when Arthur was six.

IV *un vieux . . . dans sa barque immobile* **("One old man, in his boat becalmed")**

The drunken boat of the poet's not-so-distant childhood seems to be invoked here. Back in "home port," the poet is at a standstill, but still at work, "dredging" the waters of memory.

V *Jouet de cet oeil d'eau morne, je n'y puis prendre* ("Out-of-reach toy in this dull water's eye")

The boat, an emblem of freedom, travel, and experience, is unattainable to the poet, who shuns the flowers on the bank as objects of interest or meaning.

V *Les roses des roseaux dès longtemps dévorées* ("The roses in the reeds devoured a long time ago!")

Roses—the symbol of love or passion—have rotted here or been eaten up while the poet, wishing to shake the dust off his wings and fly, stares at the motionless boat, chained to the depths of memory, "in such slime."

What Do We Care

This apocalyptic vision recalls portions of the Communard poems, *Parisian Orgy* and *Parisian War Song*. The images of earthquake, flood, and volcanic action recur in *Illuminations* where they are amplified and extended—as in *After The Flood*, *Barbarous*, and *Historic Evening*. The end of the world is presented as a drama both personal (internal) and cosmic (terrestrial).

Michael and Christine

In *A Season In Hell*, Rimbaud writes: "One vaudeville title presented horrors before me," (un titre de vaudeville dressait des épouvantes devant moi), referring to this poem and the play that inspired it.

Michel et Christine (1821) was the title of a popular "vaudeville" or melodrama by Eugène Scribe (1791–1861) that had a long and successful run during the Second Empire. Rimbaud could have seen this play in Paris or the provinces.

The action of the melodrama takes place during the Napoleonic Wars; the main characters are Michael, a peasant betrothed to Christine, a village girl, and Stanislas, a soldier in love with Christine, who sacrifices himself for the sake of the couple. Rimbaud deconstructs the plot of Scribe's play and presents a vaudeville wherein stormy skies evoke the vision of armies in flight. The sky and the earth, peasants and barbarians, sheep and wolves are the contending factions in the poet's vision, all harmonized after the storm passes, in the lightly ironic finale in which the happy couple are seen posed with the Paschal lamb, a symbol for Christ's sacrifice.

Zut alors ("So what the hell")
This opening phrase is common French slang, but may be a code word for Rimbaud's allegiance to the *"Zutistes,"* a rowdy regular gathering devoted to frank use of language, the satirizing of society, and getting drunk.

. . . cent agneaux . . . soldats blonds ("hundred lambs, blond troops")
The lambs are the clouds rolling overhead, like "blond soldiers" on the move; they're portrayed in a pastoral scene (the "idyll") that mingles the stormy sky with shepherds, sheep, soldiers, dogs, and wolves in a rapidly shifting panorama.

Sur cent Solognes longues comme un railway ("A hundred long Solognes like a railway")
La Sologne is the marshy plain that runs along the river Loire. Rimbaud is spanning a hundred marshy plains in this image—like a railway spanning rivers and miles.

L'Épouse aux yeux blues, l'homme au front rouge ("the blue-eyed Bride
and blushing man")
This is the only appearance of "Michael and Christine" in the poem.
In the play, Michael is a rustic youth much given to blushing. The
capitalization of Bride *(l'Épouse)* may indicate that Christine is an
allegory for France, "eldest daughter of the Church," as Rimbaud
recalls in *A Season In Hell.*

The Paschal lamb, eaten at Passover by the Jews to commemorate their
escape from captivity, is linked to Christ by his sacrifice that liber-
ates man from the "captivity" of death and sin, according to Ro-
man Catholic dogma.

Teardrop

The title expresses regret, tears having been utilized as the symbol for
this by classical and Romantic poets of all epochs. The inability to
quench an "essential" thirst plays into this image.

jeune Oise ("youthful Oise")
The tributary creek near Roche, flowing into the Oise near Aisnes.

mauvaise enseigne d'auberge ("a battered tavern sign")
Probably meaning nostalgia for the Green Inn; lost innocence, free-
dom, contentment.

The Black Currant River

As Steinmetz has noted, this poem is a transposition of *The Crows* to
another kind of no-man's-land. The battles were fought long ago,
but the river is still dark with blood, like black currant cordial.

les mystères révoltants ("revolting mysteries")
In subversive secrecy, the river winds and turns, sometimes flowing in
hidden places.

Qui trinque d'un moignon vieux ("who raises / Bumpers with an old
stump.")
The image of the sly peasant raising his glass with an "old stump"
conjures up the survivor of old wars getting drunk in the woods—
perhaps even toasting an old tree stump with his stump of an arm.

Comedy of Thirst

"Comedy" in French also means drama—or any theatre piece. Rimbaud
constructs part of the poem like an actor's "side" or printed part,
wherein all other action and dialogue are paraphrased or telescoped
and the actor's speeches or replies are spelled out in full.

1. *Les Parents* ("The Parents")
The poet or ME (the "actor") is given a tour of the family grounds by
his grandparents, or their ghosts.

toutes les urnes ("all the urns")
The urn has a double meaning here, inasmuch as the grandparents are
"back from the cemetery."

2. *L'Esprit* ("Spirit")
This poem refers back to the Parnassian style, with its water sprites
(Ondines) and mythological figures (Venus, et al.): "no more,"
says the ME.

Juifs errants ("Wandering Jews")
The Wandering Jew was the central figure in a widespread medieval

legend that told how a Jew, who refused to allow Christ to rest at his door on the march to Calvary, was condemned to wander over the face of the earth till the Day of Judgment. *The Chronicle of St. Albans Abbey* (1228 A.D.) quotes the Jew as saying, "Go faster, Jesus," to which Jesus replies, "I am going, but thou shalt tarry till I come again."

The allusion also shows up in Verlaine's *Romances sans paroles* ("Belgian Landscapes—Walcourt") where it refers to the two poets in their wanderings through Belgium.

Anciens exilé chers ("Beloved ancient exiles")
Ulysses, Aeneas (who sailed the seas, far from home) and/or Ovid, the Roman poet who was exiled among the Scythians on the Black Sea, where he composed *Epistulae ex Ponto* ("Letters from the Sea") A.D. 13.

. . . *fleurs d'eau pour verres* ("flowers in glasses of water")
The poet shuns the "still life" arrangement of nature favored by the Parnassians: No more bouquets, no more mythology, no more "shapes" or figurines.

Chansonnier ("Singer of Songs")
The allusion here is uncertain, but the Singer could be Apollo (another mythological figure), the god of music and lyric poetry. The god-daughter, in all likelihood then, is the muse—or the spirit of poetry—a stern mistress, like the nine-headed monster Hydra fought by Hercules. As soon as he struck off one of its heads, two shot up in its place. This muse-hydra is mouthless because the poet must speak for her while she ravishes him.

3. *Les Amis* ("Friends")
Having dealt with parents and fellow poets, Rimbaud here turns to his drinking buddies among the "Zutistes." Vomited wine eventually flows from sewer to sea.

Bitters ("Bitters")
A mixture of brandy and gin.

L'absinthe aux verts piliers . . . ("The green-pillared Absinthe . . . ")
Baudelaire's line "Nature is a temple of living pillars" *("La Nature est un temple où de vivants piliers")*—from the sonnet *Correspondances*—is here transmogrified into a paean to absinthe—the highly intoxicating green liquor to which Verlaine was addicted. Absinthe is portrayed as a sanctuary for "wise pilgrims" who seek intense intoxication without the nausea of overindulgence.
4. *Le pauvre Songe* ("The Poor Man Dreams")
The poet dreams of his future, then dismisses dreaming as a folly. The green inn reappears as an image of the inaccessible past.

5. *Conclusion* ("Conclusion")
The poet, the ME, decides that all life thirsts—better perhaps to melt and become a cloud, a mist, the dew evaporating in the morning sun.

Lovely Thoughts for Morning

Hespérides ("Hesperides")
Rimbaud equates the sun with the golden apples guarded by the daughters of Hesperus on their island at the end of the world.

Babylone ("Babylon")
The carpenters are comparable to the master-builders who made Babylon one of the wonders of the ancient world.

Vénus ("Venus")
Rimbaud here anticipates the dictum of Freud's apostate apostle Wilhelm Reich, that "Love, Work and Knowledge are the well-springs of our life. They should also govern it."

In Praise of Patience

The title *Fêtes de la patience* could also be translated as Festivals of Patience or Patient Celebrations.

Portions of this cycle (nos. 2 and 3) reappear in *A Season In Hell* in slightly revised form.

3. *Éternité* ("Eternity")

John R. Theobald in *The Lost Wine* (Green Tiger, 1980) notes: "At the age of seventeen, Rimbaud had glimpsed, this once at least, that eternity is not endless time, but a breakthrough into dimensions that nullify time altogether, the absolute now; and that he found a way, in those tight, elliptical stanzas, to communicate this awareness without a trace of didacticism: first, through an arcane fusion of sun, night, and sea; and then, through the self-denial of specious hopes, in favor of something resembling what we might attribute to the existential self-reliance . . . It is not an epiphany to recommend itself to simpler faiths."

4. *Age d'or* ("Golden Age")

In this poem, a personality alternates or disintegrates into a series of different voices (some are angelic, some are not). These voices chant a repetitive song, praising natural movement and growth—visible to the naked eye—urging the personality to sing it indefinitely ("et cetera").

D'un ton Allemand ("In a German accent")

This voice is perhaps a relative of Poe's "Angel of the Odd" (translated as *L'Ange du bizarre"* by Baudelaire in *Histoires grotesques et serieuses*) who always speaks in a German accent.

Young Marrieds

Composed on the back of a letter from the artist Forain, this lyric
dates from the 'honeymoon' period of the relationship between
Verlaine and Rimbaud, 1871–72.

aristoloches ("birthwort vine")
Any of several plants, herbs, or woody vines with aromatic roots used
in folk medicine to aid childbirth. "Devil-fingers" *(doigts du diable)*
is the folk idiom in northern France for the flowering birthwort,
linking up to the image of goblins (or little demons in the green-
ery) in the next line.

la fée africaine ("the African fairy")
The black, exotic spirit dispenses berries of like color.

les resilles ("cobwebs")
Literally "hair-nets," a common metaphor for cobwebs.

marraines mécontentes ("malcontent Godmothers")
The godmothers are disappointed that there are no children (to justify
their rôle) in this marriage. The 'godmothers' are perhaps sun-
beams that pry into every cupboard while the couple is gone.

des esprits des eaux ("water sprites")
The room is exposed to the elements; the roof leaks.

bandeaux de cuivre ("copper coronets")
Copper is symbolically powerful in the realm of alchemy, where it is in
the sphere of Venus, linked to warmth and the feminine.

au malin rat ("a knavish rat")

Symbol of hard work, the rat is also a carrier of plague. Despite the blessings of Venus, the couple's lovemaking is interrupted by a rat in the room. A *knavish* rat may imply the quarrels and spats of young marriage.

Spectres saints et blancs de Bethlehem ("O Spectres of Bethlehem, pale, sanctified / And white")

The ghosts of the slaughtered innocents—condemned by Herod the Great in an attempt to kill the baby Jesus. "Then Herod, when he saw that he was mocked of the wise men, was exceeding wroth, and sent forth, and slew all the children that were in Bethlehem, and in all the coasts thereof, from two years old and under, according to the time which he had diligently enquired of the wise men." (Matthew 3:16)

Brussels

The heading of this poem also contains the words "July" and *"Boulevard du Régent,"* indicating its time and place of composition. The fragment *Est-elle almée?* with its echoing line, "C'est trop beau!" is dated July 1872, and "Brussels" probably dates from the same year, although some critics have suggested that it was composed a year later, after the shooting incident of July 10, 1873. See note on "petite veuve" below.

Plates bandes d'amarantes ("Beds of deathless flowers")

Literally, "Flower-beds of amaranths." The amaranth is an imaginary flower that never fades; also, any of a genus of coarse herbs (including pig-weeds) cultivated for their showy flowers. The word in Greek, *amaranton*, signifies "immortality," thence the palace where these flowers grow is the abode of the immortal god Jupiter, omnipresent as far as the "Sahara-Blue," the skies of Africa.

. . . cage de la petite veuve ("a little widow's cage")

La veuve in French is not only "widow," but a species of sparrow called the widow-bird or whida-finch in English. This could also refer to Verlaine, behind bars for the attempted homicide of July 10, or to the earlier Verlaine in his cage of bourgeois respectability.

... *de la Folle par affection* ("the Madwoman's lovelorn woe")
A probable allusion to Ophelia in *Hamlet*, since *Romeo and Juliet* is touched upon in the very next line.

... *les fesses des rosiers* ("rosetree bottoms")
Literally, "buttocks of the rosebushes," a rustic expression from the Ardennes that designates the flexible trunk-branch of a rose trellis or climbing rosebush.

L'Henriette ("Miss Harriet")
Another of the poet's mystery women whose initials are H (cf. Helen, Hortense, Henrika in *Illuminations*).

paradis d'orage ("how paradise rages")
An expression also found in *Illuminations*: "Le paradis des orages" ("The paradise of storms") in "Cities II"—a kind of heaven. The pale Irish girl and the countless (thousands of) blue devils are similar symbols of melancholy.

fenêtre du duc ("the ducal window")
According to Steinmetz, Rimbaud here refers to the palace of the duke of Arenberg, an imposing Brussels edifice. By contrast, the snail or slug carries its domicile on its back, and resides in the shade of the palace.

Est-Elle Almée? / Is She A Dancing Girl?
These two quatrains are similar in style and expression to "Brussels."
The woman referred to is perhaps a member of the opera ballet; *Le Corsaire* (The Pirate) was a long-running favorite ballet by

Adolphe Adam, based on Byron's poem of the same name (1814:
The Corsair).

... *almée* ("dancing girl")

An oriental dancer (specifically Egyptian) who performs to the accom-
paniment of song. Also, according to Steinmetz, citing the
Bescherelle Dictionary, it is an Arabic word signifying cleverness
or skill *("mot arabe qui signifie savante")*. "Is She Knowing?" might
be another translation of the line.

la chanson du Corsaire ("the Wild Pirate's air")

Adam's *Le Corsaire* premiered at the Paris Opera on January 23, 1856.
There is also an opera by Verdi and several plays of the period, all
derived from Byron's tale.

Feasts of Hunger

This poem, heavily revised, reappears in *Delirium II* of A Season
In Hell. Between the opening and closing refrain (omitted in
the revision), the hungers of Rimbaud are seen to be as vora-
cious as his thirst was quenchless: he finds nourishment in the
inedible, in sounds and smells, in the stones and rubble of the
earth.

Si j'ai du goût ("If I have any *taste*")

The word is emphasized as a double entendre: Taste is not just aes-
thetic sensibility but an appetite that's omnivorous.

The Wolf Howls

This poem also appears in *Delirium II*, appended to the revised Feasts of Hunger. Again, the image of "hunger" swings between the belly and the spirit.

... autels de Salomon ... Cédron ("altars of Solomon ... Kedron")
The altars may refer to the "wisdom" of Solomon, who built the First Temple in Jerusalem (c. 10th century B.C.). Kedron is a brook that flows between Jerusalem and Mount Olivet.

Hear How It Bays

This enigmatic verse, untitled in the manuscript, resists an easy explication or explanation. Many critics, however, have noted that it seems to be a parody of Verlaine's lyrical *Romances sans paroles* or "La lune blanche" from *La Bonne Chanson*. Botanical imagery may also be disguising an allusion to alchemy and the use of urine in some experiments.

Phoebé ("the moon")
This was the name for the moon among the ancient Greeks—and thereby, used by the Parnassians and Verlaine, too.

triste et blémi ("sad and paling")
Adjectives typical of Verlaine's poetry and his extreme sentimentality.

Ô Saisons, Ô Châteaux

The general consensus regarding this poem states that the seasons cor-
respond to periods in the poet's life (and his experience); the
châteaus or castles superimpose an architectural plan—or aesthetic
map—on these moments or "seasons."

O Saisons, O Châteaux ("O Seasons, O Châteaus")
There are three different versions of the opening lines in a rough draft of
this poem (quoted in Steinmetz and in Bouillane de Lacoste ed. *Poésies*
[1939] Mercure de France). The first two are lined out and the third
remains.

(1) *Les saisons et châteaux*
Où court où vole où coule

("The seasons and the castles
Where they ran, where flew, whither flowed")

(2) *Les saisons et châteaux*
L'ame n'est pas sans defauts

("The seasons and castles
The soul not without faults")

Two final couplets and the refrain at the end of this draft are also
crossed out; I have translated them [in brackets] in a second ver-
sion of the "whole" text, *O Seasons, O Citadels.*

le Bonheur ("Happiness" / "Blissfulness")
"Le Bonheur était ma fatalité" ("Happiness was my fatality"), says the
poet in *Season In Hell* just before quoting this poem in slightly

revised form. A literal rendering of Bonheur (capitalized for emphasis) yields the term "Goodtimes," which in English is often a euphemism for sexual pleasuring.

coq gaulois ("French cock" / "cocky Chanticleer")
Literally, "the Gallic cock," which in French has a wealth of symbolic and semantic associations: patriotic, religious, and sexual. Also, the Latin word for cock or rooster is *gallus* and the Roman Catholic liturgy contains a chanted hymn that begins "Gallo canente spes redit" ("Hope returns"—or "comes again"—at cock's crow"); the song of the cock in the poem probably intends a punning play to mix worship with sexual activity, initiated at dawn, at cock-crow. Gaulois also has subsidiary meanings of "plain-spoken" or "forthright," hence the erect male sex organ, an upstanding cock.

Ce Charme! ("This Charm!")
The word refers to any strong magical incantation and is connected to the "song of the cock"—the symbolic dawn, sunrise, and sex play.

Shame

Some critics date this poem from May of 1872 (based on its regular versification), others put May 1873 as the probable date of composition, reflecting the quarrels between Verlaine and Rimbaud at that time.

. . . à vapeur jamais nouvelle (" . . . Never a fume that's fresh")
Without a clue, without any fresh or new ideas; perhaps a sarcastic jibe at the use of rhyme and stanza in this poem.

Lui ("He")
Rimbaud referring to himself—as possibly seen by Verlaine.

ses jambes! ô merveille . . . ("**his legs! Oh miracle** . . . ")
Verlaine, in many of his writings, praises or comments on the beauty
  of Rimbaud's legs (Steinmetz).

un chat des Monts-Rocheux ("**a Rocky Mountain polecat**")
A pun on Roche, site of the Rimbaud family farm. These "Rocky"
  mountains are the hills around Roche where Rimbaud prowled,
  alluding at the same time to the exotic Rockies of America.

Cuntry Matters

Conneries

Drunken Coachman

Cocher Ivre

Filthy
Drinks:
Pearly
Winks:

Bitter
Law,
Coach
Crash!

Woman
Falls,
Loins

Bleed:
Groan.
Screech!

Young Glutton

Jeune Goinfre

Silken
Beanie,
Ivory
Weenie,

Dressed all
In black,
Paul eyeballs
The pantry,

Shows bare
Tiny tongue,
Probes pear,

Readies
Breadstick
And squirts.

Paris

Paris

Al's Footwear, Pipers,
Taylor, Pleyel,
—O Tapster!—Cocoa Cremes!
—O Christs!—O Pharmacies!

Kinko, Jocko, Goodman!
Popenose, Manson, Monroe!
Matisse, Manuel, Gallicoe!
Gangster Guido—Petticoat

Of the Graces! Hatter!
Unctuous waxes!
Old bread, spirits!

Blind men!—after that, who knows?
—Town cops, Seltzer Deluxe
Right at home! Let's be Christians!

The Old Woman's Old Man

Vieux de la Vieille

Here's to the peasants of the emperor!
Here's to the emperor of peasants!
Here's to the son of Mars,
To the glorious 18th of March!
When heaven blessed Eugenia's guts!

The Sealed Lips (Seen in Rome)

Les Lèvres Closes (Vu à Rome)

All covered with Christian emblems,
At the Sistine Chapel in Rome,
There's a little scarlet skullcap
Full of dried-up ancient noses:

Noses of Theban ascetics,
Noses of the Holy Grail cant,
Where the pale night coagulates
To sepulchral ancient plain-chant.

Into that mystic shrivelling,
Every morning, they introduce

A schismatic impurity,
Dusty snuff so finely reduced.

Feast of Love (Paul Verlaine)

Fête Galante (Paul Verlaine)

Dreamy, Scapino
Strokes a bunny
Under his coat.

Columbina—
Who likes to fuck!—
Do re mi—strums

The bunny's eye-hole,
Soon enough
Tight as a drum!

The Outcast Cherub

L'Angelot Maudit

Bluish rooftops and whitewashed doorways
Just like those of nocturnal Sundays

At the edge of town: the street is white,
Totally silent, and it is night.

The houses lining the street are strange,
With window-shutters made of angels.

But look, toward the city limits,
See him running, shivering, wicked,

A black little angel staggering
From eating too many jujubes.

He takes a shit: then he disappears.
But his outcast caca still appears,

Under the vacuous holy moon,
Filthy blood in an easy cesspool.

Lily

Lys

O Swing! O lily, silver Enema-pump!
Disdainful of labor, disdaining famines!
The dawn fills you up with detergent love!
A heavenly sweetness greases your stamens!

Humanity

L'Humanité

Humanity's put shoes on big Baby Progress.

The Broom

Le balai

Here's a humble houndstooth broom, too rigid
For sweeping a room or painting a wall.
Its uses are distressing so don't laugh.
Its dull, dried-out bristles take root in some
Ancient prairie: its handle is bleached white
Like wood from an isle in the dog-star's blaze.
Its braidings resemble frozen tresses.
I love the desolate smell of the thing.

And I'd like to scrub your wide milky shores, O
Moon, wherein our dead Sisters' ghost delights.

Exiles

Exils

*   *   *

Well, if we're interested, my dear Conneau,
Less in Uncle's victories than Girly Shows . . . !
Well, it's wholesome instinct in feeble Folk!
Alas!! And who's made our bile so vile a spew?!
And who's already set to slam the bolt
Against the Wind the kids call Hullabaloo!?

*   *   *

(Fragment of a letter in verse by Napoleon III, 1871.)

Saturnine Rhetoric

after Belmontet

Hypotyposes saturniennes

ex Belmontet

What's up with this mystery so dense and gloomy?
Why, without unfurling their white sail, these gloomy
Royal skiffs of youth all at sea?

———————

Let's reverse the sorrow of our tearful places.

*   *   *

Love wants to live off her sister.
Friendship is living on his brother.

*   *   *

The scepter, which you've hardly revered,
Is just a cross of great suffering
Atop the volcano of nations!

*   *   *

Oh! Honor gushes over your manly mustache!
    Belmontet,
    archetypical Poet.

Memoirs of an Idiotic Old Prick

Remembrances du vieillard idiot

Forgive me, Father!
A youngster, at country fairs,
I never cared for dull arcades where all shots win,
But headed for the spot full of shouts, where donkeys
With droopy flanks displayed their bloody length of hose
The which I still don't comprehend! . . .

And mother then
Whose nightgown had a bitter odor, where it was
As yellow as any fruit and ripped at the hem,
My mother, who clambered noisily into bed,
—Labor's heir for all that—my mother with her ripe
Womanly thighs, with her big fat buttcheeks where the
Linen creases, gave me the unspeakable hots.

A shamefulness more crude and much calmer was when
My little sister, coming back from school,
Having long skated the ice in her wooden shoes,
Would pee, and I'd watch it escaping from her lips
Tight and pink down there, a mischievous thread of piss . . . !

O forgive me!
I dreamt of my dad now and then:
The night, the card game where the joking was obscene,
The neighbor, and I whom they pushed aside, things seen . . .
—Because a father means trouble!—and things are conceived!

His knee, sometime caressable; his trousers where
My fingers wanted to open the fly . . . —ohh no!—
To handle my father's hefty knob, dark and hard,
While his hairy hand cradled me.

Not to mention
The pot, the one with handles, glimpsed in the attic,
The calendars with ruddy covers, the basket
Of rags, the Bible and the bathroom, and the maid,
The Holy Virgin, the crucifix . . .

Oh, no one
Was so frequently troubled by sin, as if stunned!
And so now that forgiveness might be truly mine:
Since my infected senses have made me their victim,
I now confess myself, admit my youthful crimes! . . .

*   *   *

And besides!—if I might have a talk with The Lord!—
Why does puberty come late? why the misery
Of the relentless gland consulted too often?

Why the tardy shadow below my gut? Why these
Untold fears, always heaped on bliss like black gravel?

Me, I've always been stupefied! What's to know?

*　　*　　*

Forgiven?
Take back that big blue sock,
Father.
What a childhood! . . .
. . . —And let's jack off!

Old Coppées Old Copies

Vieux Coppées

1.

By the shopfronts' blazing eye, summer evenings
When the sap quakes under the shady gratings
Spread at the foot of scrawny chestnut trees,
Avoiding those gloomy groups of carefree,
Pipe-sucking, cigar-kissing stay-at-homes,
Through the narrow half-stoned lanes where I roam
—While above, an *Ibled* sign flashes red—
I'm dreaming that winter will freeze Tibet with
Its loud waters, lulling the human wave,
—And that the harsh North wind spares not a vein.

2.

To the bedside books, artistic, serene,
Obermann, Genlis, *The Pulpit* and Green-green,
Bored with bland and outlandish novelties,
I'm hoping, with old age at last achieved,
To add the tome of Doctor Venetti.
Done with public doldrums, I'll be ready
For a taste of old Charm's explicit line.
Author and artist have glossed up every
Sexual woe—and isn't it fine:
DR. VENETTI's *Love and Marriage Guide.*

3.

I sat in a third-class carriage: an old priest
Took out his pipe and calmly stuck his cropped
Grey head out the window, into the breeze.
Then, braving a rude rebuff, this Christian
Turned, energetic and sad, to ask me
For a pinch of tobacco—having been
Chaplain for some twice-condemned royalty
—To relax the tunnel's boredom, dark vein
Wide open for travel, near Soisson, Aisne.

4.

No doubt, in Spring I like outdoor cafés
Where dwarf chestnut trees are bursting with buds
Toward the narrow common fields in May.
Close by the Drinkers, the oft-scolded pups
Trample hyacinths in the flower bed.
And throughout the evenings of hyacinth
At the slab of a table dating from
1720, where a deacon carved
His Latin alias thin as scripture,
There's coughing into sober black bottles.

5. State of Siege? *(État de siège?)*

The poor coachman, under his roof of tin,
Warming an enormous chilblain in his glove,
Trolls his heavy bus along the left bank,
Nudging the farebox with his fevered groin.
Meanwhile, softly shadowed where the cops are,
The honest cab is looking at the moon
In the deep sky, cradled in green wadding,
Despite the curfew and the careful hour

When the bus returns to the Odeon
A lewd bum's howling in the crossroads dark.

6. Remembrance *(Ressouvenir)*

This year the Prince Imperial's birthday
Leaves me warm and generous memories
Of a limpid Paris where N's are a
Golden snow on palace gates, on horse-blocks,
A blast of ribbons in red white and blue.
In the public swirl of big faded hats,
Warm flowery weskits, ancient frock-coats,
And songs from oldtime workers in the bars,
On strewn shawls the Emperor walks, in black,
With Holy Señoritas, that evening.

7.

The Adolescent kid who picked up the
Balls, exiled blood in his veins, a famous
Father, watches for hope to put a bloom
On his face and stature, he wants to see
Different curtains than for Thrones and Cribs.
And, too, his fine torso doesn't aspire
To the Future's breach!—He's left the old toy.
—O that sweet dream of his! O lovely Spritz!*
His eyes are sunken, he's too much alone:
"Poor kid, his Habit is close to the bone!"

*That is, "Spritz in your own home!" (A.R.)

Smut

Les Stupra

I. Ancient Animals *(Les Anciens Animaux)*

The ancient animals all rutted on the run
With erections larded in blood and excrement.
Our forefathers proudly displayed their equipment
By the pleated sheath and seedbag of the scrotum.

In the Middle Ages, women, angel or pig,
All had eyes for a hefty codpiece on a guy;
Even a Cleaver, after his pants told a lie,
A little one, perhaps—could fall back on his rig.

Man's the equal of the noblest mammal of course;
And their enormous dong wrongfully astounds us.
But now sterility's hour has chimed: The horse

And the bull have both reined in their ardor, and no
One dares any more put his genital pride on show
In wooded groves where swarms of clowning children go.

II. Our Asses Are Not the Same
(Nos Fesses ne sont pas Les Leurs)

Our asses are not the same as theirs. I've observed
Men unbuttoning by some hedge along the way,
Pants down and whizzing shamelessly where children play;
I study the shape and form of our butt's whole curve.

Solid, pallid in lots of cases, it's furnished
With a screen of hair where the moons meet face to face;
For women only, the alluring furrowed space
Luxuriates a lengthy satiny flourish:

A wonderful and touching ingenuity,-
Such as only seen on angels in holy art,
Imitating their cheeky dimpled gaiety.

Oh! to be naked the same, seeking joy and repose,
Face turning inward toward your glorious part,
And freely murmuring till we're sobbing, we both?

III. Sonnet in Praise of the Butthole
(Sonnet du Trou du Cul)

Dark and puckered like a tiny violet eye
It breathes, obscurely lurking in a mossy froth
Still humid from love that follows the curving soft
Slope of snowy ass just past the crease of thigh.

A few glistening threads running like milky tears
Have wept past the rough hot wind pushing them away,
Getting beyond those little gnarls of ruddy clay
To lose their way where the echoing downslope veers.

In dreams I often find my suck-hole on the job;
My soul, so jealous of palpable fuckery,
Says this is its musky tear-duct, its nest of sobs.

It's the swoon-diving olive and the flute cajoled,
The pipeline where the celestial praline flows,
Feminine Promised Land in the moistening fold.

NOTES

In the company of Verlaine, Cabaner, and other bohemians, Rimbaud
was a member of the "Zutistes"—roughly, the "what-the-hell-ists"—
whose artistic credo was parody, satire, and intoxication. The con-
tents of the *Album "Zutique,"* thirty pages of "obscene" drawings
and parodistic verse, were first published in 1943.

François Coppée, Léon Dierx, L.X. de Ricard, Armande Silvestre,
and Paul Verlaine are the poets satirized or parodied by Rimbaud—
Coppée the clear favorite with over half a dozen entries.

The three scatological sonnets *Les Stupra* ("Smut") were first printed in
a small volume in 1923. The third sonnet appears in the Album
"Zutique" under the title *Ídole, Sonnet du trou du cul*; it also ap-
pears as the final poem in Verlaine's *Hombres* of 1904.

Drunken Coachman

This is Rimbaud's contribution to the many monosyllabic sonnets that
appear in the *Album "Zutique."*

Young Glutton

A sarcastic sexual snapshot of Paul Verlaine, the dandy, the aesthete,
the gourmand.

Paris

An ode to the modern Paris of 1871, made up of brand names,
  titles of commercial establishments, and the names of celeb-
  rities and criminals. I have Anglicized the French names
  with an ear to the product or personality type invoked.
  Rimbaud cites:

Alphonse Godillot	shoes
Gambier	pipes
Wolff-Pleyel	pianos
robinet	a cock, tap, or plug
Galopeau	frock coats
Mennier	chocolate
Le Perdriel	pharmacist
Veuillot	Catholic writer
Tropmann	notorious murderer who went to guillotine
Angier	playwright
Gill	artist
Mendès	writer
L'Hérissé	hatter
Enghiens	mineral water tablets

The Old Woman's Old Man

The Empress actually gave birth to a son on the 16th of March, 1857,
  not the 18th.

The Sealed Lips

The title is taken from Léon Dierx's collection of 1867, but there seems
  to be no particular poem of Dierx that is being satirized.

The Feast of Love

This smutty little aria parodies Verlaine's *Colombine* in Fêtes galantes
(1869).

The Outcast Cherub

A surreal nocturne that parodies the work of Louis Ratisbonne who
specialized in "scenes from childhood" and other sentimental tropes.

Lily

The Lily, exploited by Banville, also appeared frequently in the orna-
mental flowerings of Silvestre's verse, whose name is appended
here. Lilies, with their tapering shape and Parnassian tone, seem
to remind Rimbaud of enema pumps full of suds.

Humanity

A perfect Alexandrine that spoofs de Ricard's Parnassian call to arms:
"Salut à toi, progrès, ô soldat et prophète!" Rimbaud didn't think very
highly of the notion of "progress."

The Broom; Exiles; Saturnine Rhetoric

These fragmentary satires are domestic, political, and sexual. In *Exiles,* Conneau is the royal physician; the Uncle referred to is Napoleon I.

Memoirs of an Idiotic Old Prick

The title in French contains a pun on *membre* or "penis"—the remembrance implying an erection—hence, "old prick." Rimbaud here makes his confession to an imaginary priest, detailing the "sins" of his early sexual awakening: voyeurism, masturbation, incestuous fantasies, and guilt. (Another translation of the title might read "Repeated Erections of an Old Idiot" or "Erections Recalled by an Idiotic Old-timer.")

Old Coppées Old Copies

Parodies of poems by François Coppée (1843–1908), a Parisian war-office clerk who devoted himself to poetry. His *Reliquaire* (1866) and *Intimités* (1867) put him to the forefront of the Parnassians. *Les Humbles* and *Le Cahier rouge* were among his later volumes of poetry; he also wrote for the theatre, *Le Passant* becoming a vehicle for Sarah Bernhardt. In 1896, Coppée delivered one of the eulogies at Verlaine's funeral.

1 *Ibled*
A famous brand of chocolate in 19th century France.

2 *Doctor Venetti*
The 17th century physician Nicola Venetta was the author of *Tableau*

TRANSLATED BY DJC

de L'Amour conjugale ("Picture of Conjugal Love"), published with graphic sexual engravings. It was reissued in a four-volume edition in 1869.

3 *le réjeton royal* ("royal offspring")

The royalty here is probably Napoleon III, who was condemned and imprisoned in 1836 and 1840, preceding his German captivity of 1870.

4 *diacre* ("deacon")

According to Steinmetz, an allusion to the deacon of Paris, Saint-Menard, who died in 1727, a figure notoriously subject to convulsions.

5 [State of Siege?]

The question in the title is a play on words referring to the recent occupation of Paris by the Prussians. The honest coachman is besieged by the night, the moon, the cops, and the degenerates howling in the street. The enormous chilblain may be "Zutique" for an erection.

6 [Remembrance]

Next to this poem in the Album, Rimbaud has drawn a cartoon sketch of the Emperor dressed in black with a señorita beside him, in spit-curls, a rose on her sombrero.

7 The balls refer to an episode out of the Battle of Sarrebrück where the young prince accompanied his father to the battle camp and collected fragments of cannon balls and spent ordnance. The balls are also symbolic of puberty, which was bubbling in the prince's veins like fizzing mineral water. The capitalized "Habit" in the last line refers to masturbation. The line literally translates: "Poor youngster, no doubt he's got the Habit!"

This poem is not part of the original *Album "Zutique,"* but was copied by Rimbaud into the notebook of artist Félix Régamey in London, 12 September 1872.

Les Stupra / Smut

The word *stupra* is Latin for "obscenities" or "defilements," here Anglicized to "smut." All three sonnets were copied out by Paul Verlaine in a letter to Charles Morice, 20 December 1883; the originals of the first two have disappeared. The third, titled *L'Idole, Sonnet du Trou du Cul* ("The Idol, Sonnet in Praise of the Butthole") appears on the second page of the Album "Zutique" under the false signature "Albert Mérat," and the initials "P.V.–A.R." under that.

This version is in Rimbaud's handwriting. The first two stanzas are by Verlaine and the last two by Rimbaud.

I Ancient Animals
ange our pource ("angel or pig")
In a note to his publisher Vanier, in 1889, Verlaine asked that an epigraph be placed on the *"Filles"* section of his *Parallélements*— "Ange ou Pource. Rimbaud"; but this was never printed. This phrase may have been a code or catch-phrase between the two poets. In *A Season In Hell,* Rimbaud states at one point, in a veiled reference to Verlaine, "Thus I was in love with a pig."

Kléber ("Cleaver")
Kléber was a famous general of the French Revolution. Rimbaud perhaps refers to his manly statue on the Rue de Rivoli. I have Anglicized the name with an ear to the invisible rhyme of "beaver cleaver," American street-slang for a cocksman, a "heroic" lover of women, or the penis itself.

III *L'Idole, Sonnet du Trou du cul* (**"The Idol, Sonnet in Praise of the Butthole"**)

The work here parodied by Verlaine and Rimbaud is Albert Mérat's *The Idol,* first published in 1869, wherein he celebrated all the parts of a woman's body.

Odds and Ends

"Bribes"

I

At the foot of dark walls, beating the scrawny dogs.

II

Oh! if the bells are of bronze,
Our hearts fill up with despair!
In June, Eighteen seventy-one,
Snuffed by a creature of the dark,
We John Bawdry, we John Balouche
Died in this murky belfry
Abominating Mister Duane.

III

Behind jiggling with grotesque hiccups
A swallowed rose in a porter's belly.

IV

A brunette, she was married off at age sixteen.

*　　*　　*

So she's in love with her son of seventeen.

V

(The Complaint of an old Royalist to
Mr. Henry Perrin, Republican Journalist)

*　　*　　*

. . . You have
Lied, by my thighbone! you have told a lie,
Wild apostle. You want to make paupers
Of us? You'd like to peel our balding heads?
But me, I've got two engraved, warped thighbones!
Since for all your schooldays you sweat enough
On your coat collar to fry a doughnut,
Since you lie through your teeth, at trickery
A shorn horse drooling into an inkhorn,
You think to wipe out my forty-year siege!

I've got my thighbone! my thighbone! my thighbone!
For forty years I've been twisting it on
The edge of my beloved hardwood chair;
Its wooden impression is permanent;
And I, when I see your impure organ,

All of your subscribers, clowns, your readers,
Pulling that flabby organ in their hands,

*　　*　　*

I'll improve them, every tomorrow,
With a touch of my worked-over thighbone!

VI

(The Grocer's Complaint)

Let him go into the shop when the moon
Is mirrored in the windowpane's blue,
Let him swipe chicory tins in plain view.

VII

. . . Is it
. . . (some barrels?) . . . all stove in?
. . . No!
It's the master chef snoring like a bassoon.

VIII

. . . Among the gold, the quartz, the porcelains,
. . . a chamberpot so banal,
Indecent reliquary of old society dames,
Curls up in shame on the royal mahogany.

IX

Oh! the perennial vignettes!

X

And the drunken poet ripped the Universe to shreds.

XI

(Verses for Places)

On this throne so misshapen
That it's tied our guts in knots,

The hole was probably botched
By some truly rotten scum.

When the famous Tropmann slew Henry Kink
That assassin must've sat here to stink
Since those cunts Bading and Henry the Fifth
Get ready to enthrone their stately shit.

XII

It's raining gently on the town.

XIII

Be watchful, O my absent life!

XIV

The moonlight, when the bell chimes twelve.

NOTES

This collection of fragments and isolated verses was first published in the *Pléiade* edition (Gallimard, 1954). The title *Bribes* ("scraps" or "bits") originated with the editors of that edition.

II *Desdouets* ("Mister Duane")
The name of Rimbaud's headmaster at school. A prank of the poet's student days involved the discovery of a chamber pot in the belfry of the church, whence it was flung down to the street.

V An imaginary "letter to the editor"—the old monarchist is become a skeleton after so long in his chair (as a civil servant, perhaps). He threatens his liberal "enemies" with his thigh-bone as a club.

X There was a café—and still is—in Charleville called *L'Universe.*

XI In 1869, Jean-Baptiste Tropmann was condemned to the guillotine for murdering the entire Kink family in order to rob them. Badingue and Henry V (of France) represent political criminals.

Found Poem in English

(selected lines)

I was taken all aback—abaft—to be abashed
The fever begins to abate—to be abed
We will abide by this—What is this about
What remains over and above
Tell one where about I shall find it
I will bring it about
The thing was blazed abroad and failed
You must learn to abstain from these indulgences . . .

Back a little—Background—Backslider
He will not be Backward to undergo—
Backward fruit, children, season
Walk read backwards—This is not so bad
They baffled all our designs
The skin bagged—What do you bait with
We always bait at that inn

                    *   *   *

Hearse—hearse cloth—the throbbing of the heart
He would not have the heart to do it . . .
It lies on my heart—I have no heart for it.
Heart break he wept heartily . . .
Hedgehog—take heed—show us your heels . . .
He helped himself to the best bit
What a helpless being . . .
To fly off the hinges—speak out, I do not take hints
I have him on the hip—hipshot . . .
These manners of his will—there is a hitch . . .
No man's face is actionable . . .
This maggot has no sooner set him agog, than
The negotiations were aground . . .

All right—alluring—alm—almond
To walk alone—It is better to let it alone
Have you altered your exercises?
Nothing comes amiss to me . . .
Do you not anticipate much pleasure
I need not apologize—appendage . . .
As you love me, do not attempt it . . .
I ask nothing better than to go—to look asquint . . .

They baffled all our designs . . .
Howitz—Huckleback—Hucksteress
to huddle up work—set up a hue and cry
I huff this man—to hug a sin—a huge eater
The hulks—it is all a hum—humdrum
You humour him—hunchbacked—Hurl
this matter is hushed—Hythe . . .

NOTE

In 1872, while in London, Rimbaud obtained a Reading Room ticket at the British Museum by stating that he was over 21. He and Verlaine were both learning English. Rimbaud copied out a list of English phrases, probably culled from his reading at the British Museum. As Charles Nicholl has said, this "hand-written list ... attains the gnomic status of what was known in the 1960s as 'concrete poetry.'"

A sense of desolation and estrangement pervades this collection of lines. Rimbaud and Verlaine were both "exiled" from their former lives. Nicholl describes their situation succinctly: "The relationship was fraught but powered by the sense of adventure, of rootless freedom: they are outcasts together. They have the desperate camaraderie of the marginalized: of gay lovers, which they were; of junkies, which their alcoholism almost makes them."

This maggot

"A whimsical or perverse fancy ... a whimsical or capricious person" (Oxford English Dictionary). The obsolete term "maggotry" means "folly or absurdity."

Howitz

A field-piece or cannon (c. 1700); from the Old German *haufnitz* (a stone-sling catapult)—a howitzer.

Huckleback

Hump-backed or crump-shouldered.

Hucksteress

A female huckster; one who bargains or haggles.

To huddle up

To hurry the completion of, to finish up, or compile, in haste and
without proper care; to botch up hastily.

I huff this man

To scold, chide, or storm at; to hector or bully.

hulks

Prison ships.

all a hum

A piece of humbug, a hoax.

Hythe

Also spelled "hithe," a harbor, a small haven or landing place on a
river.

PROSE

A Heart Beneath A Cassock (1871)

The Wilderness of Love (1872)

Three Meditations on the Gospel of John (1873)

The Sun Was Still Hot (1864)

A Heart Beneath A Cassock

Secrets of a Seminarian

O Timothina Mugg! Today as I put on my holy vestments I can recall the passionate feelings—grown cold and dormant under my cassock—that made my young manly heart leap under my seminarian's hooded robe.

*   *   *

1 May 18—

Spring is here. The Abbot's vine is budding in its pot of earth: The branches on the tree in the courtyard pop tender little shoots like green droplets. The other day, leaving study hall, I saw something like the Super's nasal mushroom at an upper window . . . J.'s shoes are beginning to stink a little. And I've noticed students often going out to the courtyard to . . . These are the very same ones who live in the study like moles, roly-poly, embedded in their bellies, extending ruddy faces toward the stove, their breath as thick and warm as a cow's. They're out there in the open air for quite some time, and when they return, chuckling, they button their flies very meticulously—no, that's wrong, very slowly—in the manner of taking mechanical pleasure in that operation in and of itself quite meaningless . . .

2 May . . .

The Super came down from his rooms yesterday and, closing his eyes, with hands hidden, cringing and shivering, shuffled around the courtyard a couple of times in his priestly slippers! . . .

Right now my heart's beating time in my chest and my breast is beating against this sloppy desk of mine! Ohh! These are the times that I despise—the scholars like fat sheep, sweating in their fusty clothes and asleep in the stinking atmosphere of study, under the gaslight, in the stove's fading heat! . . . I stretch my arms! I sigh and extend my legs . . . I feel things in my head, oh! things! . . .

4 May . . .

. . . Yesterday I couldn't stand it any more! Like the Angel Gabriel I spread the wings of my heart. And the breath of the Holy Spirit swept through my whole being! I took up my lyre, my zither, and I sang:

Come to me now,
Great Mary! Thou
Mother Divine
Of Sweet Jesus
Sanctus Christus!
O pregnant virgin
So Holy and Fine
Hear this prayer of mine!

Oh! if you only knew the mysterious effluvia that shook my soul while I plucked the petals of this poetic rose! I took my harp, and like the Psalmist, raised my pure and innocent voice to the heights of heaven!!! O altitudo altitudinum! . . .

*   *   *

7 May . . .

Alas! My poetry has folded its wings, but like Galileo, crushed by outrage and torture, I'll say: And yet it moves!—Read it: the wings move! Carelessly enough, I let fall the preceding confidence . . . J. picked it up—J., the most savage of Jansenists, the Super's most rigorous toady

. . . and he took it to his master in secret. But the monster, to make me the butt of universal insult, had handed round my poetry to all his friends.

Yesterday, the Super sent for me. I went to his rooms and stood before him, full of inner strength. His last red hair quivered like a furtive glint on his bald forehead; his eyes bulged out of his flabby face, calmly, tranquilly. His nose, like a churn-handle, twitched as usual; he was whispering an *oramus*. He wet the tip of his thumb, turned some pages in his book, and took out a small greasy folded paper . . .

> "Greaaaat Maaryyy, Thoouu
> Mooother Diiiviiine!"

He was debasing my poetry! He spat on my rose! He played the clown, the Jo-Jo, the dullard, in order to smear, to sully that virginal song! He stuttered and prolonged each syllable with a concentrated hateful sneer, and when he arrived at the fifth line . . . *"Pregnant virgin!"* he stopped, wrinkled up his nose, and he—!! he blew up: "Pregnant virgin! Pregnant virgin!" he said it such a way, while his big belly swayed and quivered, in such a scary way, that I blushed and dropped to my knees, raising my arms to the ceiling, and blurted: " . . . Oh, Father! . . . "

*   *   *

"Your lyre! your zither! young man! your zither! those mysterious effluvia that shook your soul!! I'd have liked to see that! Young soul, I notice here, in this impious confession, something worldly, a dangerous abandon, temptation, anyway!—"

He stopped short, his belly shuddering from top to bottom: then solemnly said:

"Young man, do you have the faith? . . ."

"Father, what are you saying? Are you making a joke? . . . Yes, I believe everything my mother tells me . . . Holy Mother Church!"

"But—Pregnant virgin! . . . It's a conception, young man, that is, a concept! . . ."

"Father, I believe in the conception!"

"You're right, young man! It's a thing . . . "

He stopped . . . Then said: "Young J. has reported to me that in study hall he's seen you spread your legs more and more noticeably every day. He claims to have seen you completely extend your legs under the desk, in the fashion of a young man . . . disjointed. These are facts for which we need no answer . . . Come here, on your knees; come closer. I want to question you quietly. Tell me, do you spread your legs really wide in the study hall?"

Then he put his hand on my shoulder, around my neck, and his eyes grew bright, and he made me tell him things about the spreading of my legs . . . Well, all I can say is that it was disgusting, because I know what that kind of scene's about . . .

So, they'd spied on me, they'd slandered my heart and my modesty—and I had no comeback for that, the reports, the anonymous notes of one student against another, and those to the Super, authorized and ordered—And I came to his rooms, and was made to . . . under that hand of grossness! . . . Oh! the seminary! . . .

*   *   *

10 May . . .

Ohh! my classmates are downright nasty and downright lewd! In the study hall, all of these foul-mouths know the story of my verses, and as soon as I turn my head, I met the face of wheezy D., who whispers to me: "And your zither? and your zither? and your diary?" Then idiotic L. continues: "And your lyre? and your zither?" Then three or four whisper in chorus:

"Great Mary, Thou
Mother Divine!"

Me, I am a huge booby:—Jesus, don't I kick myself!—But at least I don't spy on others, I don't write anonymous notes. I keep my blessed poetry and my modesty to myself! . . .

12 May . . .

> Can't you guess at the why of love I die?
> The flower sends greetings; the bird says: hi!
> Greetings: to Spring! the angel that nurtures!
> Can't you guess why I'm on fire with raptures?
> Grandma's angel, angel of infancy,
> I'm turning into a bird; can't you see
> How my lyre quivers and I flap my wings
> Like a swallow (and soar aloft and sing)?

I wrote these verses yesterday, during recess. I went into the chapel and locked myself in a confessional and there, in dreams and silence, my youthful poetry could palpitate and fly off to regions of love.

Then, since they pick my pocket of any papers day or night, I sewed these verses into the hem of my undershirt, which is closest to my skin, and during study hall, I pull my poetry over my heart, under my clothes, and press it there for a long time dreaming . . .

15 May.

Events have crowded thick and fast, since my last entry here, and very solemn events they were, events which without a doubt will influence my future life and thought in a terrible way!

Timothina Mugg, I adore you!

Timothina Mugg, I adore you! I adore you! Let me sing to my lute, as the Divine Psalmist did on his psaltery, how I saw you, and how my heart leapt onto yours in love eternal!

Thursday was our free day; we get to go out for two hours. I went out. My mother, in her last letter, had told me: " . . . my son, go and occupy your idle hours at the home of Mister Julius Mugg, an old friend of your late father, whom you must meet someday or other before you are ordained . . . "

So I introduced myself to Mister Mugg, who greatly obliged me by sending me into the kitchen without a word. His daughter Timothina, remaining alone with me there, grabbed a towel, dried a large bowl held against her breast, and after a lengthy silence, abruptly said: "Well, Mister Leonard? . . ."

Until then, embarrassed to find myself alone with this young creature in that solitary kitchen, I'd kept my eyes lowered and invoked the sacred name of Mary in my heart. Blushing, I looked up, and right in front of my beautiful interrogator, I could only mumble a feeble: "Yes, Miss? . . ."

Timothina! You were beautiful! If I were a painter, I'd replicate your sacred features on canvas under the title: The Virgin of the Bowl! But I am simply a poet, and my words can only praise you partially . . .

The stove, with holes glowing with blazing embers like red eyes, let a thin wisp of smoke escape from the pots, the heavenly smell of bean-and-cabbage soup.

And standing by the stove, breathing that vegetable aroma through your sweet nose, and gazing at your big fat cat with your beautiful grey eyes, O Virgin of the Bowl, you wiped your vessel! The bright flat braids of your hair clung modestly to your blonde sunny brow. A blue smudge from your eyes to the middle of your cheek, just like Saint Teresa! Your nose, full of the smell of beans, flared its delicate nostrils. A light fluff meandering above your lip contributed not a little to the beautiful energy in your face. And on your chin, a lovely brown mole where fluttered a fine breezy fuzz. Your hair was discreetly pinned up at the nape, one loose curl straying . . . I looked in vain for your breasts. You don't have any: you disdain such worldly ornaments: your heart is your breasts! . . . When you whirled about to give your tabby cat a kick with a generous foot, I saw your shoulder blades jut and raise your dress and I was pierced with love as I faced the graceful, twisting, prominent twin arcs of your buttocks! . . .

From that moment on, I adored you! I worshipped not your hair, not your shoulder blades, not the lowly twisting of your posterior: What I love in a woman, in a virgin, is holy modesty. What makes me leap with love is piety and modesty. That's what I adored about you, little shepherdess! . . .

I tried to make her notice my passion, but even so, my heart, my heart betrayed me! I responded to her questions with half-uttered words. Befuddled at times, I called her "Ma'am" instead of "Miss!" Little by little I succumbed to the magical sound of her voice. At last, I decided to abandon myself, give myself over. And, at some question she asked me—I don't remember what—I threw myself backward in my chair, put one hand on my heart, and with the other grabbed a rosary in my pocket, letting its white cross dangle out. And with an eye on Timothine, the other toward heaven, I answered grievously and tenderly, like a stag to a doe:

"Oh! yes! Oh, Miss . . . Timothina!"

Miserere! miserere:—Into my eye turned delightedly toward the ceiling, a drop of brine suddenly fell from a cured ham hanging above me! And when I lowered my head, red with shame and passionately awake, I saw that in my left hand, rather than a rosary, I had a baby's brown pacifier! My mother had entrusted me a year ago to give it to the infant of Mrs. So-and-so! From the eye that I had turned to the ceiling flowed the bitter brine—but from the eye that looked at you, O Timothina, a tear flowed, a tear of love, a tear of pain! . . .

*   *   *

Sometime, an hour later, when Timothina presented me with a meal of beans and bacon omelette, entirely enthralled by her charms, I answered in a low voice: "You see, my heart is so full that my stomach is ruined!"—And I sat at table. Oh! I can still feel it, how her heart had answered the call of mine: during the brief meal, she didn't eat.

"Don't you smell something?" she said more than once. Her father didn't understand. But my heart understood: it was the Rose of David, the Rose of Jesse, the mystic Rose of Scripture; it was Love!

She brusquely got up and went over to a corner of the kitchen. And showing me the double flower of her buttocks, she plunged her arms into a pile of boots and other footwear, out of which leapt her big fat cat. She threw them all into an old empty cupboard, then returned to her seat and sniffed the air anxiously. Suddenly she wrinkled her brow and cried out:

"That smell is still here!"
"Yes, something smells . . . " her father answered rather stupidly.

(He was so profane, he didn't comprehend it!)
I realized it was nothing more than the inner turmoil of passion in my virgin body! I adored her and lovingly savored that golden omelette, and my hands kept time with the fork while, under the table, my feet trembled with joy in my shoes! . . .
But what a bolt out of the blue, like a token of eternal love, like a diamond of tenderness from Timothina, was her adorable kindness in offering me, when I left, a pair of clean white socks, with a smile and these words:
"Would you like these for your feet, Mister Leonard?"

*   *   *

16 May . . .

Timothina! I adore you, you and your father and your cat . . .

	Vas devotionis,
	Rosa mystica,
Timothina	Turris davidica, ora pro nobis!
	Coeli porta,
	Stella maris,

17 May . . .

What do I care now for the clamor of the world and the buzz of the study hall? What do I care for those who are bent over in laziness and languor by my side? This morning, every head, heavy with sleep, was glued to the table. Snores, like the trumpeting of the Last Judgment, slow, heavy snores rising up from a vast Gethsemane. But I, stoical and serene, sit upright among all these dead ones, rising like a palm tree among the ruins. Scornful of the unseemly smells and noise, I rested my head in my hands and listened to the beating of my heart full of Timothina, my eyes plunged into the azure of the sky, glimpsed through the uppermost window pane! . . .

18 May . . .

Thanks be to the Holy Spirit who inspired in me these charming verses: These verses I'm going to enshrine in my heart: And when heaven allows me to see Timothina again, I'll give them to her in exchange for the socks! . . .

I have entitled it *The Breeze:*

In its cotton-down retreat
The zephyr sleeps and sweetly breathes:
In its nest of silk and woolen
Sleeps the zephyr with cheery chin!

When the zephyr lifts its wing
In its cotton-down retreat . . .
It flies where the flower's calling,
Its soft breath smells so sweet.

O quintessential breeze
O quintessence of love:
When the dew evaporates
It scents the sky above!

Jesus! Joseph! Jesus! Mary!
Whiffs of a condor's wing,
Setting those who pray to dozing!
It passes through us and we sleep!

*   *   *

The ending is too personal and too agreeably fragrant. I will preserve it in the tabernacle of my soul. On the next free day, I will read it to my divine, my aromatic Timothina.

Let me wait calmly and be contemplative.

*   *   *

Uncertain date.—We still wait! . . .

16 June . . .

Lord, thy will be done: I shall put no obstacle before it! If you will turn away Timothina's love from your servant, you are doubtless free to do so. But Lord Jesus, do you not love also? and didn't the lance of love teach you condescension to the suffering of wretches? Pray for me!

Oh! I waited so long for the two o'clock freedom of June 15: I had restrained my soul by telling it: On that day you will be free! June 15, I combed my short modest haircut and, using a rose-fragrance pomade, I slicked it over my forehead, like the braids of Timothina. I pomaded my eyebrows; I meticulously brushed my black habit, skillfully covering certain troublesome defects in my appearance, and full of hope, I presented myself at the doorbell of Mr. Julius Mugg. He arrived after a rather long time, his skullcap tilted over one ear, a stiff lock of hair, heavily pomaded, slicing his brow like a scar, one hand in the pocket of his yellow-flowered dressing gown, the other on the latch . . . He said a curt hello, wrinkled his nose as he glanced at my shoes with their black laces, and went off leading the way, his hands in his two pockets, pulling his dressing gown out front, like the Abbot in his cassock, showing me the outline of his lower parts.

I followed him.

He went on through the kitchen, and after him I entered the parlor. Oh! that parlor! I have fixed it in my mind with pins of memory! The wallpaper had brown flowers; on the mantelpiece, a huge black wooden clock with columns; two blue vases with roses; on the walls, a painting of the battle of Inkerman and a crayon drawing, by a friend of Julius, showing a mill with its wheel shooting forth a little stream, like spit, the way all beginners draw, blackened in. Poetry is certainly preferable! . . .

In the middle of the parlor, a table with a green cloth, at which my heart saw only Timothina, although a friend of Mister Mugg was also there, a former parish sacristan, and his wife Mrs. Gampsocket, and Mr. Julius himself sat down again as soon as I entered.

I took an upholstered chair, and dreamt how a part of me was resting on a tapestry doubtless made by Timothina. I greeted everyone and, placing my black hat on the table in front of me like a rampart, I listened . . .

I didn't speak, but my heart spoke! The gentlemen continued their card game they'd begun: I noticed that each outdid the other in cheating, which surprised and saddened me. When the game was over, everybody sat in a circle around the empty fireplace. I was in one of the corners, almost hidden by Mr. Mugg's big friend, whose chair was the only obstacle between me and Timothina. I was inwardly content that so little attention was paid to me. Stuck behind the chair of the honorary sacristan, I could let my heart's feelings show in my face, unseen by anyone. So I gave myself over to a sweet abandon, letting the conversation spin on and on between those three—for Timothina hardly spoke. She cast looks of love at her seminarian, and not daring to look me in the face, fixed her bright eyes on my highly polished shoes . . . Behind the fat sacristan I gave myself over to the feelings in my heart.

I began by leaning toward Timothina, raising my eyes to heaven. She had turned around. I sat up straight again and, uttering a sigh, dropped my head to my chest. She didn't budge. I fumbled for my beads. I made my lips move, I made the sign of the cross quickly. She saw nothing. Then, beside myself, mad with love, I bent way down toward her, clasping my hands as if at communion, and sighing a long and sorrowful Ahh! *Miserere!* While I gesticulated, while I prayed, I fell from my chair with a dull thud, and the fat sacristan turned with a snicker and Timothina said to her father;

"Look, Mister Leonard is on the floor!"

Her father chuckled! *Miserere!*

The sacristan lifted me up, red with shame and weak from love, and put me back on my upholstered chair, making room for it. But I closed my eyes and tried to sleep! These people irked me, they were so unaware of the love that suffered in the shadows: I tried to sleep! But I heard the conversation turn to the subject of *me*.

I opened my eyes a little bit again.

Julius and the sacristan each smoked a thin cigar, with every delicate nuance possible, which made them look terrifically ridiculous: The sacristan's wife, on the edge of her chair, her concave chest pitched forward, behind her the waves of her yellow dress which was puffed up to her neck, fanning its unique flounce in full bloom all around her, delicately pulled the petals off a rose: A frightful smile half opened her lips to reveal her meager gums and two black and yellow teeth like the porcelain on an old stove.—You, Timothina, you were beautiful, with your white collar, your lowered eyes, your flat braids.

"He's a young man with a future. The present reflects what's to come," said the sacristan, exhaling a billow of grey smoke.

"Oh, Leonard will be a credit to the cloth," snorted his wife, showing her two buck teeth.

Politely, like a good boy, I blushed. I saw them scoot their chairs away from me and then whisper together about me.

Timothina still gazed at my shoes . . . the two dirty buck teeth looked threatening to me . . . the sacristan laughed ironically; I kept my head down . . .

"Lamartine is dead . . ." Timothina said abruptly.

Dear Timothina! It was for your worshipper, your poor poet Leonard, that you threw the name of Lamartine into the conversation. Then I raised my head, feeling that the thought of poetry alone might restore a virgin purity to these profane folk, I felt my wings quiver, and radiant, my eyes on Timothina, I said:

"The author of *Poetic Meditations* had beautiful flowers in his crown!"

"The swan of poetry is dead," said the sacristan's wife.

"Yes, but he sang his funeral song," I rejoined enthusiastically.

"Why, Leonard is a poet too!" cried the sacristan's wife. "Last year his mother showed me some of his essays from the muse . . . "

I acted with boldness.

"Oh, ma'am, I brought neither lyre nor zither with me today, but . . . "

"Oh! Your zither! You'll have to bring it another day . . . "

"But if you don't mind"—and here I pulled a piece of paper from my pocket—"I will read you some verses . . . I dedicate them to Miss Timothina."

"Yes! yes! young man! very good! Recite them, do. Go to the other side of the room . . . "

I relocated myself. Timothina gazed at my shoes. The sacristan's wife posed like the Madonna. The two men leaned toward each other . . . I blushed, I coughed, and I recited rhythmically and tenderly:

> In its cotton-down retreat
> The zephyr sleeps and sweetly breathes:
> In its nest of silk and woolen
> Sleeps the zephyr with cheery chin!

Everyone burst into laughter. The men leaned toward each other and made gross puns. But what was especially horrible was the look of Mrs. Gampsocket who played the mystic, eyes to heaven, and smiled with her scary teeth! Timothina, Timothina cracked up with laughter! This was crushing to me, Timothina holding her sides! . . .

"A sweet zephyr in cotton-down, that's nice, very nice!" . . . said Father Julius, sniffing the air.

I thought I noticed something . . . But the laughter lasted only a second: they all tried to recover their seriousness, but it burst out from time to time.

"Go on, young man, it's good, really good!"

> When the zephyr lifts its wing
> In its cotton-down retreat . . .

It flies where the flower's calling,
Its soft breath smells so sweet.

This time a roar of laughter shook my audience. Timothina gazed at
my shoes. I was warm, my feet burned as she looked at them, and they
swam in their sweat; because, I told myself: These socks which I've
been wearing for a month are the gift of her love, the glances she casts
at my feet are a token of her love: she adores me!

And then I noticed a little smell that seemed to come from my
shoes. Oh! I understood the horrible laughter of the gathering! I under-
stood that Timothina, so out of place in that nasty company, Timothina
Mugg would never be able to let her passion run free! I understood that
I too must abolish that sorrowing love which was born in my heart one
May afternoon, in the Muggs' kitchen, in front of the wriggling poste-
rior of the Virgin of the Bowl!

Four o'clock, time for me to go, chimed on the parlor clock. Be-
wildered, burning with love, mad with sadness, I seized my hat, knocked
over a chair as I fled, and crossed the hall murmuring: "I adore you,
Timothina."

And I fled to the seminary without stopping . . .

The tails of my black habit flapped behind me in the wind, like
sinister birds! . . .

*   *   *

30 June . . .

From now on, I leave my sorrow in the consoling cradle of the divine
muse. A martyr to love at eighteen and, in my affliction, thinking of
another martyr of the sex that makes our joy and our blissfulness, no
longer having the one I love, I will love religion! Let Christ, let Mary
press me to their breast. I follow them. I am unworthy to untie the
laces on Jesus' shoes; but my sorrow! but my torture! I too at eighteen
years and seven months bear a cross, a crown of thorns! But in my
hand, not a reed, but a zither! That will be a balm to my wound!

*   *   *

One year later, August 1st.

Today they put the sacred vestments on me. I'm going to serve God. I will have a vicarage and a modest servant in a rich village. I have faith. I will make my salvation and, without being a spendthrift, I'll live like a good servant of God with his servant. Holy Mother Church will keep me warm at her breast: How I bless her! bless God!

. . . As for that cruel cherished passion kept at the bottom of my heart, I'll be able to carry it faithfully. Without precisely reviving it in any way, at times I'll remember it: such things are sweet indeed!— Moreover, I was born for love and faith!—Maybe one day, returning to this town, I'll have the happiness of confessing my dear Timothina? But then, I have a sweet remembrance from her: for a year now I've not removed the socks that she gave me . . .

O God! I'll keep these socks on my feet until I reach Paradise!

-CARL

NOTES

From the middle of March 1871 until the autumn of that year, Rimbaud composed nearly a fourth of his entire literary output. *Evening Prayer, First Communion,* and *The Drunken Boat* date from this period—as well as this blackly comedic short story of self-delusion and smelly feet. The priest in *First Communion* ("a freak in black with festering shoes") is perhaps the young seminarian here portrayed at a later stage in his life.

Labinette ("Mugg")
I have Anglicized the young lady's name. *Binette* means "hoe" (the garden tool) and "face or mug," as in the common slang phrase: *Quelle binette!* meaning "what a face," or "what a mug!"

jansénistes ("Jansenists")
Named after Dutch theologian Cornelius Jansen (d. 1638), this was a sternly moralistic doctrine, maintaining freedom of the will to be nonexistent and the redemption of mankind limited to only a part of humanity. Jansenism is Catholicism's answer to Calvinism.

Césarin ("Julius")
A literal version of this name in English might turn out something like "Little Caesar," so I have named Timothina's father after the first of the Caesars.

Madame de Riflandouille ("Mrs. Gampsocket")
I have compounded a Dickensian surname for the sacristan's wife out of *riflard* (a large umbrella, or "gamp") and *douille* (A "socket," hose, or casing). According to Benjamin Ivry, the lady's name in French "means 'to pare sausages made of chitterlings,' another phallic reference"—the zephyr of course, being the primary "phallic reference."

The Wilderness of Love

Les Déserts de l'amour

Notice

These are the writings of a young, wholly youthful *man* whose life developed somewhere it doesn't matter where: without a mother, without a country, indifferent to all you might know, avoiding all moral authority like many a pitiful young man who's already fled. But he himself, so troubled and restless that he headed for death as toward a fatal, terrible purity. Not having loved women—though full-blooded!—his heart and soul and all his energies were sublimated in sad and strange delusions. From the ensuing dreams—his loves!—which came to him in bed or in the streets, and from their continuation and their finale, some sweet religious considerations may be derived. Perhaps you remember the endless sleep of the fabled Mohammedans—still brave however circumcised! Yet these bizarre sufferings possess a disquieting authority, so that it's sincerely hoped that this Soul, wandering among us all, and seeking death it would seem, will encounter in that very moment sober consolation and dignity.

A. Rimbaud

I

Certainly, it's the same landscape. The same rustic house of my parents: even the same room where, above the doors, there's a Russian-leather pastorale with a coat-of-arms and lions. For suppers, there's a little room with candles and wine and antique paneling. The dining table is very grand. And servants! there were quite a few of them, as far back as I can remember.—One of the old friends of my youth was there, a priest in his priestly robes; just now, for the chance to be at large, at liberty. I remember his purple room with its yellow paper window panes; and his hidden stash of books that had gotten drenched in the sea!

Me—abandoned in this endless country house: reading in the kitchen, drying the mud on my clothes in front of the guests, engaging in small talk: deathly distressed by the murmur of the morning's milk and the last century's night.

I was in a very dark room: what was I doing? One of the maids came up close to me: I'd have to say she was a bit of a pup: nonetheless, she was beautiful, and of a motherly nobility hard for me to describe: pure, knowing, wholly charming! She pinched my arm.

I don't remember her face very well any more: much less her arm, the skin of which I rolled in my two fingers; nor her mouth, on which mine had seized, like a desperate wavelet forever lapping away at something. I turned her over in a basket of cushions and sail-cloth, in a dark corner. I remember nothing more than her white lace panties.

Then, O despair! the wall vaguely became the shadow of trees, and I was plummeting into the loving sadness of the night.

II

This time, it's the Woman that I saw in the City, and with whom I spoke, who speaks to me.

I was in a room, in the dark. Someone came to tell me that she was at my place: I saw her in my bed, all mine, in the dark! I was flustered, mainly because it was my parents' house: gripped with anguish too! I was in rags and she, a woman of the world, who was giving herself to me, would have to leave! A nameless anguish: I took her, and I let her tumble from the bed, half-naked; and in my indescribable swoon I fell with her and rolled with her on the carpets in the dark. The family lamp reddened the neighboring rooms one after another. Then the woman disappeared. I shed more tears than God could ever ask of me.

I went out into the endless City. O fatigue! Drowning in the dull night, in the flight of happiness. It was like a winter's night with a snowfall smothering the world once and for all. The friends to whom I cried out: where is she? falsely replied. I was there in front of the windows where she passes every evening: I was running through a shrouded garden. They made me leave. I wept enormously at all this. Anyway, I went down to some place full of dust and, sitting on a pile of lumber, I shed every tear in my body that night.—And my empty tears still came back to me, always.

I understood that she belonged to her everyday life; and that a good turn would take longer than a star to come round again. She hasn't come back, and will never come back, the Adorable One who visited my room—something I'd never have presumed. Truly, this time I wept more than all the children of the world.

NOTES

According to Starkie *(Rimbaud,* p. 179), Les Déserts de l'Amour dates from
    1872, shortly after the poet arrived in Paris. The Notice or preface
    seems to indicate that a work of some length was planned, but after
    two parts were completed, he seems to have abandoned it. He gave
    the manuscript to Forain, one of the "Zutistes," sometime in 1872.

"He may have assigned to woman a high and noble place in his aes-
    thetic doctrine, nevertheless, in practice, he seems to have held
    the conviction that woman, as he knew her, was loathsome and
    repulsive, and that love, like everything else, needed renovating.
    This did not necessarily mean that the only alternative was homo-
    sexuality, but rather that the relations between the sexes needed to
    be changed." (Starkie: *Rimbaud* p. 181)

Notice: *Mahométans legendaire* ("fabled Mohammedans")
According to Muslim legend, seven youths, accompanied by their dog
    Katmir, fell asleep for 309 years in the cavern in which they had
    been walled up by a wicked emperor. They remained standing for
    the whole time, not moving, eating, nor drinking.

Three Meditations on the Gospel of John

Trois Méditations Johanniques

I

In Samaria, many folk had made plain their faith in him. He didn't see them. Samaria, the upstart, the egoist, was more strictly observant of protestant law than Judea of the ancient tablets. There, universal wealth permitted all enlightened discussion. Sophism, the slave and soldier of routine, had, after having flattered them, cut the throats of many prophets.

They were sinister, those words of the woman at the well: "You're one of the prophets, you know what I've done."

Women and men believed in prophets in those days. Nowadays they believe in statesmen.

A few steps from the strange city, unlikely to physically menace it, what if he'd been taken for a prophet, since he'd shown up there so whimsically, what might he have done?

Jesus had nothing to say to Samaria.

II

Light and charming, the air of Galilee: the inhabitants received him with a curious delight: they had seen him, roused to holy anger, driving the money-changers and sellers of game from the temple. Miracle of youth, pale and furious, they thought.

He felt his hand in the hands laden with rings, and on it the lips of an official; the official was on his knees in the dust: his head was attractive enough, though half-bald.

Traffic spun through the city's narrow streets, rather a lot of it for this town; everything that evening seemed to be in need of too much gratification.

Jesus drew back his hand; it was a proud movement, childlike and feminine. "You people, if you don't see miracles, you don't believe."

Jesus hadn't performed any miracles yet. He had, at a wedding, in a green and rosy dining room, spoken a little boldly to the Holy Virgin. And no one had spoken of the wine of Cana at Capernaum, neither in the marketplace nor at the docks. Maybe the townfolk.

Jesus said: "Go, your son is in good health." The official went on his way, like one carrying some buoyant prescription, and Jesus continued through the streets less frequented. Orange bindweed and some borage displayed their magical gleam between the paving stones. At last in the distance he saw the dusty prairie and the buttercups and the daisies begging mercy of the day.

III

Bethsaida, the pool of the five colonnades, was a troubled spot. It resembled a sinister lavatory, always afflicted with rain and gloom; and the beggars are restless on the inner steps—grown pale in the glimmer of storms, precursors of hellish lightning, joking about their blue-eyed blindness, about the white or blue bandages wrapped around their stumps. O military washroom, O popular bathhouse. The water was always black, and no cripple ever fell into it, even while dreaming.

It was there that Jesus made his first serious move, among the squalid cripples. There was a day in February, March or April when at two o'clock in the afternoon the sun spread a great scythe of light over the shrouded waters. And back there, far behind the cripples—as if I might have seen what all this solitary sunbeam awakened from buds, from crystals, from worms, in that reflection like a white angel lying on its side—all the infinitely pale reflections came to life.

All the sins, the demon's nimble and tenacious offspring, that, for hearts a little sensitive, made these men more frightful than monsters, wanted to fling themselves into that water. The cripples descended, no longer jeering, but with longing.

The first one in will come out cured, they said. Not so. The sins hurled them back onto the steps and forced them to search for other sites: because their Demon can only stay in a place where alms are assured.

Jesus entered just after the noon hour. No one was washing up or watering animals. The light in the pool was as yellow as the last leaves on the vine. The Divine Master leaned against a column: he watched the sons of Sin: the demon stuck out his tongue in their tongue, and laughed at the world.

The Paralytic, who'd been lying on his side, arose, and with a singularly confident step, he was seen by the Damned to cross the gallery and disappear into the city.

NOTES

These scenic "meditations" were probably composed around the time Rimbaud began work on *A Season In Hell*. *Bethsaïda* was the first to appear in print, in 1898, in the Mercure de France edition of *Works* edited by Berrichon and Delahaye. The other two, discovered by Henri Matarasso, were first published in 1949.

I The first part of "In Samaria" may be missing, since the story seems to begin with no set-up, and Jesus is referred to as "him" with no antecedent. The woman at the well (John 4:7–26) perceives Jesus as a prophet (4:19), a "sinister" recognition because of the mortality rate among prophets in Samaria.

II *à la Sainte Vierge* ("to the Holy Virgin")
This alludes to the conversation at the wedding feast at Cana (John 2:1–12), where Jesus changed the water into wine.

II *Allez, votre fils se porte bien* ("Go, your son is in good health")
Jesus' response to the official, John 4:50, quoted word for word.

III "Now there is at Jerusalem by the sheep market a pool, which is called in the Hebrew tongue Bethesda, having five porches. In these lay a great multitude of impotent folk, of blind, halt, withered, waiting for the moving of the water. For an angel went down at a certain season into the pool, and troubled the water: whosoever then first after the troubling of the water stepped in was made whole of whatsoever disease he had." (John 5:2–4)

III *le Paralytique se leva* ("The Paralytic . . . arose")
In Rimbaud's version, the mere presence of Jesus cures the man. Compare John 4:5–9.

The Sun Was Still Hot

I

Prologue

The sun was still hot; yet it hardly lit up the earth any more; like a torch before it, flickering feebly, so the sun, earthly torch, was going out and its body of fire let fly a final and feeble glimmer that lit up the trees' green leaves, the little flowers beginning to fade, and the gigantic summit of pines, of poplars, and centuries-old oak trees. The cooling wind, that is, a cool breeze, agitated the leaves of the trees with a rustling like the silvery waters of the brook that flowed at my feet. The ferns curved and bent their heads to the breeze and I fell asleep, not before slaking my thirst at the brook.

II

I dreamt that I was born in Rheims in the year 1503.

Rheims was then a little city, rather, a town, famous nevertheless for its beautiful cathedral, witness to the coronation of King Clovis.

My parents were not too rich, but very honest: their only worldly possession was a little house, which they'd always owned, added to that, a few thousand francs and some little gold that my mother had put aside.

My father was an officer [a Colonel in the Royal Guard]. in the army of the king. He was a tall, thin man, dark hair, beard, eyes, skin of an even complexion. Although he was barely 48 or 50 when I was born, he'd certainly have been taken to be 60 or 58. He was a lively character, outgoing, with a short temper, unwilling to endure anything displeasing to him.

My mother was quite different: a sweet, calm woman, upset by

283

very little, who nevertheless kept the house in perfect order. She was so easygoing, my father would make her laugh like a teenaged girl. I was the favorite. My brothers were less valiant than I, even though they were bigger. I had little love for studying, that is for reading, writing, and arithmetic; but when it came to helping around the house, cultivating a garden, running errands, that was happiness!—I enjoyed that.

I remember one day my father had promised me twenty cents if I did well for him on a long-division problem. I began it, but could not finish. Ah! how many times he promised me pennies, toys, sweets, even once five dollars if I'd read him something.

Despite all this, my father sent me off to school as soon as I was ten.

"Why learn Greek and Latin?" I'd say to myself. I don't know. Besides, there's no need for it. What does it matter if I pass my exams? What's the use of passing your exams? No use at all, not so? Yes, though: it's been said, no diploma, no employment. But I don't want employment; I'll have a private income. Even if you wanted a job, why learn Latin? No one speaks this language. Sometimes I see some Latin in the newspapers, but, thank God, I'll never be a journalist.

Why learn history and geography? It's true, you have to know that Paris is in France, but no one asks at what degree latitude. As for history: learning the lives of Chinaldon, Nabolassar, Darius, Cyrus, Alexander, and their other buddies remarkable for their diabolical names, it's torture. Why should I care that Alexander was Great! What does it matter? . . . .How does anyone know if the Romans really existed? Maybe their language, their Latin, is a forgery; and, even if they did exist, let them leave me alone and keep their tongue to themselves. What evil have I done them that they put me to the torture?

Let's take a look at Greek: This dirty tongue is spoken by no one, no one in the world! . . . Ah! bloody rot in bloody rotten! Rot damn! me, I'll be monied; it's no good wearing out the seat of your pants on a bench, bloody rot-a-tot-god!

You've got to pass an exam to shine shoes, to get a job shining shoes; for the jobs that are open are for shining shoes or herding pigs or cattle. Thank you God! I want none of it myself, bloody rot'n'god! And with that, you get slapped around in payment. They call you an animal, which isn't true, half a man, et cetera.

Ah! bloody rotten rot! . . .

(To be continued)
Arthur (1864)

NOTES

This sketch, from the poet's school notebooks, portrays his discontent
at ten years old, dreaming himself into another era, dreaming of
an absent father (four years gone), bridling at the burden of school-
work, dreaming of the future.

Rheims . . . Clovis
Rheims, located northeast of Paris, was the traditional site of the coro-
nation of the kings of France. Clovis I (466?–511) of the
Merovingian dynasty was crowned there in 481 A.D.

A Colonel in the Royal Guard *("Colonel des Cents-Gardes")*
Rimbaud's footnote. Literally, "Colonel in the Hundred Guardsmen."

Chinaldon, Nabolassar, Darius, Cyrus, Alexander
The name *Chinaldon* is obscure, but probably from ancient history.
Nabolassar (d. 733 B.C.) was king of Babylonia; the Chaldean
calendar, used for centuries, dated from his coronation. Darius
was the name of three great kings of Persia, the last of whom met
defeat at the hands of Alexander the Great (331 B.C.). Cyrus the
Great (d. 529 B.C.) was the founder of the Persian Empire.

Bloody rot in bloody rotten! . . . etc. *(saperlipote de saperlipopette!")*
Rimbaud is ringing variations on the slang word *sapristi*, which derives
from sacristi or sacrée hostie: God's sacred body/blood.

Dream

Rêve

(from a letter to Ernest Delahaye dated 14 October 1875)

Scene: the barracks at night:

You get hungry in the barracks—
And that's a fact . . .
Explosions, gaseous blasts,
A spirit says: I am Gruyère!
Defeever says: Gimme air!
The genius says: I am Brie!
The soldiers carve up their bread:
What a life, whoopee!
The genie says—I am Roquefort!
—It'll knock us dead!
—I am Gruyère, I am the Brie . . .
etc.

—Waltz—
Aren't we a pair, Defeever and me,
etc.

NOTE

This last example of rhymed verse from the poet's hand—less a poem
than a ditty on farting (or belching)—brings his literary output to
a Rabelaisian conclusion. All the poet's "hungers" here become so
much "cheesy" air.

In his letter, he tells Delahaye that he expects to be called up for mili-
tary service very soon and appends this "Dream." A couple of
paragraphs later, he contemplates a college degree ("I've got to buy
the books soon") and military instruction for " . . . two or three
enjoyable seasons. And anyway," he says, "the hell with my 'craft
and art,'" *Au diable d'ailleurs ce "gentil labeur."*

This is Rimbaud's ultimate farewell to poetry. Soon he would begin the
wanderings that led him to Africa and a life of toil and hardship.
As Steinmetz has aptly put it: "The genius of *Illuminations* here
becomes a secular figure stating the names of cheese. He offers no
gift other than stench."

PART THREE

Illuminations

"The poems . . . were . . . something to help him to escape from sordid reality and to find his own form of life. The poems express his manner of escape . . . to . . . a magic land of his own . . . not bound by ordinary laws of logic . . . fantastic pictures . . . come to life, in which the known and the unknown mingle and blend . . . "

Enid Starkie
Arthur Rimbaud, Chapter VI

"Illumination is conscious awareness of the soul. In order to have illumination, we must have sincerity and humility."

Sri Chinmoy

ILLUMINATIONS

After The Flood

Après le Deluge

Once the concept of The Flood had settled,
A rabbit pulled over in the clover, in the swinging bluebells,
and said his prayer to the rainbow through a spider's web.

Oh! the precious stones in hiding—the flowers peering out
already!

Stalls were setting up in the broad muddy street and boats
were hauled toward the sea piled high like in old engravings.
Blood ran, at Bluebeard's,—through slaughterhouses,—in
circuses,
where the seal of God made windows pale. Blood and milk
both flowed.

Beavers got busy. Brandied coffees were steaming in cheap
cafés.

In the big house with still-dripping windowpanes, the
children
in mourning gazed at marvelous pictures.

A door slammed,—and in the village square a boy swung
his arms, along with weather vanes and steeplecocks every-
where,
under the dazzling downpour.

Madame XXX funded a piano in the Alps. Mass and
first communions were celebrated at a hundred thousand
cathedral altars.

Caravans departed. And the Hotel Splendide was built
in the chaos of ice and the polar night.

Since then, the Moon's been listening to jackals howling
across
the deserts of thyme,—to idyll poetry from peasants groan-
ing in the orchard.
Finally, in the budding violet grove, Eucharis told me it
was Spring.

—Well up, lagoons: Foam, roll out over the bridges and
through the woods:—black shrouds and organs—
thunder and lightning, rise up and roll:
Waters and sadnesses, rise up and raise the Floods.

Because ever since they dissipated—oh! precious jewels
hiding in the ground, and flowers opening!
—it's all a bore! and the Queen,
that Sorceress who lights her ember in the pot of earth,
will never tell us what she knows, and what we don't know.

Childhood

Enfance

I

This black-eyed idol, with yellow mane,
without family or fame
is nobler than any Mexican or Flemish fable:
Her domains, impudent azures and insolent greenways run
along beaches, fiercely named by the boatless waves
in Greek, Slav, Celtic.

At the edge of the forest—
dreaming flowers
tintinnabulate, explode, illuminate—
the girl with orange lips,
her knees crossed in the flood of light
rising in the meadow, her nakedness shadowy,
pierced and dressed by rainbows,
the greenery, the sea.

Women stroll to and fro on terraces
neighboring the sea:
Little girls and giant ladies,
awesome negresses in the grey-green foam,
upstanding jewels in the succulent soil of thickets
and frosty little gardens—Young mothers, big
sisters with glances full of wanderlust,
sultanas, princesses in swaggering
tyrannical drag, and strange little girls
and people sweetly pathetic.

What an annoyance! the hooey
of "darling heart" and "precious body!"

-CARL

II

There she is, the little dead girl, behind
the rosebushes.—The young mommy, lately passed away,
descends the stony steps.—The cousin's carriage crunches
on the sand.—Little brother (fresh from Hindustan!)
is there in front of the sunset in a field of pink marigolds.
—The old folk have all been buried upright in that
wall of scented clove.

A flurry of golden leaves encircles the general's
house. They've gone South.—You follow
the red road all the way to the deserted inn.
The chateau's up for sale, shutters hanging in the lurch.—
The priest must've taken the key to the church.—
All around the grounds keepers' cottages stand forlorn.
The outer walls are so high that one sees
no more than treetops rustling in the breeze.
Besides, there's nothing much to see there anyway.

The fields rise again to villages devoid
of cocks, of anvils. The floodgate is lifted.
Oh! the wayside shrines and windmills
of the wilderness,
the islands and the haystacks!

Magical blooms were buzzing.
The hillsides cradled them.
Elegant, fabulous animals roamed free.
Clouds gathered over the ancient sea
made up of an eternity of burning tears.

III

In the woods there's a bird whose song
will make you stop and blush.

There's a clock that will not strike.
There's a wetland with a nest of pallid creatures.

There's a cathedral descending
and a lake ascending.

There's a little cart abandoned in
the brambles, or rolling madly down the hill,
beribboned.

There's a troupe of little actors
in costume, visible on the way through
the edge of the wood.

Finally, when you're hungry and thirsty,
there's someone to chase you away.

IV

I am the saint in prayer on the terrace,
like the placid cattle grazing down
to the Palestinian sea.
I am the scholar in his gloomy armchair.
The branches and the rain batter the library windowpane.

I am the walker on the highway through the
stunted woods; the rumble of the floodgates drowns
my footsteps. For a long time I watch
the sunset's melancholy golden wash.

I might well be the runaway kid on the jetty,
leaving for the high seas, the little farmboy
following that path heading up to touch the sky.

The road's uneven. The knolls are covered
with shrubbery. The air is motionless.

How far away now the birds and brooklets.
It can only be the end of the world I'm headed for.

V

When will they ever let me rent this whitewashed tomb,
with its lines of mortar in relief,
—down far, far underground.

I lean my elbows on the table, the lamp lighting brightly
these tabloids that I'm an idiot to read again,
these books devoid of interest.—

At an enormous distance far above
my subterranean room, houses take root
and fogs are gathering. The mud is red or
black. Monstrous city, night without end!

A little above me are the sewers. On all sides
nothing but the density of the globe. Maybe
chasms of azure and fire-pits. Maybe
on these levels moons and comets, seas and fables meet.

In the bitterest hours I picture
sapphire balls, and metal ones.
I am master of the silence.
Why does something like a skylight
whiten at the corner of the ceiling?

Tale

Conte

A Prince became annoyed to find himself employed
perfecting nothing but vulgar giveaways.
He could foresee astonishing revolutions of love,
and suspected his wives capable of more than
easy compliance made easier with blue skies and lavish
apparel.
He wanted to see the truth, essential desire and
gratification's hour.
Even if it was just a godly aberration, he wanted it. He
possessed
at least plenty of human ability.

All the wives who'd known him were assassinated:
What havoc in the garden of beauty!
Under the blade, they blessed him. He didn't order
any new ones.—The wives reappeared.

He killed all those who followed him, after
the hunt or after drinks.—All of them followed him.
He amused himself cutting the throats of magnificent animals.
He set fire to the palaces. He flung himself on the people
and hacked them to pieces.—The multitude,
the roofs of gold, the beautiful animals existed all the same.

Can a man achieve ecstasy in destruction, grow younger
through cruelty? The populace was mum.
Nobody offered to air his own views.

One evening he rode off proudly. A Genie appeared,
of ineffable beauty, unspeakably so.
From his look and his pose arose the promise

of a love so various and complicated! of indescribable happiness,
unbearably so! The Prince and the
Genie probably annihilated each other
in the best of health. How could they help but die of it?
Together thus they died.

Yet this Prince passed away in his palace at the usual age.
The Prince was the Genie. The Genie was the Prince.

The music of the mind gives way to our desires.

Pageantry

Parade

What solid, husky dudes! Quite a few have exploited
your societies. Without cares and in so little hurry
to put to work their brilliant expertise and
their experience of your moralities. What manly men!
Eyes glazed over, like the summer
night—reds and blacks, tricolored, steely, pricked with
golden stars; faces twisted, livid, pallid,
ablaze: what raucous revelry! That brutal
swagger in their glittering rags!—Some of them are kids
—how'd they look to Cherubino?—equipped
with fearsome voices and some dangerous
tools. They've got orders to take the town from the rear,
decked out in disgusting *luxury.*

O the ultraviolent Paradise of maddening grins!
Far better than your Fakirs
and other showtime buffooneries. In costumes
improvised with all the taste of a bad dream,
they play sad love songs, tragedies
of hoodlums and demigods more spirited
than history or religion ever got to be. Chinese,
Hottentots, Gipsies, idiots, hyenas, Molochs,
old dementias and sinister demons, they mix
the motherly popular fare with bestial postures
and caresses. They'll explain the latest pieces
and the "good girl" singalongs. Master
jugglers, they transform the place and the people,
resorting to irresistible hocus-pocus. Their eyes
flame, the blood sings, their bones enlarge,

the tears and blushing trickles flow. Their
mockery or their terror lasts for a minute,
or months to go.

I alone have the key to this savage pageantry.

Antiquity

Antique

Graceful son of Pan! All around in
that head of yours, crowned in
flowering buds and berries,
your eyes like rolling jewels
are moving to and fro.
Smudged with ruddy dregs
your cheeks go hollow.
Your fangs gleam.
Your chest resonates like
a guitar whose twanging
tingles up and down your golden arms.
Your heart beats in that belly
where the doubled sex is sleeping.
Walk the night, smoothly moving this thigh,
that other thigh and
this leg, the left.

Being Beauteous

Right before the snow a Beautiful Being looms.
Deadly whistlings and circles of heavy music
make it rise, this beloved body,
spreading and wavering like a ghost:
Scarlet, blackened wounds explode
in the loveliest naked parts. The very colors of life
deepen, dance and disengage around
this Vision in the making.
And thrills rise and roar and the crazy savor
of these effects is full of deadly keening
and the raucous music that the world,
so far behind us, hurls at our mother
of beauty—she recoils, she rises. Oh!
Our bones redressed in fresh and loving bodies!

Oh the ashen face, the badge of tantrums, the crystal
embrace! The gun barrel on which I must fling myself
through the scrimmage of trees and the lilting breeze.

Lives

Vies

I

Oh the towering gateways to the holy land,
the terraces of the temple! What's happened to
the Brahmin who taught me the Proverbs? Then and there,
again I see the same old things.
I recall the silver and sunlit hours
near the rivers, the countryside's hand
on my shoulder and our caresses standing in the
peppered fields.—A flight of scarlet pigeons
thunders round my thought.
—Exiled here, I had a stage whereon
the dramatic masterworks of every literature
were played. I could show you untold wealth.
I watch the tale of your discovered treasures.
I see the sequel! My wisdom as much
derided as a chaos.
What's my nothingness compared
to the amazement that awaits you?

II

I am an inventor far more
worthy than all those who've preceded me:
A musician even, who's discovered something
like the key of love. At present
a country gentleman from a bitter land beneath a sober sky,
I try to be moved by the memory of my beggarly
beginnings, of my apprenticeship or else my arrival
in wooden shoes, a few disputes, some five or six widowings
and several drinking sprees where my willpower kept me

from rising to the fullest harmony of my cronies.
I don't regret my old share in hijinks divine:
The sober atmosphere of this bitter landscape
fortifies my dreadful skepticism.
But since this skepticism is no longer
workable,—and after all, I'm devoted to
a new disorder—I expect to become
a really nasty madman.

III

In an attic where I was locked up at twelve years old
I came to know the world:
I illustrated the human comedy.
I learned history in a kitchen closet.
At some nightly festival in a Northern town I hit on all the
women out of the Old Masters.
In a stale back-alley in Paris,
I was shown the classic skills.
In a magnificent dwelling, entirely surrounded by the Orient,
I completed my life-work and passed my illustrious retirement.
I have brewed my own blood.
My duty's been done.
It no longer needs a thought.
I'm really from beyond the grave
—and finished with obligations.

Taking Off

Départ

Enough seen. The Vision was met with
in every air.
Enough had. City rumblings, evenings, and under
the sun, and always.
Enough known. The arrests of a lifetime.—O Rumors
and Visions!
Taking off into fresh affections and the latest buzz!

Royalty

Royauté

One beautiful morning, among some really sweet people,
a gorgeous couple shouted aloud out in public:
"My friends, I want her to be queen!"
"I want to be queen!"—
She was laughing and trembling. He was telling their
friends about a revelation, about an ordeal finally ended.
They swooned, the one against the other.

As a matter of fact they did become royals all morning,
while
bright crimson banners were hoisted over the houses,
and the whole afternoon, while they made their progress toward
the palm-tree gardens.

For One Reason

À Une Raison

One stroke of your finger on the drum
sets every sound free,
begins a new kind of harmony.

One step of yours, that's the wake-up call
for the new men who are on the move.

Your head turns away: the novelty of love!
your head turns this way—the latest thing is love!

"Fix our prizes and sift our afflictions,
beginning with Time," those children sing to you,
"Elevate our lucky substance and our prayers,
wherever, we don't care," they implore you.

Having always arrived,
you'll take yourself everywhere.

Morning Rapture

Matinée d'ivresse

Oh *my* Delight! Oh *my* Beauty! Harrowing fanfare,
never tripping me! Enchanted rack! Hooray
for the unheard-of work and for the body of marvels,
for the very first time! This stuff came on
in childish laughter, that's the way it'll end up after.
This venom will still be running in all our veins even when,
the fanfare fading, we're sent back to the dissonant
olden days. O now made worthy of these tortures!
Let's fervently embrace that superhuman promise
made to the body and soul at our creation:
That promise, this dementedness!
For elegance, for knowledge, for violence!
Someone promised us
to bury the tree of good and evil in the shade,
to banish tyrannical moralities so we could parade
our purest love. That stuff kicked in
with a little nausea, and the way it ends
—since we couldn't just seize eternity
on the spot—it ends with a whiff of chaos.

Laughter of children, sensibility of slaves,
virginal austerity, horrified
by these shapes and faces here below,
you're blessed by the sleepless night's remembrance.
It used to come on with every farmboy antic,
and look! it ends with angels flaming in ice.

Brief intoxicated insight, sanctified!
Even if it's just a masquerade in our favor.
We avow you, methodology!
We're not forgetting how you glorified all our yesterdays.

We believe in this poison. We be leaving it our lives every day from now on.

Now is the time of *Assassins*.

Phrases

Phrases

When the world's distilled into a lonely dark
wood before our four astonished eyes—into
a beach for two faithful children—
into a house of music for our bright affection,
—I will find you.

Let there be just one old man left here below,
calm and beautiful, surrounded by "unheard-of luxury,"
—and I will be at your knee.

Let me have realized all your memories—let me
be that girl who knows how to gag and bind you,
—I will stifle you.

*   *   *

When we're most intense—who'll flinch?
Most giddy—who'll stoop to ridicule?
When we're at our wickedest, what would they
do with us?
Dress yourself up, dance and laugh.—I could
never throw Love out the window.

*   *   *

My buddy, little miss beggar, you big brat!
It's all the same to you, these unhappy
women and this hack work, and my
writer's block. Endear yourself to us with
your fabulous voice, your voice!
Matchless flatterer of this vile despair.

*   *   *

An overcast morning in July. A taste of ashes
floating in the air—odor of greenwood sweating on the grate—
flowers drenched—promenades plundered—the mist from off
the canals across the fields—After all, why not playthings
and incense?

*   *   *

I have stretched ropes from steeple to steeple; garlands
from window to window; chains of gold from star to star,
and I dance.

*   *   *

Fumes keep rising from the far lagoon. What
sorceress looms erect against the empty sunset? What
violet foliage is going to fall?

*   *   *

While public funds flow into brotherly
festivities, a bell of rosy fire tolls in
the clouds.

*   *   *

Enlivening a pleasing taste for Chinese ink,
a powdery blackness softly showers over my wakefulness
—I lower the flames of the chandelier, I fling myself
on the bed, and
turning toward the dark I see you, my babes!
My queens!

Workers

Ouvriers

Oh, that warm February morning! The unseasonable
South Wind came up, reviving memories of our poverty's
absurdity, of our youthful misery.

Henrika wore a checkered brown-and-white
cotton skirt, last fashionable a century ago,
a bonnet with ribbons and a silken scarf. It was
far sadder than mourning. We were taking a stroll
in the suburbs. The weather was overcast, and that wind
out of the South stirred up all the foul odors of spoiled
gardens and dried-up fields.

This didn't weary my woman as much
as it wearied me. In a leftover puddle from the flood
of the month before, on a steep enough pathway, she made me
take a look at some tiny little fishes.

The city, with its fumes and factory noises, followed us
a long way along the road. O
That other world, land blessed by sky and shadow!
The South Wind took me back to the pitiful episodes of my
childhood, my summers of despair, the terrible plenty of power
and knowledge that fate forever turns away from me. No!
We'll not be summering in this greedy land
where we'll never be more than a pair of needy lovers!
I don't want this hardened arm hauling *one cherished image*
anymore.

Bridges

Les Ponts

Out of grey skies of crystal: A bizarre design of bridges,
these here upright, those bulging, others descending obliquely
at an angle to the first, and these shapes reflected in
the other lit-up circuits of the channel, but all so very
thin and airy that the banks, loaded with domes,
dip and diminish. Some of these bridges are laden yet
with shabby bars. Others support poles
and signposts and flimsy railings. Minor chords
cross over them and swiftly fade; lines climb the banks.
One picks out a red vest, maybe other outfits
and musical instruments. Are these the popular songs,
shreds of lordly concerts, remnants of national anthems?
The water is grey and blue,
as wide as an arm of the sea.

—A toneless ray, dropping from the highest
sky, annihilates this comedy.

City

Ville

I'm an ephemeral, quite content citizen
of a metropolis considered modern because every known taste
has been evaded in household furnishings and exteriors,
and in the city's design as well.
You'd hardly point out any traces of a single monument to
superstition here. Morals and language finally get reduced to
their simplest expression. These millions of folks,
who feel no need to get acquainted, organize
their education, their careers and their old age
all so much alike, their lifetimes look a lot shorter
than found in statistical foolishness for continental
populations. As it is, out my window, I see
additional specters rambling through
the dull, eternal smutty fog—our shady wood,
our summer night!—the latest Furies, in front
of my cottage that's my home and heartland, since
everything here's like this,—Death without tears,
our busy little servant girl, a desperate Love,
and a cute Crime squealing in the mud on the street.

Beaten Paths

Ornières

On the right, the summer's dawn rouses the foliage and the fogs
and the hubbub out of this corner of the park, and
the slopes, left,
contain in their violet shadow the wet road's
countless running ruts. A parade of enchantments. Here they go:
Wagons laden with gilded wood animals, tent poles
and motley backdrops, drawn by twenty dappled circus ponies
at full gallop, and the kids and the men on their
most astonishing animals;—
twenty cars, embossed, bedecked
with flags and flowers like old-fashioned carriages or fairy tales,
filled with children dolled up for a suburban pastoral play:
—Even coffins under their canopy of night pitch
ebony plumes, passing swiftly to the trot of huge
blue-black mares.

Cities I

Villes I

These are CITIES! This is a people for whom these
dreamy Alleghanies and Lebanons were raised!
Cabins of crystal and wood glide by
on invisible rails and pulleys. The ancient craters
ringed by colossi and palm-trees of copper, melodiously
roar among the flames. Lovers' festivals
echo across the canals strung out behind the cabins.
The chase of chiming bells clamors in the gorges.
Unions of gigantic singers rush up in
robes and regalia as dazzling as
daylight on the summits. On the platforms among
the canyons, Rolands blow their own horns.
Over the catwalks of the chasm and the tavern rooftops,
the fever of heaven raises flags. A crumbling blaze
of glory overtakes the upland fields where
angelic centauresses amble amid the
avalanches. Above the level of the highest peaks,
a sea troubled by the eternal birth
of Venus, laden with choirs of waves and the
murmur of precious pearls and shells;—the sea
sometimes darkening with deadly brilliance.
On the slopes, a gathering of flowers, tall as
our guns and trophies, bellowing. Processions
of Mabs, in russet iridescent dresses, climb
the ravines. Up there, at the foot of the waterfall and the
brambles, deer suckle Diana. The Bacchae
of suburbia burst out sobbing and the moon burns and howls.
Venus penetrates the caves of saint and smithy.
Groups of belfries carol the plans of the populace.
Strange music flows from castles built of bone.
Every legend evolves and zealots rip through

backwater towns. The paradise of
storms calms down. Savages dance nonstop
at the all-night festival. And, for an hour, I went down
into the bustle of a Baghdad boulevard where
companions were singing the joys of the latest labor,
under a heavy breeze, going round unable
to evade the fabled phantoms of the mountains where they had
to gather again.

What fine embrace, what beauteous hour will bring me back
to that region, source of my slumbers and my
slightest movements?

Vagabonds

Vagabonds

Pitiful brother! What atrocious all-nighters I owed him!
"I didn't fervently seize on this venture.
I made fun of his disability.
Because of me, we'd go back into exile, into slavery."
He supposed me oddly unlucky
and oh-so bizarrely innocent,
and he added some disquieting causes.

I responded with mockery to this doctor satanical,
and ended up heading for the window.
Beyond the landscape traversed with bands of rare music,
I created phantoms of future nocturnal luxury.

After this vaguely hygienic distraction,
I'd lay me down on a pallet. And nearly every night,
as soon asleep, my needy brother would rise,
with rotting mouth and ripped-out eyes—
as good as he dreamt—and drag me through the room
screaming his peevish idiot's dream.

I had, in fact, made a vow in all
sincerity of spirit to restore him to his
primal state as a son of the Sun,
—and we did wander, nourished by cavernous wine
and roadside biscuit, me pressing on
to discover the place and the formula.

Cities II

Villes II

The official Acropolis exaggerates modern barbarity's
most colossal ideas. Impossible to convey
the dull day produced by the sky's immutable grey,
the imperial splendor of the buildings and the snow forever
on the ground. With a monstrous taste for magnitude,
they've reproduced all the marvels of classical architecture.
I go to art shows in places twenty
times more vast than Hampton Court.
What paintings! A Nebuchadnezar of Norway's
designed the ministry stairways; the underlings
I saw there were already haughtier than Brahmins,
and I trembled at the look of colossal guards
and construction foremen. By the arrangement
of the buildings into squares, closed courts and terraces,
they've shut out all the cabbies. The parks display
primitive nature improved with splendid art.
The high-class district has some puzzling parts:
An arm of the sea, without boats, rolls out its
blue sleet blanket between embankments lined with giant
candelabra. A short bridge leads to a side-door
immediately under the dome of the Holy Chapel.
This dome's an artistic steel armature
about fifteen thousand feet across.

At certain points on copper gangways,
platforms, and stairs that wrap around
the markets and the pillars, I believed I'd be able to judge
the depths
of the city. One wonder I wasn't able to figure out:
What levels are the other districts above or below the Acropolis?
For the stranger in our midst, exploration
is impossible. The commercial district's

a circus in one style, with galleries of arcades.
One sees no boutiques, but the snow
on the road is crushed flat; a few Hindu fatcats, as rare as
Sunday morning strollers in
London, dash for a coach made of diamonds.
A few red velvet couches: they serve up icy drinks,
variably pricey for eight hundred to eight
thousand rupees. At the thought of finding some theatres
in this circus, I tell myself the shops must
contain some pretty somber dramas. I think
there's a police force. But the laws have got to be
so very strange, I give up trying to imagine
any grifters here.

Suburbia, as elegant as a lovely street
in Paris, is favored with luminous weather; the
democratic element numbers some few hundred
souls. Here again, the houses aren't in rows.
Suburbia loses its way bizarrely in the countryside,
the "County" that fills the everlasting west
with forests and vast plantations where
savage gentlemen pursue their chronicles
under the light they've created.

Wakefulness

Veillées

I

Here's enlightened repose, not feverish nor languid,
on the bed or in the meadow.

Here's the friend, not fiery nor faint-hearted. The friend.

Here's the beloved, not tormenting nor tormented. The
beloved.

Wind and world unlooked for. Life.

—Was it really this?

—And the dream quickens.

II

Lights relume the tree by the building.
Out of both extremities of the room, some ordinary decor,
harmonic elevations merge.
The wall facing the watcher is a
psychic series of cutaway friezes,
of atmospheric bands and geologic
accidentals—Rapt and speedy dream
of group love with beings
of every character caught in the act
of all appearances.

III

The lamps and carpets of the vigil make the noise

of waves all night, along the hull and around
the steerage.
The sea of the night-watch, like Emily's breasts.

The tapestries, halfway up, of lacy thickets,
emerald-tinted, where the doves
of wakefulness dart.

The slab of dark hearth, with real suns by the
shores: ah! pits of enchantments; only a vision of dawn,
this time.

Mystique

Mystique

On the sloping rubble
angels twirl their fleecy
robes in the emerald steely grasses.

Fields of flame frolic up to the summit
of the hill. At left, the ridge of humus has been
trampled by every homicide and every battle
and every news of disaster prolongs their trajectory.
Behind the crest, on the right, the orient line,
advancement.

And while the tableau's top border
is formed by the whirling, leaping uproar
of those conches from the seas and the nights of humanity,

the flowering sweetness
of the stars and the sky and the
rest of it descends over the facing slope—like a petticoat
against our face—and makes the bottomless pit below
turn blue and flower there.

Dawn

Aube

I've embraced the dawn of summer.

Nothing budged in front of the palace yet. Still waters
ran dead. The camp of shadows hadn't quit
the way into the woods. I walked on in, reviving
the warm and vivid wind, and precious jewels were watching
and wings were soaring noiselessly.

The earliest adventure was, in a path already
filled with cool and creamy splendors, a flower that whispered
its name to me.

I laughed at the golden wasserfall
dishevelling through the pines:
At the silvery summit I recognized the goddess.

Then I raised her veils one by one. In the roadway,
flailing my arms. Near the field where I
squealed on her to the cock. Uptown, she flew between
steeples and domes, and running like
a beggar on marbled embankments, I chased her down.

On the high road, near a laurel grove,
I wrapped her in her gathered veils
and had a little taste of her immense quality.
The sunrise and the child took a tumble
at the bottom of the woods.

On waking it was noon.

Flowers

Fleurs

From a golden ledge—among the
silken cords, the grey gauzes, the green
plush and the crystal discs blackening
like bronze in the sun—I see the
foxglove open over a swirling carpet
of silver, of eyes and heads of hair.

Shards of yellow gold are scattered
over the agate, pillars of mahogany
hold up a dome of emeralds, white
satin bouquets and slender pricks
of ruby surround the rose in water.

Like a god of immense blue eyes
and snowy limbs, the sea and the
sky seduce the mob of robust
young roses on the marble terraces.

Vulgar Nocturne

Nocturne vulgaire

One breath blows open operatic breaches
in the walls—scrambles the twister of
corroded rooftops—scatters the boundaries
of hearth and home—eclipses the crossways.

—Climbing down the ivy,
having steadied my foot on a rainspout—
I slipped into this carriage,
its epoch indicated well enough
by the convex glass, the padded panelling,
the contorted upholstery. Hearse of my slumber,
isolated, shepherd's hut of my shenanigans,
The vehicle veers onto the grass
of the overgrown highway: And in a flaw
at the top of the right-hand window glass,
pallid lunar shapes, petals, nipples twirl.

—The deepest green and blue invade the scene:

Unharnessing near a patch of gravel.

—Wouldn't you whistle up a storm here,
for Sodomites—and Salemites—
and savage animals and armies.

—(Coach-boys and dream-steeds will be taking
their way back under the choking smother
of old trees, in favor of my plunging
at eye-level into the silken stream)

—And off we go, whipped across the rippling
water and spilling drinks,
rolling on to the howling of watchdogs . . .

—One breath scatters the boundaries of hearth and home.

Seascape

Marine

Silver and copper the chariots—
Prows of steel and silver—
Thrashing the spray,
Whipping up the tumbleweeds.
The currents of the prairie
And the vast beaten paths of the backflow
Unwind, spiralling easterly,
Around the pillars of trees—
Around the pilings of the pier,
Whose tilted view slams
Into whirling clouds of light.

Winter Festival

Fête d'hiver

The waterfall chimes behind those
comic-opera bungalows.
Girandoles—above the groves
and lanes by the river Meander—prolong
the greens and reds of sunset.

Nymphs out of Horace in
Empire hats and hairdos—
Siberian circle-dances,
Chinese girls out of Boucher!

Anguish

Angoisse

Can She finesse an excuse for my
continually crushed ambitions—?—Can a rich
finale repair ages of want?—can one successful
day numb the shame of our fatal
inability?

(O palms! diamonds! Love, power!—Higher
than the sum of joy and fame! in every way, every
where—Demon, god—this youthful being
here: Me!)

Can the accidents of scientific fairy-dust and the
trends of a brotherly trust be cherished
like a gradual return to the outset of
innocence? . . .

All the same, the Vampire who renders us tame expects
us to entertain ourselves with her leftovers,
or else for us to be more amusing:

Rolling in bruises,
through the tedious breeze and the sea;
in torments, through the silence of murderous
wind and water; in tortures that laugh out loud,
in their cruel turbulent silence.

Metropolitan

Métropolitain

From the indigo straits to the seas of Ossian,
over the rose and orange sands washed by the wine of skies,
crystal boulevards rise and criss-cross,
hastily filled by poor young families
who buy supplies at the fruit-stand. Nothing too rich.
—This is the city!

Out of the asphalt desert a line of panic's in flight,
shrouded in a fearful fog in
spreading layers across the sky, bending back,
recoiling and descending, made of
the most sinister black smoke the grieving Sea can draw
—a welter of helmets, wheels, boats and buttocks
—this is the battle!

Raise your head: this wooden bridge an arc;
the last garden in Samaria; these illuminated masks
under a lantern whipping in the cold night wind;
the foolish water-nymph in her drunken dress
at the bottom of the river;
the luminous skulls among the
potted plants—and other phantasmagoria
—this is the countryside.

Roads bordered with iron fences, with
walls, hedges poking out, and with
harrowing flowers called hearts and sisters.
Damascus damned by lassitude—
possessions of enchanted aristocracies
ultra-Rhenish, Japanese, Guaranas, ready
again to receive the music of the ancients

—and there are taverns that'll never
open again as it is;—there, some of
them are princesses, and, if you're not
too overwhelmed, there's the study of the stars
—this is the sky.

In the morning where you struggled with Her
amid the snowy brilliance, these green lips, those glaciers,
the black tapestries and blue rays,
and the purple perfumes of the polar sun,
—this is your power.

Barbarous

Barbare

Long after the days and the seasons,
and all creation and the nations,

the signal in the flesh bleeding
over the silk of seas and icy flowers;
(they don't exist.)

Rescued from those old heroic fanfares—
that still attack us, heart and head—
far from ancient assassins—

oh! the signal in the flesh
bleeding over the silk of seas and icy flowers;
(they don't exist.)

Deliciousness!

Infernos, weeping through the roaring frost—
delicious things!—the fires in that
windy rain of diamonds hurled
from earth's eternally carbonized
core for us—O world!

(Far away from old retreats and ancient flames,
the ones we listen for, the ones we feel.)

Infernos and foam. The music, whirling
out of cyclones and crashing icicles on the stars.

O Sweetness, O world, O music! And there,
the shapes, the sweatings, the heads of hair
and the eyes, hovering. And the white, scalding
tears—O sweetness!—and the feminine voice
having reached volcanic depths and icy grottos.

The signal . . .

Bargains

Solde

For sale: whatever the Jews won't sell,
whatever nobility and crime haven't sampled,
whatever outcast love and hellish honesty the masses ignore:
Whatever neither time nor science need have a name for .

Voices revived: Brotherhood aroused out of all
choral and orchestral forces and their instant application:
the matchless happenstance of releasing our feelings!
For sale: Bodies beyond price, adornments
of every race worldwide, every sex, whole families!
Riches gush in every direction.
Discount diamonds duty-free!

For sale: Chaos for the masses,
satisfaction guaranteed for amateur snobs,
horrible death for lovers and believers!

For sale: habitations and migrations,
sports, bedazzlements and flawless comforts:
And the buzz, the trends, and shape
of future things they bring!

For sale: the uses of calculus and crazy
leaps of harmony! Serendipity with easy
terms above suspicion, Immediate Delivery!

The senseless, infinite rush for
invisible splendors, intangible delights—
and their secret madness for every vice
with its hideous grinning for the crowd.

For sale: Bodies and Voices,
the immense unquestioned opulence
that will never sell out.
The vendors haven't run out of bargains yet!
The salesmen needn't figure their totals too soon!

Fairy

Fairy

For Helen, juicy embellishments conspired
among the virginal shadows and the heartless brilliance,
in the silence of the stars.
The summer's fever was conferred
upon mute birds and the following indolence
on a barge of priceless mourning over the waters of dead
love affairs, of drowned perfumes.

—The next moment from the song of women gathering wood
to the rumble of the torrent before the forest's ruin.
From the clangor of the flocks to the echo in the valleys
and the outcry on the steppes.—

For Helen's infancy there was a shivering in furs
and shadows,—and the hearts of the poor and the legends
of the sky.

And those eyes of hers! and her dancing—better still
than precious flashes, than cool authority, than the pleasure
of the matchless time and place.

War

Guerre

As a child, certain skies refined my outlook:
All of their characteristics colored my appearance.
The Phenomena made a stir.—At present,
the endless bending of moments, and the infinitude of
mathematics
pursue me through the world where
I submit to every secular success, with respect
for childhood's weirdness and its overwhelming affections.
—I contemplate a war, for right or might, out of surprising
logic.

It's as easy as a musical phrase.

Youth

Jeunesse

I. Sunday
(Dimanche)

Paperwork put aside, the sky's descending inevitability
and the rummaging of memories and the seance of its rhythms
possess the house, the head and the world of spirit.

—A horse trots off along suburban turf,
past garden plots and tree lots, pierced with sooty
pestilence. A wretched actress somewhere
in the world sighs, yearning for improbable
spontaneities. Desperadoes languish after
outrage, booze and bloody wounds. Little kids
choke back their curses by the riverside.—

Get back to that study,
to the buzz of a devouring labor
that gathers in and flowers again
among the masses.

II. Sonnet
(Sonnet)

Man of common mettle,
was not the flesh a fruit hanging in the orchard?
O childish days! the body a treasure to squander?
O loving, the peril or power of Psyche?
The hills of the earth were fertile once with princes, artists,
and their descendants and their offspring pushed us
into crimes and grief: the world, your wealth and your peril.

But now, that labor complete, you and your schemes,
you, your fidgeting, are just a song and dance—
neither fixed nor at all forced, though they make for a
double-event
that's inventive and a hit with humanity,
fraternal and variable, through a universe devoid of imagery:
—Power and parity reflecting the dance
and the voice only now receiving praise . . .

III. Twenty Years Old
(Vingt ans)

The teaching voices banished . . .
the body's brightness bitterly
sedated . . . —Adagio—Ah!
The infinite self-love of adolescence,
the studious optimism:
How the world was drunk with flowers that summer!
Arias and etiquette are dying out . . .
a choir for soothing uselessness
and absence!
A choir of glasses of nocturnal song . . . In fact,
the nerves get shot in a hurry.

IV

You're still at St. Anthony's temptation:
Your sporting zeal cut short,
your childish pride's obsessions,
your terror and depression.

But you will set yourself to work:
All the possibilities
of harmony and architecture
will swirl up around
your center.

Perfect beings, unforeseen,
will offer themselves
to your experience.

All around you the curiosity
of elderly crowds and idle riches
will surface dreamily.
Memory and instinct will feed
your creative compulsion.

As for the world, what'll become of it
when you leave?
In any case, nothing currently on view.

Promontory

Promontoire

The golden dawn and the shivering evening find
our brig at sea and facing this Villa with its
dominions that form a promontory as vast as
Hesperus or the Peloponnese or the great isle
of the Japanese, or even Araby! Temples are lit
by returning parades; immense vistas of modern
coastal defenses; dunes illuminated by
flowering blazes and bacchanalia; the grand canals of
Carthage and Embankments of a cock-eyed Venice;
sluggish eruptions on Etnas and fissures full of
flowers and glacial waters; lavatories enclosed
by poplars from Germany:
Sloping parks leaning oddly beyond the tops of Japanese Trees;
the circular façades of the "Royal" or
the "Grand" out of Scarbro or Brooklyn; and their flanking
elevated railways tunneling and dominating the design of
this hotel, chosen from the most elegant
and colossal historical buildings of Italy, from America,
and out of Asia, whose windows and terraces, now rife
with lights and liquor and rich breezes,
are open to the refreshment of travellers and aristocrats—
who allow at daily hours, all the seashore tarantellas
—and even the valley ritornellas
made famous in art, which wonderfully decorate
the façades of the Palace. A Promontory.

Stages

Scènes

The ancient Show of Shows pursues its unities and divides
into Interludes:
From Broadways to little stages.

A long wooden pier stretches from one end to another of a
rocky field
where the lowbrow crowd shuffles along under barren trees.

Down corridors of gauzy black following strolling footsteps among
the lanterns and the leaves.

Birds from the mysteries swoop down over stonework pontoons,
moving past the little islands covered with boatloads of onlookers.

Lyric scenes accompanied by flute and drum take their
bows in cozy nooks
up under the ceilings around modern club-rooms
or ancient Oriental auditoriums.

Magic's maneuvered at the summit of an amphitheater
crowned by thickets—
or shifts its shape and modulates for the Booboisie in the shade
of a forest of moving trees over the crest of cultivation.

Musicals have been segregated onstage by the ridge of ten
intersecting flats
erected from the footlights to the balcony.

Historic Evening

Soir Historique

Any evening, for example, when the naive tourist finds himself
recoiling from our economic horrors, the hand of a master
animates the grasslands harpsichord;
some people play at cards in the depths of the pool,
evocative mirror of queens and concubines; they've got the saints,
the veils, harmonious threads and legendary tone-colors
over the setting sun.

He shudders at the passage of huntsmen and hordes: On
the lawn, stages drip with drama. And the puzzlement of paupers
and morons over those silly plots!

In his captivated vision—Germany shambles toward the moons;
Tartary deserts flash and flare;—Old revolts are
swarming in the center of the Celestial Empire, over stairways
and kingly thrones—a pallid little world and flat,
out of the West, Africa goes for a build-up. After that,
a ballet of well-known evenings by the sea, a worthless chemistry,
and a few impossible tunes.

The same old middle-class magic drops us everywhere the
mail stops.
The totally elemental physicist feels it's no longer possible
to undergo this personal atmosphere,
this fog of remorse in the flesh, already an affliction duly
noted.

No! the instantaneous sterilizer, of oceans blown away,
of subterranean fires, of the planet swept away,

and systematic exterminations—convictions not so very slyly
indicated
in the Bible and by the Norns
—that's a chore for the serious to oversee.

Meanwhile, it's not just the stuff of Legend!

Bottom

Reality becoming too thorny for my epic
personality—I found myself, despite all that, at my lady's place,
a huge grey-blue bird soaring toward the borders
of the ceiling, and trailing plumage in the gloom of the
evening.

I became, at the foot of the canopy supporting her
adorable jewels and her material masterpieces, a great
bear with purple jaws and shaggy, shabby fur,
with eyes for the crystal and the
silverware.

Everything became shadowy and a glowing aquarium.

In the morning—dawn of a wrangling June—I ran
to the fields, an ass, braying and brandishing
my beef until the Sabines of the
suburbs came to fling themselves on my harnessed breast.

H

H

Every perversity violates the nastier poses of Hortense.
Her solitude is the erotic mechanism; her lassitude,
love's dynamic. Under the watchful eyes of kids
she's been, for countless ages, the hottest hygiene
of the races. Her door's wide open to misery.
There the morals of the up-to-date
evaporate in her passion or out of her action.
—O shuddering spasm of inexperienced loves on the bleed-
ing dirt and
through the bright, clear hydrogen! you hit upon Hortense.

Motion

Mouvement

The ricochet down the chute of rapids
The whirlpool astern
The rampant swiftness' glide
The current's enormous thrust,
Led on by unheard-of lights
And chemical innovation
The voyagers whirl through waterspouts into the
Maelstrom's valley.

These are the world-conquering
Fortune-hunting chemical personnel:
Sports and comforts come along for the ride.
They bring off the education
Of races, classes and animals on this Vessel:
Repose and vertigo
To the floodlit glow
In terrifying nights of study.

For out of the babble among the systems,
—The blood, the flowers, the fire, the jewels—
Out of the shaky reckonings on this pitching deck
—One sees, rolling like a levee
Beyond the motorized hydraulic highway,
Monstrous, lit-up endlessly—their haul of learning:
—They've ransacked harmonic ecstasy
And the heroism out of discovery.

Among the most amazing atmospheric incidents
A young couple disembark alone
—Is this primitive savagery forgivable?—
And sing and assume position.

Devotions

Dévotion

To Sister Louise Vanaen de Voringhem:—
Her blue nun's bonnet turned towards the Northern sea.
—Pray for the castaways.

To Sister Leona Woods d'Ashby: Bow wow!—
the summer grass abuzz with stink.
—Pray for the fever of mothers and children.

To Lulu—the demon—who's kept a taste
for church-going from the time of Girrrlfriends
and her unfinished education.
Pray for the men!—To Madame X.

To the adolescent I used to be. To that saintly
old man in hermitage or mission.
To the spirit of the poor. And a very high clergy.
As well as to every cult in any place full of
memorial cults, and amid such results
that one must succumb to the moment's yearning,
Or else to our characteristic, serious vice.

This evening, pray to Circeto of the glacial heights,
fat as a fish and illuminated like the ten months
of ruddy night—(amber and spunk, her heart),
—for my only prayer's as muted as these regions
of night and will go before a more violent bravery
than this polar chaos.

Pray at all costs in every weather,
even on metaphysical trips.—But more so *then.*

Democracy

Démocratie

"The flag heads for squalid landscapes
and our rigmarole muffles the drumroll.

"Deep at the core
we'll nourish the most barefaced whoring.
We'll butcher the logical revolutionaries.
"Off to spicy and distempered lands!
—in the service of the most colossal
military-industrial exploitations.

"'So long' to this place, no matter where.
Recruits of good intent, we have a savage philosophy:
Ignorant of skill, conveniently getting laid;
let the world go blow.
That's real progress! Forward, march!"

Spirit

Génie

He is tenderness and he is now, because he's thrown the
house open
to frosty winter and the murmur of summer—he
who has purified food and drink, he who is the charmer of
fugitive places and the superhuman delight of stillness.
He is tenderness and the future,
the power and the love that we—standing by
in rage and boredom—we see passing
through the stormy sky and the flags of ecstasy.

He is love, the perfect and reinvented measure,
marvelous and unforeseen reason, and eternity:
Beloved machine of fatal accomplishments.
We have all known the dread of his giving out, and of our own:
O joyous vigor, liveliness of our senses, affectionate egotism
and passion for him, he who loves us for the sake of his
life eternal.
And we call him back to us and he travels on . . .

And if Adoration moves on, ringing, his promise rings:
"Away with these superstitions, these bodies of old,
these engagements and ages.
This is the epoch that sinks without a trace!"

He will not go away, he will not descend again from heaven,
he will not accomplish the redemption of women's rage
and men's amusement and all their sin:
Because he's done, he exists, and is loved.

O his breathless, headlong racing: the
terrible swiftness of the flawless form and action.

O fertility of the spirit and immensity of the universe!

His body! the dreamt-of redemption, the shattering
of grace crossed with new-found violence!

The sight of him! the sighting! all the old grovelling
and pain are *lifted* at his passing-by.

His light! the abolition of all sonorous and moving
suffering in a music more intense.

His stride! Migrations more enormous
than ancient invasions.

O he and we! pride more benevolent than
wasted charities.

O world! and the clear-cut melody of new misfortunes!

He has known us all and loved us all.
May we be able, this winter's night, from cape to cape,
from the storm-tossed pole to the castle,
from the crowd to the seashore,
from look to look, powers and feelings failing,
to call to him, and see him
and send him on his way, and under the tides
and on the snowy desert heights,
to follow his vision, his breath,
his body, his light.

NOTES

The original manuscript of *Illuminations* is a series of unnumbered
pages without dates of composition. These were most likely com-
posed between 1872 and 1874 in Paris, Brussels, and London,
although this has by no means been established with any degree of
finality.

The present translation is based on the text of the Bibliothèque de
l'Image edition of 1998, which reproduces the existing manuscript
in facsimile with a printed line-for-line version on the facing pages.
For the most part, I have followed the lineation of these handwrit-
ten copies in order to "open up" the prose line and allow for a
simulation of the original's rhythmic pulse. The manuscripts of
"Soir Historique" and "Génie" are at present inaccessible and those
of "Démocratie" and "Dévotion" are presumed lost—at any rate,
missing—so I have lineated these four prose poems in a manner
to match the rest. As Paul Schmidt has observed in his introduc-
tion to *Complete Works* (Harper and Row, 1976), "a prose poem in
French is poem first and prose secondarily; a prose poem in En-
glish is in the opposite case." By following (and sometimes veering
from) the author's handwritten lineation, I have attempted to re-
verse this case, to let these astonishing visions unfold as 'poem
first and prose secondarily.'

Notes and commentary are based on the excellent example provided
by Jean-Luc Steinmetz for G.F. Flammarion (1989). Nick Osmond's
Introduction and Notes for the Athlone French Poets' *Illumina-
tions* (1976) contain a close reading of the text and, where helpful,
he is quoted in the following notes.

According to Verlaine, who received the manuscript from Rimbaud in
1875, the work's title is in English and should be pronounced,
"Illuminécheunes." In his original 1886 edition, Verlaine appended
the subtitle *"gravures colorées,"* which he rendered into English as
"coloured plates" or "painted plates."

Rimbaud himself, in any case, provides the solitary title *Illuminations* once (in parentheses) after "Promontory" in the manuscript.

*   *   *

To look is the key function I have pursued in rendering these visions into contemporary American English. Rimbaud's imagery, however dense and multi-layered, seems to me primarily visual, and the question to which I most often returned when faced with a tangle of possibilities was, "What is he seeing?"

While this might seem a simplified response to Rimbaud's idea of the poet as a "voyant" or "seer," it is grounded in the natural and observable. In his book *Rimbaud and Jim Morrison: The Rebel as Poet*, Wallace Fowlie comments on *Illuminations*: "The art of the prose poems is oracular. Nature is the starting point for Rimbaud as it was for Baudelaire ('la nature est un temple'). In these pages of Rimbaud, a natural object ends by symbolizing human life. They appear today the most serene and the most philosophically penetrating of all that Rimbaud wrote."

Après le Déluge / After The Flood

The cycle begins with a poem of changes—a revolution, a new world created, a parade of life-and-death activities and quasi-religious intensity.

l'idée du Déluge ("the concept of The Flood")
This is the concept or thought of a Biblical Flood rather than its historical or 'factual' reality. The vignettes that follow expand in subject matter and scope (from the rabbit at his prayers to the Queen of the Night bent over her cosmic cauldron), concluding with an invocation for future floods, summoned to relieve or redeem human boredom and vexation. Boredom, says Baudelaire in *Au Lecteur*, is "our wickedest

vice"—"C'est l'Ennui ... ce monstre délicat ... " (It's Boredom ...
that fastidious monster ...)

les 'mazagrans' ("Brandied coffees")

A *mazagran* is a coffee drink mixed with brandy and sugar, served in a
glass or a mug without handles; it originated in Algeria and is
named for the decisive battle that put the Algerians under French
rule in 1840.

les estaminets ("cheap cafés")

An *estaminet* is what might be termed a 'dive' in Anglo-American slang—
a joint serving only coffee and alcohol.

Eucharis me dit que c'était le printemps ("Eucharis told me it was Spring")

Eucharis is the Eucharist or Communion, the sacrament of the
Catholic faith that renews Christ's sacrifice of his body and
blood (The Easter Story). Also, in Greek, Eucharis is a woman's
name meaning 'full of grace.' In the classic French novel
Télémaque by François Fenelon (1651–1715), Eucharis is a
companion of the nymph-goddess Calypso, daughter of Atlas,
who rescues Odysseus after his ship-wreck and keeps him on
her island for seven years (Homer's *Odyssey*, Books I–IV). An-
other translation of the line could read "Grace told me it was
Spring."

la Reine, la Sorcière ("the Queen, the Sorceress")

In contrast to Easter (and/or mythic nymphs of graceful bearing),
Rimbaud here evokes Hecate, the Queen of the Night, a ruler
over the souls of the dead. Hecate's function as a bringer of
wisdom and a source of good luck to sailors and hunters over-
laps that of Diana (Artemis), goddess of the hunt; she is asso-
ciated with the moon as well as sorcery and black magic (q.v.
Shakespeare *Macbeth* III:5 and *Hamlet* III:2). Ghosts and de-

mons are at her service and she haunts the night with a pack of howling dogs.

Enfance / Childhood

The unifying line in these five poems is the rite of passage from childhood to maturity. These rites are sexual, religious, personal, familial, scientific: women are seen as types of various idols; ghostly families gather; surreal or empty landscapes dominate the scene; the poet longs for escape into nature, or for solitary meditation in complete isolation.

I The yellow-haired idol is another of the mysterious female figures that appear throughout *Illuminations* (cf. Helen, Henrika, Harriet, the sisters and Circeto of "Devotions").

The poem seems to equate childhood's early years with faraway enchanted lands populated with exotic women (nudes, giantesses, sultanas, princesses, et al.).

"The Girl With Orange Lips" episode has been set to music by Earl Kim in his song cycle *Where Grief Slumbers* (1982).

II A ghostly family reunion at a deserted house opens out to vistas fallen into disrepair and desertion.

In the village, "devoid of cocks, of anvils," there is no livestock, no activity—hence, no people, no sex. Symbolically, the rooster is associated with the sun, masculinity, fertility, and victory over darkness; the anvil is often seen as the feminine, receptive counterpart of the hammer, which is a masculine symbol—together they represent the active and passive roles of complementary, opposing images.

III Wandering in the woods, the child observes phenomenal scenes.
The forest seems a cathedral of trees reflected in the sky-blue wa-
ters of a lake. He glimpses woodland creatures in their hidden
habitations. A troupe of strolling players—apparently of the
commedia dell'arte in their recognizable costumes (Pierrot,
Punchinello, Columbine)—lose control of their little cart on a hill-
side.
IV These are aspects (child-like) assumed: the saint, the scholar, the
walker, the runaway. The birds and brooks of earlier enchanted
landscapes recede into the distance at childhood's end.

V In the city, the vista closes in on the poet; he delves underground for
a sense of solitude and space. The outer world keeps intruding.

Conte / Tale

Nick Osmond notes that " ... all the *Illuminations* are related to the
fairy-tale genre in the sense that they deal matter-of-factly with the
fantastic ... But 'Conte' ... has a density and mystery not usual
in fairy-tales."

The Prince may represent Verlaine or Rimbaud, or Rimbaud's creative
ambition, "the self which plays the conscious, controlling role in
the creative act." (Osmond)

The acts of violence are dream-like and their effects immediately can-
celed in an almost humorous manner, subjects popping back up
like jack-in-the-boxes after being 'killed.'

La musique savante manque à notre désir ("The music of the mind
gives way to our desires")
The mind's music (art, creation, destruction) is organized by, or at the
mercy of that which we desire.

Parade / Pageantry

What exactly is the "savage pageantry" here presented? A foreign festi-
val, a troupe of players, a religious ceremony? The poet 'alone' has
the key. Street-hustlers, vagabonds, religious hucksters, con art-
ists, traveling actors—all of these are possible interpretations of
these "solid, husky dudes."
The last line, *"J'ai seul la clef de cette parade sauvage,"* serves as a recur-
ring theme in Benjamin Britten's song cycle "Les Illuminations"
(1939).

comment regarderaient-ils Chérubin? ("how'd they look to Cherubino?")
The translation here could easily read "how might they look to a Cherub?"
or "how would Cherubino see them?" The term *Chérubin* both
means cherub (angel) and is the name of a character in
Beaumarchais' comedy, *The Marriage of Figaro* (1781), an adoles-
cent just awakening to love—naive, charming, ignorant, and
dreamy. In Mozart's opera (1786), Cherubino is sung by a woman
(mezzo-soprano) to indicate that his voice has not yet changed.

On les envoie prendre du dos en ville ("They've got orders to take the
town from the rear")
In French slang, the phrase *prendre du dos* means "to take [it] from the
rear"—to sodomize or bugger or to 'get screwed' physically, finan-
cially, or emotionally. Another possible translation of the line could
read: "Someone dispatched them to take it from the rear in town"
or "They've been sent as envoys to bugger the town." The phrase
combines images of active and passive copulation plus the image
of an aggressive military action that captures (captivates) the whole
town.

Molochs ("Molochs")
Moloch was a bloodthirsty god of the ancient Ammonites, mentioned
   in the Bible (Jeremiah 32:35), who demanded the fiery sacrifice
   of children.

Antique / Antiquity

The title has two meanings in French: (1) a masculine noun referring
   to the style of Greek and Roman art; and (2) a feminine noun
   meaning a work of art, per se, dating from antiquity.
Rimbaud here plays with a conventional 19th Century poetic formula—
   the idealization of (and a sentimental nostalgia for) " . . . the glory
   that was Greece, / And the grandeur that was Rome" (E.A. Poe, *To
   Helen*). A goat-legged satyr belonging to the clan of the great god Pan
   is described in fantastical detail from top to bottom; then, at the
   poet's direction, the faun strolls right off the page and into the night.

In Greek myth, phenomena such as trees, rivers, and mountains were
   considered to be alive with divine spirit; they were widely vener-
   ated as familiar deities. Pan, a god associated with intoxication
   and sexual freedom, was a symbol for this 'pantheism'—a univer-
   sally animated cosmos.

Ta poitrine ressemble à une cithare ("Your chest resonates like a guitar")
The faun's chest resembles a *cithern* or hand-held harp (like a zither),
   vibrating like the body of an acoustic guitar (another kind of 'hand-
   held harp.')

Being Beauteous

Rimbaud stretches his English title in two directions—referring to a
being of great beauty or to the state of being beautiful. Auditory
and visual hallucinations abound; life and death are commingled
in a swelling and diminishing.

The "raucous music" of society and human striving, with which the
world assaults the creative muse, causes beauty to recede and then
rise anew. Those who 'see' the epiphany are clothed in new inspi-
ration, in "fresh and loving bodies." Lovers' quarrels and sudden
death "through the scrimmage of trees and lilting breeze" are an-
other kind of terrifying 'beauty.'

l'écusson de crin ("the badge of tantrums")
Literally, "the shield [or badge] of horsehair." Figuratively, *un crin* is a
bad-tempered person (from crin-crin, a scratchy fiddle), and the
phrase "être comme un crin" means to be irritable—hence "tan-
trums." This image falls between "the ashen face" (anger) and "the
crystal embrace" (brittle, hard, angular)—heading for the quasi-
suicidal threat or epiphany in the last phrase of the poem.

Vies / Lives I–III

These are a series of 'autobiographical' allegories in which the speaker
(or poet) is by turn, among other things, an adept, a lover, a stage
director, an apprentice, a cynic, a musician, and more. There is a
sense of striving and failure in all three "Lives"; his thoughts are
confused by "flights of scarlet pigeons" (passions? drugs?), skepti-
cism haunts him, mortality and madness take their toll.

Départ / Taking Off

In Rimbaud's manuscript, this poem is on the same page following "Lives III"; it is both a summary of the three preceding poems and a sequel (or epilogue) to them. The poet leaves his present existence for new inspirations and fresh experience. *"Départ"* is not so much an organized departure as an abrupt absence or sudden leave-taking—'cutting out,' as one slang expression has it; "taking off" or 'splitting.'

La vision s'est recontre à tous les airs. ("The vision met with in every air.")
This is but one of the many possible translations of this line. *L'air* can mean the atmosphere, the winds, as well as aspects of a face or personality—or a melody, an aria, or simply the open air as in 'out-of-doors.' Another version of this line might read: "The vision was encountered on every breeze," or "The vision was met with in all weathers."

Les arrêts de la vie ("The arrests of a lifetime")
Literally, "the stoppages of life" or "the holdups of a lifetime," in the sense of one's progress being interrupted, delayed, or halted, as in 'arrested in mid-flight' or 'at a stand-still.' There is also a possible allusion to Rimbaud's many brushes with the police.

Royauté / Royalty

This is another fable like *"Conte/*Tale," with a traditional 'fairytale' opening line ("Un beau matin . . ."); it portrays the ecstatic union of a man and a woman who have passed a crisis in their lives together. The woman is proclaimed a Queen by her husband or lover; the woman, "laughing and trembling," agrees with his pronouncement. The "really sweet people" who may indeed be their friends or simply passers-by, go along with this royal decree and fête the couple all day long with banners and parades. Some critics have opined that the Queen is a purely symbolic figure personifying Rimbaud's genius; others claim that the poem simply celebrates sexual happiness and the transcendent love that transforms the couple.

À Une Raison / For One Reason

The figure of Reason (good sense, judgment, sanity, cause) is presented as an idol—a god-like figure, or (in late 20th Century parlance) a pop star or cult personality such as Jimi Hendrix, Elvis Presley, or Jim Morrison of the Doors. There are both military and religious connotations at work; the 'god' or 'leader' may be seen as a musician of sorts, a drummer (perhaps, like the Catman of KISS, an icon), and human-kind as a marching army ("on the move"), as a horde of adoring children. The leader/hero/god marks time "on the drum" and finally transcends both time ("Having always arrived") and space ("you'll take yourself everywhere").

... *le nouvel amour!* (" ... the novelty of love! / ... the latest thing is love!")
This is often translated as "the new love," but *nouvel* means also "recent, novel, fresh, new-fangled, or modern," hence the two different phrases used here to translate Rimbaud's single, multi-layered phrase.

Matinée D'Ivresse / Morning Rapture

The title of this *Illumination* is often given as "Drunken Morning," but the substance being abused ("this venom") is more likely hashish than alcohol. What Rimbaud seems to be after is not so much a clinical description of the drug's effects, but the degree of insight that might be acquired by devotion to its uses ("sensibility of slaves . . . sanctified").

The hallucinatory parade of images includes Creation, the Garden of Eden, love, rustic foolery and flaming angels, dancing, chastity, the laughter of children, torture, and the legendary Assassins out of Ancient Persia.

Chevalet féerique ("Enchanted rack")
This image carries multiple meanings in the original, linking images of music and art and torture. A *"chevalet"* is not only a rack (the medieval instrument of torture), but a bridge (on a stringed instrument such as the violin); it is also an artist's easel and a sawhorse, trestle, or bench. The phrase has subsidiary meanings of "magical bridge," "imaginary painting," or "enchanted workshop."

une débandade de parfums ("a whiff of chaos")
Literally, "a stampede of perfumes" as a result of the sensory intensification of the "venom" on the user's faculties.

veille ("sleepless night" . . . "insight")
In Rimbaud's usage, according to Osmond and others, "the word seems to stand for the hyper-alertness of hallucination rather than simply the state of being awake." Compare the use of the word in *"Veilles/* Wakefulness."

le temps des Assassins ("the time of *Assassins*")
This refers to the Persian and Syrian *Hashishin* of the 12th Century,

TRANSLATED BY DJC

from which the modern word 'assassin' derives. These were the devoted followers of Hasan-i-Sabbah (c. 1170), also known as The Old Man of the Mountains, a great Islamic revolutionary whose power base spread from the Caspian Sea to Egypt. All those who held land or power and were not followers of Hasan's sect were in danger of being killed by his agents—the so-called Hashishin.

Hasan utilized hashish in a program of mind control to train and educate "young men, selected from the most robust inhabitants of the places he ruled, so as to make them executioners of his barbarous decrees. The whole object of their education was to convince them that by blindly obeying their chief's orders, they could assure themselves after death of the enjoyment of every pleasure that can flatter the senses . . ." (*Dynasty of the Assassins*, A. Sylvestre de Sacy, 1809). Believing that they had already glimpsed life in heaven, thanks to Hasan's powers (organized hashish 'dream trips'), these Assassins were utterly fearless and willingly died to achieve their task.

Rimbaud may have been familiar with Baudelaire's *Hashish Poem* of 1860. Certainly by November of 1871 (according to Delahaye's account), he was known to be smoking the substance. Delahaye asked Rimbaud what he'd seen after the poet abruptly awoke from a drug-induced sleep. ". . . Nothing at all . . ." he replied, "some white moons, some black moons, chasing each other."

Baudelaire writes: "I like to consider this abnormal mental condition as a real grace, a magic mirror in which man may see himself as beautiful—that is, as he ought to be and might be; a sort of angelic excitation." *(Hashish Poem)*

Baudelaire goes on to say that the "magic mirror" can become a distorting mirror and that frequent dependence on the drug results in mental slavery and a twisted sensibility.

See *Tales of Hashish: A Literary Look at the Hashish Experience*, edited
and annotated by Andrew C. Kimmens (William Morrow and Co.,
1977) for a more detailed history of hashish and its literary heri-
tage.

Phrases

Here, a series of phrases like musical fragments are divided into two
sequences—the first a kind of love lyric and the second a progression
of ecstatic celebrations that arise out of fog, moisture, a sweating
fire, and misty landscapes. Images of music, singing, dancing, festiv-
ity run through the entire poem. Or, as Nick Osmond has it, "Phrases"
is not a single poem, but "a series of related inspirations."

deux enfants fidèles ("two faithful children")
This line is generally considered to be a parody of the phrase "*deux
enfants . . . deux jeunes filles*" in the last stanza of *Verlaine's Forgot-
ten Songs (Ariettes Obliées)* IV:

> "Let us become two children, let us be two little girls,
> Admiring nothing and astonished by it all . . . "
> *("Soyons deux enfants, soyons deux jeunes filles,
> Éprises de rien et de tour étonnées . . . ")*

Ma camarade, mediante, enfant monstre! ("My buddy, little miss beggar, you big brat!")
These epithets, according to most critics, refer to Verlaine. This whole
"Phrase" refers to the poverty-stricken life led by the two poets in
London, to Rimbaud's erratic progress on his work *("ces
manoeuvres")* and Verlaine's glib sympathy ("ta voix").

"The Voice" was used by Rimbaud as shorthand for 'verbal harmonies'
in poetry; and Verlaine used it in this sense in his *Ariettes Obliées.*

les fleurs rouies ("flowers drenched")
Rouissage is the process of soaking hemp to separate the fibers so it can be
   made into rope. The flowers here are 'soaking wet' or 'drenched' like
   hemp. This may be a veiled allusion to hashish ("playthings and incense"),
   which is derived from the budding flowers of the hemp plant.

Ouvriers / Workers

A pair of poor working-class lovers walk to the suburbs of a factory
   town. The speaker of the poem grows more alienated from his
   companion as their walk progresses.

Henrika
An imaginary character (like Helen in "Fairy" or the sisters in
   "*Dévotion*"); or perhaps Verlaine in yet another guise?—Possibly a
   young woman in whom Rimbaud took an interest.

the flood of the month before
The Thames River flooded in January of 1873; Verlaine and Rimbaud
   were in London in February of that year.

des orphelins fiancés ("a pair of needy lovers")
Literally, "betrothed orphans." A betrothal is a contract for a future
   marriage, usually arranged by the parents. Rimbaud's original phrase
   implies the poverty and isolation of the two workers; no parents,
   no dowry.

Les Ponts / Bridges

This landscape is a surreal mixture of the literal and the fantastical; the bridges are both architectural and musical, simultaneously. *Pont* is a bridge (literally) and a link (figuratively) in French, as in English.

Ville / City

The blankness and anonymity of modern city life are satirically enumerated by Rimbaud, along with a sense of disassociation and distaste as the poem proceeds.

notre ombre des bois, notre nuit d'été ("our shady wood, our summer night")
The factory fumes and smog of the city are the urban equivalents of shade trees and balmy nights.

des Eriunyes nouvelles ("the latest Furies")
New-style deities of vengeance. The Furies were also known as the Eumenides (kindly ones) and Semnai (the holy ones). "Erinyes" is Greek for Furies. In the old mythology, they were spirits of punishment who avenged without pity wrongs done to kindred, especially murder within the family. According to Hesiod, they were daughters of the Earth-mother, conceived from the drops of blood spilled when Cronos (Time) castrated his father Uranus (Heaven).

TRANSLATED BY DJC

Ornières / Beaten Paths

According to the memoirs of Rimbaud's childhood friend Ernest
Delahaye, an American circus passed through Charleville in 1868
and 1869, when Rimbaud was fourteen. The "Big Parade" be-
comes a metaphor for life itself.

les milles rapides ornières ("countless running ruts")
Literally, the phrase translates "the thousand running ruts," but *mille*
(one thousand) and *vingt* (twenty) are the numbers traditionally
used in French to convey the idea of 'very many' or 'innumerable';
hence, "countless."

Villes / Cities (I)

. . . *ces Alleghanys et ces Libans* (". . . these Alleghanies and Lebanons")
These two mountain ranges are halfway round the world from each
other, one in the eastern United States, the other in the Middle
East.

Rimbaud probably knew Edgar Allan Poe's "A Tale of the Ragged Moun-
tains" in Baudelaire's translation (retitled "*Les Souvenirs de M. August
Bedloe*" in Histoires extraordinaires). In Poe's tale, Bedloe, who
makes "habitual use of morphine," takes a lengthy stroll in the
Ragged Mountains, "une branche des Montagnes Bleues, Blue
Ridge, partie orientale des Alleghanys," as Baudelaire notes. Deep
in the mountains, Bedloe sees a vision of a fantastic "eastern-style
city such as we read of in the Arabian Tales, but of a character
even more singular than any there described." Poe's ensuing exotic
vista contains the germinal tone and vivid perspective enlarged
upon by Rimbaud.

Here are a few phrases from Poe's luxuriant paragraph: "On every hand
was a wilderness of balconies, of verandas, of minarets, of shrines,
and fantastically carved oriels. Bazaars abounded; and . . . silks, mus-
lins . . . jewels and gems . . . idols grotesquely hewn, drums, banners
and gongs . . . And amid the crowd, and the clamor . . . roamed a
countless multitude of holy filleted bulls . . . From the swarming streets
to the banks of the river, there descended innumerable flights of steps
leading to bathing places . . . Beyond the limits of the city arise . . .
gigantic and weird trees of vast age . . ."

les Rolands sonnent leur bravoure ("Rolands blow their own horns")
Roland (Orlando) was Charlemagne's nephew and the bravest knight of
his court; he is the French equivalent of Lancelot or Gawain in the
Arthurian legends. He was killed in battle, blowing his horn to
signal Charlemagne that they'd been ambushed by the Moors. *Le
Chanson de Roland* is France's great medieval epic poem, compa-
rable to England's *Beowulf* and Sumeria's *Gilgamesh*; it mytholo-
gizes Roland's final battle in the Pyrenees and his brave death in
the mountain gorges.

Rimbaud's text literally translated reads "Rolands trumpet their brav-
ery." In the *Chanson*, Roland's bravery was of such extremity—
and proud obstinacy—that he delayed blowing the signal until it
was clear that the battle was lost and reinforcements would not
save them. I have transmogrified the 'trumpet' image into a com-
mon English phrase that points up Roland's egotistical 'bravery.'

Mabs en robes rousses, opalines ("Mabs, in russet, iridescent dresses")
Mab, or Maeve in Gaelic, is the Celtic Queen of Fairies. She is de-
scribed at length by Mercutio in Shakespeare's *Romeo and Juliet*
(Act I Scene 4). Romeo speaks of dreams and Mercutio answers:

"O then I see Queen Mab hath been with you.
She is the fairies' midwife, and she comes

> In shape no bigger than an agate stone
> On the forefinger of an alderman,
> Drawn with a team of little *atomi*
> Over men's noses as they lie asleep . . . "
> [and so on for 35 more lines]

Mab is the midwife (pronounced by Shakespeare as 'middif') who assists at the birth of men's dreams.

. . . *les cerfs tettent Diane* (" . . . deer suckle Diana")
In Greek and Roman mythology, deer were sacred creatures to the hunting goddess, chaste Artemis or Diana. The mythic-ironic-maternal image here conjured by Rimbaud is that of a holy virgin tendering her breasts to wild animals like human (or divine) infants.

Baccantes de banlieus ("The Bacchae of suburbia")
This is similar to "the Sabines of the suburbs" from "Bottom" (q.v.); in these two phrases, Rimbaud combines a mythological subject with contemporary reality.

The Bacchae were women devotees of Dionysus (or Bacchus) who ran wild in the hills once a year at the Dionysian Festivals of pre-classical Greece. These rites eventually evolved into the drama festivals of Aeschylus and Sophocles' time. In Euripides' play *The Bacchae*, Prince Pentheus of Thebes is torn apart by these god-frenzied women, including his mother Queen Agave, when he spies on their secret rites. Maddened, the Bacchae believe he is a sacrificial lion-cub as they rip off his arms, legs, and head.

Venus entre dans les cavernes des forgerons et des ermites ("Venus penetrates the caves of saint and smithy")
The goddess of love, Venus, was married to Vulcan, god of the forge—a blacksmith—who fashioned a fine steel net to snare

his wife and Mars, god of war, together in bed. In Flaubert's novel *The Temptation of St. Anthony* (Chapter V), Venus attempts to seduce the holy hermit in his cave. Rimbaud here evokes two classical scenes—the goddess of love and beauty visiting both the husband's hellish smithy and the ascetic's cell. Love 'enters into' every scene.

Toutes les légendes evoluent et les élans se ruent dans les bourgs ("Every legend evolves and zealots rip through backwater towns")
The second image (*élans*) is multi-layered, perhaps a kind of pun. Two different ideas are conflated in *élan*, which is actually two distinct words spelled identically, the first one meaning a leap or bound—a 'surge of emotion,' spirit or vivacity (hence 'zeal' or 'zealot')—and the other meaning "elk" or "moose." The zoological translation is often favored, but "legends and zealots" seems to connect more smoothly with Rimbaud's progression of gods, animals, people, phantoms, and dreams.

Quels bons bras, quelle belle heure ("What fine embrace, what beauteous hour")
Like the opening of *Matinée d'ivresse* ("Morning Rapture"), this line seems to evoke or echo the poet's experience with hallucinogenic substances: "Oh *my* Delight! O *my* Beauty!"

Vagabonds

The vagabonds of the title are Rimbaud and Verlaine, companions in misery, living hand to mouth, the relationship disintegrating but not yet broken up.

satanique docteur ("doctor satanical")
In a letter written five years later, in 1878, Verlaine recognized himself

in this phrase. The reference is to the Faust legend, with Verlaine in the role of Doctor Faust and Rimbaud as Mephistopheles.

vin de cavernes ("cavernous wine")
Water from out of the ground, spring water flowing from a rocky cave.

Villes / Cities II

The official Acropolis
The Acropolis of ancient Athens was the highest part of the city, the seat of government and worship; home of the Parthenon. Any modern acropolis would be the financial district and government agencies grouped together.

Hampton Court
The London residence of British kings and queens in the 17th Century; now (as in Rimbaud's day) a museum.

Nebuchadnezar
King of Babylon, c. 550 B.C. Nebuchadnezar was responsible for the famous Hanging Gardens of Babylon, one of the Seven Wonders of the World (according to Herodotus). Built on terraces and consisting of flowers and fruit trees on various levels, these gardens were designed to please a favorite wife, reminding her of the mountains of her homeland. Nebuchadnezar also expanded the city walls, high and wide, making them broad enough for two chariots, each drawn by four horses, to meet and pass while patrolling the city. A hundred years later, Herodotus claimed that Babylon still surpassed any other city in the world for splendors and magnitude.

. . . haughtier than Brahmins
". . . haughtier than [illegible]" would be a literal rendering of the manuscript here. The original word is crossed out and its re-

placement, written directly on top of it, seems to be "Brahmins." This reading—a Brahmin is a Hindu of the highest caste, traditionally assigned to the priesthood—is congruent with the later images of "Nabobs" and "rupees."

. . . an arm of the sea
The Thames River.
. . . the dome of the Holy Chapel
St. Paul's Cathedral in London.

A few Hindu fatcats
"Nabobs" in the original; a class of wealthy native officials in colonial India. Hence, any rich or influential person. Rimbaud's use seems to be specific, in the original sense; note the "rupees" charged for ice-cold drinks.

. . . any grifters here
Des aventuriers is literally "adventurers," but in French carries the implication of graft or illicit dealings, fraud, phony speculation.

Veillées / Wakefulness

This *Illumination* is made up of three distinct poems describing the progress of an all-night vigil, perhaps under the influence of hashish or absinthe.

Section I portrays a dream-state of love and friendship and equilibrium, while Section II is a theatrical series of pictures or hallucinations brought on by the night's wakefulness. Section III intensifies the sonic and visual aspects of the hallucinatory vision until dawn enlightens these "pits of enchantments" and the sunrise finds the poet alone in his room.

*   *   *

In a letter from Paris, dated June 1872, to his friend Ernest Delahaye
back in Charleville, Rimbaud described his all-night vigils.

" . . . Nowadays, I work all night. From midnight to five o'clock in the
morning. Last month, my room, on Monsieur-le-Prince Street,
overlooked the garden of St. Louis School. There were huge trees
under my narrow window. At three in the morning, the candle
would pale: all the birds twittered at once in the trees: it's done.
No more work. I had to watch the trees, the sky, caught by this
incredible first hour of the morning. I'd look at the school dormi-
tory, absolutely dumbstruck. And already, the abrupt racket, sono-
rous, delicious, of the carts on the boulevards. I smoked my ham-
mer-head pipe, spitting over the attic eaves because my room's
right under the roof. At five o'clock I'd go downstairs to buy some
bread: it was time. Workers out walking everywhere. It was time
for me to get drunk at the wine-merchant's. I returned to eat, and
to go to bed at seven a.m. when the sun drives the wood-lice out
from under the roof-tiles. The early summer mornings and the
evenings of December, these always enchant me here.

"But for the moment, I have a lovely room over a bottomless court-
yard, about ten feet square.—Victor-Cousin Street makes a cor-
ner on Sorbonne Place by the Bas-Rhin Café . . . —There, I drink
water all night I don't see morning, I don't sleep, I suffocate. And
there it is!"

Mystique

A series of visions where Rimbaud pulls cosmic imagery (angels, stars,
etc.) down to earth (the sloping rubble, humus, the hills) and fixes

it into a picture frame ("the tableau"), transforming hell (the bottomless pit) into a heaven (blue and flowering).

comme un panier ("like a petticoat")
The word *panier* is often translated here as 'basket,' but another meaning of the word is 'hoop petticoat' in French. This seems to fit the action more precisely, the sweetness of the night sky descending softly like a curving expanse of delicate material.

Aube / Dawn

These images are at once intimate and extravagant; the poet embraces dawn as if it were a goddess. The encounter is physically intense, simultaneously innocent and sexually knowing.

As the sunlight spreads over the landscape, the poet scrambles after, finally catching "her" on the high road near a laurel grove (sacred to Apollo in Greek myth).

wasserfall blond ("golden wasserfall")
The German word for waterfall is used perhaps for exotic or ironic effect. This could be the goddess (dawn) shaking her long blond hair (the rays of the rising sun) through the trees.

Fleurs / Flowers

The flowers are a mixture of the organic and inorganic; they are both vegetable and mineral. The poet creates a new hybrid that in the final section is personified as a "mob of . . . young roses" seduced by the sea and sky, which have likewise been transformed into "a god."

The opening phrases hint at a kind of 'magic theatre' with the poet or "voyant" perched high in the balcony overlooking audience and stage. Osmond notes that "The theatre, here as elsewhere, is an image for the visionary scene."

Nocturne Vulgaire / Vulgar Nocturne

The title can be taken in at least two senses: as a 'crude' nocturne or as an 'ordinary' or 'commonplace' one. The nocturne as a musical composition was popularized by Chopin in his set of 21 pieces for the piano. In general, it refers to any 'night-piece,' literary, pictorial, or musical.

Rimbaud may have been responding to a poem of Verlaine's called *"Nocturne parisien,"* or the poet may have seen Whistler's infamous "Nocturne in Blue and Silver," which was on exhibit at the Dudley Gallery in 1872, or at Whistler's one-man show in 1874. Rimbaud was in London both years and it is surmised (out of "Cities II") that he went to art galleries and exhibits while there.

The poem is an escape-by-night that gradually turns into a drunken escapade.

brèches opéradiques dans les cloisons ("operatic breaches in the walls")
The term *opéradiques* is coined by Rimbaud out of the English word. In this opening image, the home is blown apart theatrically, with scenic special effects of weather, wind, and light.

éclipse les croisées ("eclipses the crossways")
Croisées means both 'windowpanes' and 'crossroads'; the English 'crossways' denotes both the squares of the windowpanes (the cross-bars of a multi-paned window) and the cross-roads or point of decision, as well as something that lies athwart another thing.

les Sodomes—et les Solymes ("Sodomites—and Salemites")
The inhabitants of the Biblical cities of Sodom (wicked) and Jerusalem (holy).

Postillons et bêtes de songe ("Coach-boys and dream-steeds")
Bêtes de songe is literally 'dream-beasts' or 'beasts of dreaming,' with a punning wordplay in the original on *bêtes de somme*, French for "beasts of burden." The postilion and horses make their first appearance late in the poem and this passage seems to indicate that the whole nocturne is a dream-state, or that the runaway has fallen asleep in the carriage.

Marine / Seascape

Rimbaud's visionary technique verges on the cinematic here, with the sea becoming the desert becoming the sea, ad infinitum, into "whirling clouds of light" or "cyclones of light." Ships' prows are like plows, the shifting sands like tidal backflows, the pilings of a pier like a forest, and vice versa. This poem and *Mouvement* ("Motion") are both composed in free verse, not prose.

Fête D'Hiver / Winter Festival

A picture postcard of a celebration featuring musicals, fireworks, and costumed dancers. The time frame of the vignette hints at a 'classical' era with its mention of the river Meander, nymphs, Horace, and the empires of Rome and Napoleon.

Girandoles
A radiant, showy composition; a stationary fireworks display.

du Méandre ("the river Meander")
A river of ancient Phrygia (modern Turkey), from which we get the
   English word 'meander' (to wind or saunter about at random), as a
   result of the river's many curves and wandering bends. It flows
   into the Aegean Sea two hundred miles northeast of Crete.

Nymphs d'Horace ("Nymphs out of Horace")
In Greek myth, nymphs were female personifications of rivers, trees,
   mountains, etc.; according to *The Oxford Companion to Classical
   Literature*, "they were vague beings, young and beautiful, fond of
   music and dancing, long-lived but not immortal, usually gentle,
   occasionally formidable."

The most famous and formerly oft-quoted of the Roman lyric poets,
   Horace (65 B.C.–8 B.C.) lived to see his *Odes* become a standard
   textbook in the schools. In Rimbaud's day, Horace's poetry was
   still part of regular school curriculum.

Coiffées au Premier Empire ("Empire hats and hairdos")
During the First Empire under Napoleon, French women affected a
   return to 'Roman Empire' hairstyles and headdresses.

Chinoises de Boucher ("Chinese girls out of Boucher")
Eighteenth Century French artist François Boucher (1703–1770) painted
   many Chinese scenes and subjects; he also designed the sets and
   costumes for the famous *Fêtes chinoise* of Noverre, chief dancer-
   choreographer of the era.

Angoisse / Anguish

The "anguish" is apparently Rimbaud's at having failed to change life through the systematic "*dérèglement de* tous les sens" ("disorder of *all the senses*") as he set forth in this "Lettre du Voyant" to Paul Demeny in 1871.

He thinks about calling on Anguish as he would a goddess, to intercede for him with some higher power; he recalls his youthful promise; he then sees Anguish as a vampire who orders all of us to debauch and debase ourselves for her amusement ("Rolling in bruises . . . ").

Métropolitain / Metropolitan

The visionary world in this *Illumination* progresses from the city (with its "poor young families") to the countryside to the world at large: a free-flowing metaphor for the poet's takeover (or makeover) of the universe. The "Her" of the last part is perhaps another aspect of the feminine divine, like the summer Dawn or the "she" of Anguish.

Ossian
The legendary Gaelic bard and warrior, c. 390 A.D., son of the mythic Fingal. *Ossian's Poems*, published in 1790 by James MacPherson, were primarily MacPherson's work, based on mere fragments of the actual Ossian's verse. Before these were exposed as a fraud, they enjoyed a huge vogue in continental Europe. Popular prints of the early 19th Century often showed the bard, harp in hand, posed overlooking a stormy sea.

Samaria
One of the three subdivisions of ancient Palestine, between Judea on the south and Galilee on the north. See Luke 10:25–37 and John 4:5–30.

Damascus

A major trade-route city of ancient times, located 133 miles north of Jerusalem. The road to Damascus was the famous scene of St. Paul's conversion (Acts 9:1–27 and 22:1–16). Damascus also has a special place in Islamic tradition; the Prophet Mohammed described it as "a chosen land," an eternal refuge for holy men. Several hundred Muslim wise men and prophets are said to have lived and died on the slopes of Mount Qassyum, which overlooks the city. Saladin and two other great kings are buried near the Ummayad Mosque.

In Rimbaud's image, it seems even a holy city is "damned by lassitude" when the "enchanted aristocracies" and the populace are too lazy or indifferent to heed the saints and prophets all around them.

Guaranies ("Guaranas")

The original inhabitants of central South America, colonized by the Jesuits in the 18th Century. Q.v. Roland Joffe's 1986 film *The Mission*, starring Robert De Niro and Jeremy Irons. There is also an opera *Il Guarany* (1870) by Antonio Carlos Gomes (1836–1896) and a choral symphony by Philip Glass (b. 1937) entitled *Itaipu* ("The Singing Stone" in Guarani).

Barbare / Barbarous

The vocabulary and image-world of this *Illumination* echo "Matinée D'Ivresse": the fanfares are now far away in time and space, as are the assassins—and the angels that were flaming in ice have been turned into flowers. "They don't exist."

Nick Osmond comments: "The poems' vision is built up from two extremes which progressively fuse."

Le pavillon en viande saignante ("The signal in the flesh bleeding")
A *pavillon* is either some kind of heraldic tent or a flag or emblazoned
banner, hence the 'insignia' or "signal" of meat or flesh. Whether it
is the signal (or tent or flag) that is bleeding or the flesh (meat) is
uncertain in the original. Rimbaud clashes opposites in every
phrase.

Solde / Bargains

A sales pitch, the artist as salesman offering stock on hand at reduced
prices.

ce que le temps ni la science n'out pas à reconnaître ("whatever neither
time nor science need have a name for")
Literally, "whatever neither time nor science need recognize." The recog-
nitions of time and science involve classification, enumeration, nam-
ing, counting. Hence, the opening list of 'bargains' is made up of
things that "don't exist." The Jews were supposed to be able to sell
anything and everything; human activity runs the gamut from 'nobil-
ity' to 'crime'; and "outcast love and hellish honesty" are the grist of
tabloids, rumor, scandal, and gossip—the sure delight of a herd men-
tality.

The list of items then turns to all the aspects of the world that have not
yet been fully exploited.

Fairy

A myth or legend re-imagined, the mystery of feminine beauty, allure.

Hélène ("Helen")

The fairy's name. She is Rimbaud's invention; also perhaps Helen of
   Troy (a demon or spirit in the Faust legend) whose mother Leda
   was impregnated by Zeus in the guise of a swan—a "mute bird"
   whose only song is a hiss when disturbed or excited. See W.B.
   Yeats' 1923 poem "Leda and the Swan."

Helen of Troy's birth inaugurated all the vast Homeric legend, both
   Iliad and *Odyssey*, the Trojan War, the wrath and death of Achilles,
   Odysseus' wanderings, the death of Agamemnon at the hands of
   his wife Clytemnestra (Helen's sister), and the eventual domestica-
   tion of the Furies into the Blessed Ones.

In the earliest versions of the Faust legend—the German *Faustbook* of
   1587 and Christopher Marlowe's *Dr. Faustus*—as well as Part II of
   Goethe's epic, Helen is conjured up via the devil's power to serve
   as Faust's paramour.

"Whereupon he fell in love with her, and made her his common Con-
   cubine and bedfellow, for she was so beautiful and delightful a
   piece." (*The English Faust-book*, 1592)
"Was this the face that launch'd a thousand ships / And burnt the
   topless towers of Ilium?" (Marlowe: *Dr. Faustus*, 1593/1604)

"What is left for me but to surrender to you my self and all that my
   delusion made mine?" (Goethe: *Faust* Part II Act 3, 1827)

Guerre / War

The war of the title is a mental rather than a military action—an assault
   on conventional attitudes conceived out of "surprising" or unconven-
   tional logic.

The child prodigy's "outlook" is refined or sharpened by "certain skies" (different aspects of the world). War is declared on received wisdom and the order of worldly success *("tous les succès civils")*.

*   *   *

In the manuscript, the title of "Fairy" is followed by Roman numeral I, while *"Guerre"* is preceded by numeral II. No connection between the two poems is otherwise apparent, unless the 'mental war' is meant to echo the Trojan War, which, with its body of legend, has been the subject of diverse musical settings; those of Gluck and Berlioz may have been known to Rimbaud. ("I contemplate a war ... It's as easy as a musical phrase.")

Jeunesse / Youth

I. *Dimanche* / Sunday
Sunday is presented as a time of idleness and dreaming.

Les calculs de côté ("Paperwork put aside")
Literally, "Calculations/Schemata to the side"; the artist puts his organized intellectual activity aside to allow for spontaneous daydreaming.

The horse (taking off), the actress (yearning), the Desperados (languishing after violence and intoxication), and the little kids (cursing) are all aspects of the poet and his quest, presented in a series of 'flashbacks' or inner visions.

II. Sonnet
The poet achieves his rite of passage from adolescent awakening (sexual and creative) to adult accomplishment (song and dance) that unites humanity in a cooperative endeavor/appreciation (music, dance, acting).

The poem is set forth in 14 lines like a sonnet, but unrhymed.

le péril ou la force de Psyché ("the peril or the power of Psyche")
The ancient Greek myth of Psyche and Eros is told by Apuleius in
Books 4–6 of *The Golden Ass*: Psyche was so beautiful that Venus
became jealous of her, and sent her son Cupid or Eros to make
Psyche fall in love with some ugly beast. However, Eros himself
was smitten, and became her lover. He put her in a palace and
visited her only at night, in the dark, telling her never to try to look
upon his face. Her jealous sisters, envious of her 'mystery lover,'
told her he must be a monster who would surely devour her. Psyche
hid a lamp one night and after Eros fell asleep she used it to look at
him. A drop of hot oil awakened him and, furious at her disobedi-
ence, he left her. Solitary and full of remorse, Psyche wandered the
earth in search of her lover. In the end, Zeus took pity and con-
sented to their marriage, and Psyche was brought to heaven. The
tale is often interpreted as an allegory of the soul's journey through
life and its eventual union with divine love. Psyche means 'soul' in
Greek; Eros means 'passion/love' (hence 'erotic' or 'eroticism').

In Rimbaud's version, the intervention of self-consciousness (peril) in
the pure, innocent enjoyment of sex (power) is Psyche's downfall.

III. *20 ans* / 20 Years Old
The crisis of maturity coupled with nostalgia for youthful optimism
and a world of flowering possibilities is told from the viewpoint of
impending manhood. Everything moves slowly now ("Adagio") ex-
cept for the nerves, which "get shot in a hurry."

St. Anthony's temptation
Saint Anthony the Great, patron saint of swineherds (4th century A.D.),
was the founder of a brotherhood of ascetic monks who lived in
the desert, fasting and praying. The story of his temptation by the
Devil, who appeared to him in every conceivable shape, both hor-

rific and beautiful, is well-known in classic western art (e.g.,
Matthias Grünewald's painting and the eponymous novel of Gustav
Flaubert; the tale is treated ironically in *Thaïs* by Anatole France).

The Youth seems to complain that he's still at the 'St. Anthony' stage,
capable of succumbing to temptation. He sets forth a formula for
success and forecasts that the future will be unlike anything "cur-
rently on view."

Promontoire / Promontory

The poet creates a new world out of the jumbled fragments and tech-
nologies of the old, piling it all onto a promontory that is also a
vast resort hotel like a palace. Compare the *"Hotel Splendide"* in
"After The Flood"; see also Gilbert Sorrentino's *Splendide-Hôtel.*

Hesperus . . . Peloponnese
Greek "Hespera," the Western Land; from the Greek point of view,
this denoted the Italian peninsula; from the Roman, Spain.
"Peloponnesos" is the southern part of Greece, connected to the
main peninsula by the Isthmus of Corinth.
Carthage . . . Venice
Cities on the sea. Carthage was a strategic trade city on the Tunisian
coast of North Africa, founded by the Phoenicians in 814 B.C.
The Carthaginians dominated the southern Mediterranean until
the Romans destroyed their empire in 146 B.C. The city was re-
built as the capital of the Roman province of Africa by Julius and
Augustus Caesar; by the 2nd century A.D., Carthage had become
the largest city in the west after Rome.

Venice was the major trade city of the Italian peninsula during the
Middle Ages and into the Renaissance; a 'gateway' to the Orient, it
dominated Mediterranean trade for centuries.

Etnas
Mount Etna, Europe's highest active volcano, located in Sicily, is here pluralized in the poet's vision.

Scarbro . . . Brooklyn
The 'Royal' was a large resort hotel with a curving façade, popular in 19th Century England; the 'Grand' was a famous New York hotel of the same era. Both hotels were near the coast. Rimbaud's knowledge of them probably came from travel-guides or pamphlets he saw in London.

elevated railways
The famous 'el' train of 19th Century New York City was one of the technological marvels of the age.

Scènes / Stages

Des oiseaux des mystères ("Birds from the mysteries")
In the manuscript, the word *"mystères"* is written over the word "comédiens," indicating that perhaps these are actors in bird-costume, or trained birds. "Mystères" probably refers to the medieval Mystery Plays, a class of drama usually relating incidents from the life of Christ. The birds may be seen as a flock of doves (Matthew 3:16, Mark 1:10, Luke 3:22, John 1:32) released en masse.

les Béotiens ("The Booboisie")
Literally, "the Boeotians" (pronounced Bay-Oceans), from Boeotia, the central plains country of Greece, northeast of Athens. This is essentially 'cattle country,' famous for its wheat and horses. The ancient Athenians considered the Boeotians dull and thick-witted as well as artistically backward: rustic, uncultured boobs. In French the term is used in much the same way speakers of English use

'Philistine'—but the French carries with it the sense of 'country hick.' H.L. Mencken's apt coinage "Booboisie" (out of 'boob' and 'bourgeoisie') seems to match best with Rimbaud's usage.

des futaies mouvante ("a forest of moving trees")
Perhaps an allusion to Shakespeare's *Macbeth* Acts IV and V ("Great Birnam Wood to high Dunsinane Hill / Shall come against him." . . . "and now a wood / Comes toward Dunsinane." . . . "I say, a moving grove.") or to the Gospel of Mark (8:24): "And he looked up, and said, I see men as trees, walking."

Soir Historique / Historic Evening

This "Historic Evening" marks the 'success' of the poet's quest to change the world. Like the naive tourist, retiring from the world of "economic horrors," he sits back and puts himself in the hands of a master, becomes an audience of one. Theatrical and musical images describing the world ensue—but they eventually grow "pallid and flat" and come to exemplify "middle-class magic," art as mere manipulation of images, and parlor tricks.

The final images of destruction reject simple visionary tricks and private fantasy—: Nothing less than the end of the world (as we know it) and the systematic extermination of mankind will do to fill the void left by this rejection. But even that, Rimbaud seems to say, is not enough for a Legend's fulfillment.

"Any old evening was good enough for the irresponsible activities of the naive tourist," says Osmond, "but the evening when the revolution begins will be an historical one."

Tartary deserts
The land of Central Asian nomads. Genghis Khan and his successors

established the Kingdom of Tartary in the early 13th Century, and
from 1238 to 1462 dominated Eastern Europe.

Celestial Empire
Ancient China. This is a translation of the Chinese *Tien Chao*, literally
   "Heavenly Dynasty," alluding to the belief that the old emperors
   were directly descended from the gods. The Chinese themselves
   were sometimes referred to as 'Celestials' in the 18th and 19th
   Centuries.

. . . in the Bible and by the Norns
Visions of a cataclysmic 'End of the World' scenario are found in the book of
   Revelations *(Apocalypse)* and Nordic mythology (*Götterdämmerung*), where
   the three Norns, or Fates, foretell the Twilight of the Gods as a mighty
   catastrophe: a final battle, fire, and flood.

Bottom

my epic personality
A poem of transformations. The title refers to the character in
   Shakespeare's *A Midsummer Night's Dream* who undergoes a trans-
   formation under the spell of mischievous Puck. He is given the
   head of an ass and Titania, Queen of the Fairies, enchanted, falls
   in love with him. The poet here is changed from bird to bear to an
   ass, braying in the field.

the Sabines of the suburbs
'The Rape of the Sabine Women' was a popular subject for poets and
   painters from Antiquity on; the paintings by Paul Rubens and J.
   Louis David are examples from the 17th and 18th centuries.

After the founding of Rome, c. 753 B.C., Romulus had difficulty pro-
   viding wives for all of his followers, so he invited the men of the

neighboring tribes to a celebration of games. While the men were at the games, Roman youths raided the Sabine territory and carried off all the women they could lay their hands on.

Rimbaud's usage (Like "Bacchae of suburbia" in "Cities") combines the mythological and the modern, with the implication that these are 'women of easy virtue' or 'wild women' that will engage with many partners of all kinds.

H

The poet is apparently entranced by some mysterious beauty named Hortense who is provocatively posed. These poses are perhaps photographs of an erotic or pornographic nature; Daguerreotype nudes—from the academic to the ultragraphic—were produced in Paris as early as 1855. "For devotees of amorous images there were boudoir scenes with *suggestive* poses. And for collectors of pornography, even plates with downright filthy scenes were readily available." (Michael Köhler, ed., *The Body Exposed*, Edition Stemmle 1995)

The unspoken activity in both the poem and the probable photos is masturbation: orgasm directed on the image. The enigmatic H might be Hortense or Hashish, or even Hydrogen, whose scientific symbol is the letter H. No single reading explains this poem.

Mouvement / Motion

The river moves both horizontally and vertically, the ship weaving and bobbing, moving swiftly down the ramps of water ("the chute of rapids").

A ship's company of chemically-motivated scientists, fortune-hunters, carry the baggage of civilization with them, ransacked from everywhere; they have plans for changing the world.

The young couple (in a reversal of the 'two by two' of Noah's ark) "disembark alone" to sing their song and assume (an amorous?) position . . . The couple could represent Rimbaud and Verlaine, who jumped ship from the aesthetic mainstream ("the babble among the systems")—or any pair of lovers that abandon society's organized program for a life of spontaneous action and expression.

Dévotion / Devotions

The title refers to religious fervor or intensity, which can take the form of prayer. The poem is a kind of litany, a series of supplications to various "holy women," saintly figures.

The poet's prayer, which is as dark or "muted" as the vast night of the midnight sun, will finally confront a more intense struggle than snow, ice, and darkness—especially when the struggle or journey is 'metaphysical' (a *trip* in the psychedelic or religious sense).

À ma soeur Léonie Aubois d'Ashby. Baou—("To Sister Leona Woods d'Ashby: Bow-wow!")
The names of these religious ladies are a strange mix of Flemish and French and English, hence "Woods" for "Aubois." The bark of a dog seems the best translation of the otherwise inexplicable "Baou"; this conjures forward the image of flies on dogpiles in the tall summer grass, a mixture of sound and smell and swelter ("the summer grass abuzz with stink").

À Lulu-démon ("To Lulu—the demon")
A forerunner of Frank Wedekind's "Lulu" (from his play *Pandora's Box*,

1902; transformed into a film of 1929 by G.W. Pabst, starring
Louise Brooks; later becoming Alban Berg's 1935 opera *Lulu*).

Lulu is a charming but amoral temptress who seduces both men and
women with innocent aplomb. Wedekind's Lulu meets her demise
at the hands of Jack the Ripper.

du temps des Amies ("from the time of Girrrlfriends"

Lulu's taste for church-going stems from an inadequate convent educa-
tion, perhaps coupled with passionate schoolgirl friendships that
imply lesbian attraction. In 1867 (four years before he met
Rimbaud), Verlaine anonymously had published a book of 'lesbian
poems' entitled *Les Amies*; Rimbaud seems to slyly allude to it
here.

Circeto . . . grasse comme le poisson ("Circeto . . . fat as a fish")

This religious figure is invented by Rimbaud out of Circe, the en-
chantress who waylays Odysseus in Book X of the *Odyssey*, and
Ceto, the daughter of Pontus (sea) and Gaia (Earth), who is pro-
tectress of aquatic animals such as the seal.

As a seal-goddess, native to Arctic climes, Circeto (human-animal-
divine) would be "fat as a fish." The six months of the polar night
here become ten, another example of the poet's manipulation of
natural phenomena.

la nuit rouge ("ruddy night")

The long darkness of the midnight sun where the sky is red instead of
black.

Démocratie / Democracy

The poem is spoken by a recruit who brags about his exploits in the service of 'democracy.' Colonialization and subjugation, rape and pillage are carried out under the banner of "democratic intervention."

des revoltes logiques ("the logical revolutionaries")
The troops will slaughter the leaders of revolts that logically occur out of repression.

Au revoir ici, n'importe où ("'So long' to this place, no matter where")
The soldiers move from country to country (no matter where); the phrase "Au revoir"—'See you later' or 'Goodbye'—could also refer to the place in its original (pre-'democracy') state.

Génie / Spirit

The Spirit (or Genius) is eternity, love, the perfect and reinvented measure of a life, and marvelous reason—all things in humankind's experience or comprehension that tend toward the numinous or a transcendent sensibility.

Il est l'affection ("He is tenderness")
Wallace Fowlie, in his Introduction to *Rimbaud: Complete Works, Selected Letters*, remarks "In comparison with . . . [*A Season In Hell's* crisis] . . . of a metaphysical order, *Les Illuminations* leads us into a very concrete world of rooms and landscapes and cities where the poet attains a harmonization between desire and reality. *Génie* is the fusion of an ideal being and a human being. This prose poem is both a climactic piece in Rimbaud's art and the apotheo-

sis of a world. In it the poet is engineer showing us the plans of a future universe.

"Was he prophet? genius? mythical figure? He was a poet, but no ordinary poet. He was a child expressing himself in the language of a man. *Génie* combines the virile tenderness and the virile vigor of a man."

PART FOUR

RIMBAUD'S LIFE: A CHRONOLOGY

1854
October 20, six o'clock in the morning: Jean-Nicolas Arthur Rimbaud born in Charleville, Ardennes (northern France), second son of Captain Frédéric Rimbaud and Vitalie Cuif.

1860
His father, an infantry captain, deserts the family; Arthur is six years old with an older brother (Frédéric, Jr.) and two younger sisters (Vitalie and Isabelle). The mother becomes head of the house-hold, schooling the children at home.

1865
In the spring, Arthur begins attending public school. His mother hires a private tutor who stimulates his love of classical literature and encourages his writing.

1870
First poem published (January issue of *Revue pour Tous*). His adolescent reading includes works of Victor Hugo, Baudelaire, Poe, and Jules Verne, from the library of his teacher Izambard.

August 6: Having skipped over several years' classes, he graduates from school at age fifteen, winning all scholastic prizes.

August 28–October 29: War declared between France and Prussia. Izambard leaves town; Arthur's older brother runs off to join the army. Rimbaud runs away from home twice, first to Paris, then Brussels. The Prussians invade and occupy Charleville in December.

1871
February 25: He runs off to Paris again, which is in turmoil from the Franco-Prussian War.

March 10: Rimbaud back in Charleville.

April-May: Returning to Paris on foot, he joins a regiment of Communard street commandos. Paris is bombarded, under siege by royalist forces in Versailles.

May 13–15: Back in Charleville. *Lettres du voyant* (see ff.)

August: *Le Bateau Ivre*. He spends his days with Charles Bretagne, a local eccentric who dabbles in music, literature, and the occult. Bretagne prompts him to contact Paul Verlaine, an old friend, who has made a name for himself in Parisian literary circles. Rimbaud sends a letter with five poems.

September 10: Rimbaud arrives in Paris at Verlaine's invitation. Verlaine introduces him to the Parisian literary set with mixed results. In October, Rimbaud abruptly leaves the Verlaine household to live on his own. He sleeps in alleys and earns money by selling trinkets on the streets. In November, Verlaine tracks him down and arranges housing and financial support for him. The relationship between the two becomes an affair. Their behavior scandalizes Verlaine's wife and in-laws.

1872

Rimbaud commences work on *Illuminations*. He and Verlaine experiment with drugs and drink. He lives in various attics and spare rooms, aided by Verlaine's connections. Profoundly disappointed by their lack of 'seriousness,' he manages to attack, insult, or alienate Verlaine's entire circle of friends. Verlaine and his wife Mathilde have a baby. Rimbaud goes back to Charleville for a term. He and Verlaine correspond; he returns to Paris in the summer.

July: Verlaine abruptly leaves his wife and infant son and runs off to Brussels with Rimbaud. In September, after a failed reconciliation between Verlaine and Mathilde in Brussels, the two runaways move to London. Rimbaud works on *Illuminations;* Verlaine composes *Romances Sans Paroles.*

1873

January to March: In London, the two poets live on money sent by Verlaine's mother. In April they go to Brussels. Rimbaud then visits the family farm at Roche, where he begins *Une Saison en Enfer.*

May 27: Verlaine and Rimbaud return to London. In late June, after a quarrel, Verlaine deserts Rimbaud, leaving him stranded in London.

July 3: Verlaine apologetically writes asking Rimbaud to meet him in Brussels, where he is staying with his mother. Rimbaud arrives in Brussels on July 8. On July 10, a drunken Verlaine shoots Rimbaud, wounding him in the wrist (see "Chronicles of Belgium," ff.). Verlaine is arrested on July 11 after threatening to shoot Rimbaud again. Rimbaud is bedridden; the bullet is removed July 17.

July 19: Rimbaud drops all charges against Verlaine, who is still in jail.

July 20: Rimbaud goes home to Roche, resumes work on *Une Saison en Enfer.* He more than likely suffers withdrawal pains from absinthe, opium, and hashish, substances now absent from his regular diet.

August 8: Verlaine is sentenced to two years in prison.

Mid- to late-August: Rimbaud completes *Une Saison en Enfer.* In September, his mother finances its publication, and it is printed in Brussels.

1874

In January, Rimbaud returns to Paris, where he is snubbed by the literary crowd who blame him for Verlaine's imprisonment and disgrace. *Une Saison* is ignored by the critics and publishers.

February: Poet Germain Nouveau becomes friendly with Rimbaud. In March, Nouveau and Rimbaud move to London, taking a room in a boarding house. They support themselves by working in a cardboard box factory and by giving occasional French lessons. Together, they make a fair copy of *Illuminations*. According to Starkie, Rimbaud composes new pieces for the work at this time, probably among them "Workers," "Metropolitan," and "Promontory," as well as "Democracy," "Anguish," "City," and "Cities" I and II.

June: Nouveau leaves for Brussels.

July 6: Rimbaud's mother and sister Vitalie come to visit him in London; they stay three weeks. Rimbaud fails to find serious employment in London. He returns home to Charleville in December.

1875
In January, Rimbaud goes to Stuttgart to study German and finds work as a French tutor. Verlaine is released from prison in Belgium.

In February, Verlaine comes to Stuttgart in order to see Rimbaud again. Rimbaud gives the completed manuscript of *Illuminations* to Verlaine, and tells him he's finished with literature. They never meet again. In late August, Rimbaud is back at the family farm.

1876
Family discord at Roche. Rimbaud leaves home to pursue varied jobs between Vienna and Amsterdam. In mid-May, he joins the Dutch Army. In June, after basic training, he sails for the East Indies with his regiment. After 13 days of active service on Java, he deserts August 15. Back on the coast two weeks later, he ships out with a British merchant vessel under the alias 'Edwin Holmes.' He arrives in Europe on December 6 and is back in Charleville December 9.

1877

Spring in Hamburg, where he joins the Cirque Loisset as a cashier. The circus tours Denmark and Sweden. By late summer, he sets sail for Alexandria, but, stricken with 'gastric fever,' lands in Italy. He recovers, spends time in Rome briefly, and returns home to Roche.

1878

In October, he leaves Charleville, crossing the Alps on foot to Genoa. He then sails to Alexandria, where he lands a job as a quarry foreman on Cypress.

1879

In June, he contracts typhoid fever on Cypress and returns home.

1880

In the spring, he goes back to Cypress. Because of some 'difficulty,' he abruptly quits his job. In June, he sets out for Arabia, sailing down the Red Sea to Aden. He finds work with Alfred Bardey, an exporter dealing in coffee, ivory, and animal hides. In December, Rimbaud sets up a second company trading post in Harar, Abyssinia (Ethiopia).

1883

Rimbaud writes a description of the interior of Abyssinia, being one of the first Europeans to set foot there. In Paris, Verlaine publishes an article on Rimbaud's poetry. "We entirely (if with black sadness) approve his abandoning poetry, provided, as we do not doubt, that this was a logical, honest, and necessary step for him." (Verlaine: *Les Poètes maudits)*

1884

Rimbaud's report on Abyssinia, submitted by his employer, is published by the Societé de Géographie. The Societé requests further information; Rimbaud does not reply. There is war in Abyssinia, and Harar is evacuated.

1885
Rimbaud is in Aden with his Abyssinian mistress; he sends her home in October, quitting his job with Bardey.

1886
Rimbaud starts up a gunrunning operation in Tajoura, East Africa. *Illuminations* is published by Verlaine who, thinking that he's dead, refers to him as "the late Arthur Rimbaud."

1887
Rimbaud makes a tidy profit in the gun trade, and returns to Aden. He summers in Cairo, then goes back to Aden in the fall.

1888
He resumes work in the import-export trade with a new employer back in Harar. In Paris, Verlaine publishes a second article on Rimbaud.

1889–90
Business in Harar. In his spare time, Rimbaud studies mechanics, astronomy, engineering, and hydraulics. He is friendly with King Menelik's cousin, Ras Makonnen, father of Ras Tafari, the future Haile Selassie.

1891
Unable to work because of the pain from a swollen tumor on his right knee, Rimbaud leaves Harar in April. On May 20, his condition much worse, he arrives in Marseilles, where his leg is amputated. He returns home to Roche in June, on crutches. In August, he returns to Marseilles, planning to sail to Africa, but his condition worsens again and he becomes paralyzed. His sister Isabelle stays at his bedside.

Rimbaud dies at 10 o'clock in the morning, November 10 at age 37 in the Hospital of the Immaculate Conception, Marseilles. He is buried in Charleville. His mother allows only the immediate family to attend the services.

The first major collection of his poetry is published in Paris on that same day.

RUMORS AND VISIONS

From the *Lettres du voyant*

To Georges Izambard, May 13, 1871 (excerpt)

" . . . Right now, I'm debauching myself as much as possible. Why? I wish to be a poet, and I'm working to turn myself into a *seer* [a visionary]: you'll not understand this at all, and I hardly know how to explain it to you. It's a matter of arriving at the unknown by the disordering [or derangement] of all the senses. The sufferings are enormous, but one must be strong, to be a poet, and I have recognized that I'm a poet . . . It's not all my fault. It's wrong to say: I think. One should say: I am 'thought up' . . .

"I is somebody else. Too bad for the wood that finds itself to be a violin . . . "

To Paul Demeny, May 15, 1871 (excerpt)

"Romanticism has never been fairly judged. Who's to judge? The Critics!! The Romantics? who prove so well that a song is seldom the work of the singer—that is to say, a thought sung and understood by the singer.

"For *I* is an Other. If brass wakes up to find it's a trumpet, it's not to blame. This is obvious to me: I am midwife to the birth of my thought: I watch it and listen to it: I give the downbeat: the symphony makes murmur in the depths, or leaps in one bound onstage.

" . . . But it's a matter of making the soul monstrous: in the fashion of a freak show, if you will! Imagine a man planting and cultivating warts on his face.

"I say that one must become a *seer*, make oneself into a visionary.

"The Poet makes himself a *seer* by a long, immense, and organized deregulation of all the senses. All shapes of love, of suffering, of madness; he searches out himself, exhausting all the poisons inside him, in order to keep only their quintessences. Indescribable torture, where he needs all his faith, all his superhuman powers, where he becomes among all men the great sick one, the great criminal, the great accurst—and the Scholar supreme!—because he reaches the Unknown! Since he's cultivated his soul, already rich, richer than anyone's! He arrives at that which is unknown, and even if, driven insane at the end, losing sight of his visions, he has seen them. Let him die, leaping through nameless, unheard-of things: they come, other horrible workers: they start from that horizon where the other collapsed . . .

"The poet therefore is truly a thief of fire.

"He's responsible for humanity, even the *animals*. He will have to have his inventions smelled and handled and heard; if what he fetches up from down-below has form, he bestows form; if it is formless, he gives formlessness. A language must be found.—In short, every word being an idea, the time for a universal tongue will come! You'd have to be an Academic—deader than a fossil—to compile a dictionary in any kind of language. Feeble minds, beginning to think about the first letter of the alphabet, would soon go crazy!

"This language will be of the soul for the soul, summing up everything, the smells, the sounds, the colors, thought latching onto thought and pulling. The poet would define the quantity of the unknown arising in his time in the universal soul: then he'd give more—more than his thought's formula, more than commentary *on his march toward Progress!* Enormity becoming the norm, absorbed into everything, he would become a veritable multiplier of progress!

"As you can see, this future will be materialistic.— Always full of *Number* and Harmony, these poems will be built to last.—In a way, it would be something of a return to Greek poetry.

"Eternal art will have its uses, just as poets are citizens. Poetry will no longer give rhythm to action; it *will be in advance.*

"These poets will exist. When the infinite servitude of Women is broken down, when she lives for herself and through herself, man—up till now abominable—having set her free, she will become a poet, she too! Woman will discover the unknown! Will her world of ideas differ from ours?—She will find strange, unfathomable, repulsive, delicious things; we'll receive them, we'll understand them.

"While waiting, let us demand *something new* from poets: ideas and forms. All the smart guys will soon enough believe they've satisfied this demand, but it's not so!
"The first romantics were *seers* without wholly realizing it . . . The second Romantics are very much visionaries: . . . But since inspecting the invisible and hearing the unheard-of is not the same as recovering the spirit of dead things, Baudelaire is the primary visionary, king of poets, a true god! Still, he was trapped in an artistical milieu; and his highly praised use of

form is trivial. Inventions of the Unknown demand new forms.

" ... The new school, called Parnassian, has two visionaries: Albert Mérat and Paul Verlaine, a real poet.— And that's it.

" ... Therefore I'm working at turning myself into a *visionary.*"

THE COMPRACHICOS AND THE

FREAKSHOW

(. . . à l'instar des comprachicos, quoi! /
. . . in the manner of a freakshow, if you will!)

Rimbaud says "the soul must be made monstrous," succumbing to a Faustian hubris here, in that he claims hegemony over the soul—the poet as parent-guardian-kidnapper-cum-creator of the soul. In Victor Hugo's *L'Homme qui rit* (1869), the "comprachicos" were kidnappers of children who mutilated or deformed them in order to exhibit them for money.

> "I've always been fascinated by freakish things," says American artist Joe Coleman, discussing certain aspects of his own work.[1] "Freaks are physical embodiments of internal torment, and I find great power in that. Exhibitions of freaks of nature are considered politically incorrect these days, of course, but the carny-sideshow aesthetic hasn't disappeared—it's on television now, on programs like the Jerry Springer Show[2]."

[1]*LA Weekly,* 17 December 1999, p. 45.

[2]A televised, staged "group therapy" session featuring folk of dynamic and often grotesque dysfunction, popular in the USA at the end of the 20th Century.

RIMBAUD'S LAST LETTER

Dictated to his sister Isabelle, 9 November 1891—never sent

To the Director of Shipping:

Item: A single tusk
Item: 2 teeth
Item: 3 teeth
Item: 4 teeth
Item: 2 teeth

Dear Sir:

I am writing to inquire if I don't have anything left on your accounts. I want to change services today from this one— the name of which I don't recall—but in any case, to one run by the Aphinar Line. They ship everywhere from here: And I, disabled, unlucky & unhappy, I can't find anything, as the first dog you meet in the street will tell you.

So let me know the cost of the Aphinar service to Suez. I am completely paralyzed: so I want to find myself ready to ship out early and soon. Tell me at what hour I need to be carried aboard . . .

NOTE

At the end, still hoping to reach Africa, Rimbaud dictated this letter to his sister Isabelle the day before he died.

Charles Nicholl, in the final chapter of *Somebody Else*, comments, "Where or what Aphinar is no one is sure. The phrase he uses is le service d'Aphinar, which seems to mean 'the ship from Aphinar' but could equally mean 'the Aphinar shipping line', so one cannot be quite sure if Aphinar is a place or a company, or even a particular captain. One cannot even be sure that 'Aphinar' is what Rimbaud said: it is only Isabelle's transcription. Was it rather al Finar, the Arab word for 'lighthouse', and was this phantom ship which he wished to board 'in good time' the one that would carry him away from the light and into the darkness?

"We have no answer to this or to any other question arising from this most hermetic of Rimbaldien texts. The answer is known to the dogs in the street but they cannot, after all, tell us."

TO ARTHUR RIMBAUD

by Paul Verlaine

24 August 1889

Mortal, angel AND fiend, as much to say Rimbaud,
You deserve first place in this book of mine,
Even though some scribbler has labeled you ribald
Babyface, grassy snake, drunken small fry.

Spiralling incense and the lute's harmonies
Greet you in the temple of memory;
Your radiant name will be sung in glory,
Because you loved me as it had to be.

Women will see you tall, strong, never old,
So handsome, your beauty rustic and sly,
So desirable, your indolence bold.

History has carved you triumphant in death,
Even delighting in life's pure excess,
Your snow-white feet propped up on Envy's head!

À ARTHUR RIMBAUD

by Paul Verlaine

24 Août 1889

Mortel, ange ET démon, autant dire Rimbaud,
Tu mérites la prime place en ce mien livre,
Bien que tel sot grimaud t'ait traité de ribaud
Imberbe et de monstre en herbe et de potache ivre.

Les spirales d'encens et les accords de luth
Signalent ton entrée au temple de memoire
Et ton nom radieux chantera dans la gloire,
Parce que tu m'aimas ainsi qu'il le fallut.

Les femmes te verront grand jeune homme très fort,
Très beau d'une beauté paysanne et rusée,
Très désirable, d'une indolence qu'osée!

L'histoire t'a sculpté triomphant de la mort
Et jusqu'aux purs excès jouissant de la vie,
Tes pieds blancs posés sur la tête de l'Envie!

NOTE

Verlaine's memorial verse from 1889 when he assumed Rimbaud was dead. (Published in *Le Chat Noir*, August.)

CHRONICLES OF BELGIUM

(excerpt translated from the Flemish by Marcel F. Vogelÿ)

"*Verlaine Shoots Rimbaud, July 10, 1873:* The French poet Paul Verlaine (age 29) shot his friend and fellow poet Arthur Rimbaud (19 years old) at the Hôtel de Courtrai in the Brouwerstraat (Brussels), firing two gunshots. Verlaine was drunk at the time. The first bullet hit Rimbaud at the front of his left forearm close to his wrist. The second one missed him and hit the wall 30 cm [about a foot] above the floor. Verlaine had bought a 7 mm revolver and a box of 50 bullets that morning at the shop belonging to Montigny in the St. Hubert Gallerie. Around noon he returned to the hotel with the revolver, quite drunk. The two friends had breakfast together at the Brouwershuis with a lot more booze and then returned to their hotel. A fight started after Rimbaud announced he was going back to Paris and demanded some money from Mrs. Verlaine [Verlaine's mother] for a railway ticket."

TO KNOW THE UNKNOWN

L'inconnu: (noun) an unknown person, a stranger; the unknown, that which is unknown.

—Cassell's New French Dictionary (1903)

"Knowing has two poles, and they are poles apart: carnal knowing, the laying on of hands, the hanging of the fact by head or heels, the measurement of mass and motion, the calibration of brutal blows, the counting of supplies; and spiritual knowing, invisibly felt by the inside self, who is but a fought-over field of distraction, a stage where we recite the monotonous monologue that is our life, a knowing governed by internal tides, by intimations, motives, resolutions, by temptations, secrecy, shame, and pride."

—William H. Gass, *Finding a Form* (essays)
("Autobiography" p. 179), Alfred A. Knopf, 1996

*   *   *

Oh, Death, old captain, hoist the anchor! Come, cast off!

Pour us your poison wine that makes us feel like gods!
Our brains are burning up!—there's nothing left to do
But plunge into the void!—hell? heaven?—what's the odds?
We're bound for the Unknown, in search of something *new*!

—Baudelaire: *Le Voyage* (excerpt)
transl. Edna St. Vincent Millay

*   *   *

"In 1870 France suffered one of its most humiliating na-
tional defeats at the hands of the emerging German nation
under Bismarck. At the same time, the American South
was being subjected to occupation under the guise of Re-
construction, which would teach it an unquiet, resentful
stoicism and firmly entrench the poetics of loss and defeat,
articulated by Poe, as the literary ethos of the region. Out
of the Franco-Prussian War came the end of Napoleon III's
empire and the beginning of the Third Republic, the long-
est lived of all France's republican governments. Elections
to empower a National Assembly, held at German insis-
tence, revealed a split between Paris and the rural masses
that had existed since the Revolution of 1789: of more
than six hundred deputies only two hundred were republi-
can and the rest monarchist. Civil war broke out between
the assembly and Parisian republicans, who had suffered
siege by the Germans for four months, refusing to give up
long after Napoleon III had. The Paris commune was set
up as a rival republican government, lasting from March to
May, 1871. With defeat imminent, the *communards* en-
gaged in an orgy of destruction, setting fire to public build-
ings and murdering the archbishop of Paris. The National
Assembly's recriminatory measures made the communards
seem demure and retiring by comparison: 330,000 people
denounced, 38,000 arrested, 20,000 executed, 7,500 de-
ported.

"The preceding events coincided with the emerging
poetic consciousness of Rimbaud. In August, 1870, he fled
his home for the first time, only to be arrested on August
31 at the Gare du Nord. A second flight ended in a return
to his mother under police escort. In December, 1870, the
community of Mézières, a suburb of Charleville, where the

Rimbaud family lived, was heavily bombed. In late February, 1871, Rimbaud fled Charleville for the third time and stayed in Paris for two weeks during the time when the Commune was formed. Thus war, and not only with the Germans, but civil war, was well known to Rimbaud before his seventeenth birthday. He knew it as defeat, devastation, the triumph of the peasant mentality he had come to despise so vehemently in Charleville. He wrote in a letter to Georges Izambard, his teacher, "On est exilé dans sa patrie!" ("We are exiled in our own country!") [Wallace Fowlie (ed. and trans.), *Rimbaud: Complete Works, Selected Letters* (Chicago, 1966). In citing Rimbaud, I have used Fowlie's dual language edition. (J.H.)]

"In Rimbaud's poem, "Les Corbeaux," Poe's raven has become the muse of war and devastation. In "Chant de Guerre Parisien" Rimbaud had already established the destructiveness of war as a metaphor for the derangement of poetry.

> Thiers et Picard sont des Eros,
> Des enleveurs d'héliotropes;
> Au pétrole ils font des Corots:
> Voici hannetonner leurs tropes

Thiers and Picard are Cupids, / Thieves of heliotropes; / They paint Corots with gasoline: / Here their tropes are buzzing about

"The warriors lay waste to the landscape, 'painting' it with fires, bombs, and gasoline, turning flowers into lucent figures, transforming heliotropes into *helio*, 'towards the sun', and trope, 'turning'. Fire translates the referential object into a real enactment of its name (a misconstrual, a pun) for the name refers to the way in which the stems bend so that the plant receives a maximum of light, not its potential for combustion; the name is overdetermined). So

Thiers and Picard are poets after all: "Ils sont familiers du Grand Truc!" ("They are familiar with the Big Trick!"). In the letter in which this poem was included, he wrote that "je m'encrapule le plus possible . . . . Il s'agit d'arriver à l'inconnu par le dérèglement de tous les sens" ("I am degrading myself as much as possible . . . . It is a question of reaching the unknown by the derangement of all the senses"). What many readers of Rimbaud have missed entirely is that he is talking about reaching the unknown as ignorance, as misconstrual, not as transcendence, not as any positive sense of an inconnu that could be assimilated to Catholicism or any wish to totalize. "Il arrive à l'inconnu, et quand, affolé, il finirait *par perdre l'intelligence de ses visions*, il les a vues!" ("He reaches the unknown, and when, bewildered, he ends *by losing the intelligence of his visions*, he has seen them!" [emphasis mine]). Poetry involves the exhaustion of knowledge as such, the repudiation of signification and of the pure signifier, which, like fire, destroys the referent. And poetic vision must reach beyond language. It must apply the more apparent fluidity of words to the immolation of the 'real'. Literature is no more or less than an exaggeration of perception. The comforting illusion that the indeterminacy, the grotesqueness, of poetry can be confined to purely linguistic phenomena is just that—an illusion."

—Jefferson Humphries, *Metamorphoses of the Raven*
Chapter III, pp. 68–70
Louisiana State University Press, 1985

" . . . there's good. There is a truth. There is a reality. It can't be expressed logically with math, science or words. It's beyond and between and underneath and all around any words you could ever express. It's the reality that Nietzsche, Aristotle, Socrates and all those other guys I was reading to try to figure things out were missing. If you're trying to describe the truth, then stop using words; just shut up and sit there. If you stop thinking, analyzing and criticizing, if you meditate or take psychedelics, you can start expressing the truth. That's what I love about music: it's nonverbal communication, with frequencies of energy traveling through the air and filling your brain with electrical impulses."

—Sean Lennon (interview)
1998 June *PAPER*

"The object of all art is to obtain a partial revelation of that which is beyond human senses and human faculties—of that in fact which is spiritual . . . The human, visible, audible and intelligible media which artists (of all kinds) use, are symbols not of other visible and audible things but of what lies beyond sense and knowledge."

—Ralph Vaughan Williams
(1920) essay cited in notes to
EMI British Composers CD 567221-2

"Our senses speak only of our place of exile. To recover *the true life,* the veil of the senses must first be rent. This is the true function, a negative one, of hallucinations and deliriums. And thus here is suggested, beyond physical aspects forced to destroy each other, the possibility of a supreme encounter which is, this time, the Vision. (. . .)

"Thus the *unknown* is both light and rhythm, our only true act, a rapture; and in any case the violent denial of language in its rational uses."

—Yves Bonnefoy: *Rimbaud*
(transl. Paul Schmidt)
Harper & Row, 1973

RIMBAUD'S ALCHEMY

"Looking backward historically, we can say that what we see now as two things, and which for the sake of clarity we try to keep apart—namely a difference between what in Jungian terms we call the collective unconscious and what in physics we call matter—were, in alchemy, always one: the psyche."

(. . .)

"We generally think of active imagination as talking to our own personified complexes, and trying in our imagination and fantasies to personify certain of our complexes and then have it out with them, allowing the ego complexes or the ego to talk to these inner factors."

—Marie-Louise von Franz
Alchemical Active Imagination (1969)
Shambhala 1998

CRITICAL COMMENT

" . . . Crane's poems [like those of Rimbaud] are a fresh vision of the world, so intensely personalized in a new creative language that only the strictest and most unprepossessed effort of attention can take it in. (. . .)

"He shares with Rimbaud the device of oblique presentation of theme. The theme never appears in explicit statement. It is formulated through a series of complex metaphors which defy a paraphrasing of the sense into an equivalent prose. The reader is plunged into a strangely unfamiliar *milieu* of sensation, and the principle of its organization is not immediately grasped. The logical meaning can never be derived . . . ; but the poetical meaning is a direct intuition, realized prior to an explicit knowledge of the subject-matter of the poem. The poem does not convey; it presents; it is not topical, but expressive."

—Allen Tate: *White Buildings: Poems by Hart Crane*
(Introduction)
Liveright, 1926 (1972)

" . . . Much of the supposed obscurity of Rimbaud's poetry disappears as soon as the reader becomes aware that he's face to face with an awesomely nimble cabalist, a sleight-of-hand artist who can create heavens and hells, or annihilate them, with equal ease. Analogies explain nothing, but perhaps Rimbaud's *Illuminations* can best be understood in terms of an ingenious kaleidoscope. The weirdly contrived phrases and clauses—fragments of colored glass and jewelry, oddments of flesh and nightmare and blood-smeared bone—are carefully arranged by the kaleidoscopist's hand

to enchant your eye. But as soon as the entire picture fills
the eye-line, a tap of the poet's finger makes everything
collapse."

—Bertrand Mathieu (translator's postscript)
Rimbaud: A Season in Hell & Illuminations
BOA Editions, 1991

... "Ah! a moment, father," I interrupted, "do not go so
fast; tell me something of the mystics."
—"Monsieur," said he, "devotion warms a heart easily
aroused to passion, and the heart affects the brain, which is
warmed also; the result is ecstasies and raptures. This is the
delirium of devotion; often it reaches perfection; which means,
it degenerates into quietism; you know that a quietist is a
combination of the madman, the devotee, and the libertine.
"Yonder are the casuists, who reveal to the day the secrets
of the night; who shape in their imagination all the de-
mons which love can produce, collect, compare, and make
them the eternal objects of their thoughts; happy for them
if their hearts are not affected as well, and do not become
the accomplices in the irregularities so artlessly described
and so nakedly painted.
"You see, monsieur, that I think freely, and say what I think
... If I chose, I might speak of all this with admiration; I
might repeat again and again: 'This is divine; that is wor-
thy of veneration; there is something marvelous in this;'
and then one of two things would happen: either I should
deceive you, or you would cease to respect me."
We had to adjourn the conversation to the next day, as the
dervish was called away on business.

—Montesquieu: *Persian Tales* (1721)
Letter CXXXIV; H.M. Caldwell Co., Athenaeum, 1897

"Je est un autre"

"Introspection, observation and the records of human be-
havior in the past and at the present time, make it very
clear that an urge to self-transcendence is almost as wide-
spread and, at times, quite as powerful as the urge to self-
assertion. Men desire to intensify their consciousness of
being what they have come to regard as 'themselves,' but they
also desire—and desire, very often, with irresistible violence—
the consciousness of being someone else. In a word, they
long to get out of themselves, to pass beyond the limits of that
tiny island universe, within which every individual finds him-
self confined. This wish for self-transcendence is not identical
with the wish to escape from physical or mental pain. In
many cases, it is true, the wish to escape from pain reinforces
the desire for self-transcendence. But the latter can exist with-
out the former. If this were not so, healthy and successful
individuals, who have (in the jargon of psychiatry) 'made an
excellent adjustment to life,' would never feel the urge to go
beyond themselves. But in fact they do . . . .

   "If we experience an urge to self-transcendence, it is
because, in some obscure way and in spite of our con-
scious ignorance, we know who we really are. We know
(or, to be more accurate, something within us knows) that
the ground of our individual knowing is identical with the
Ground of all knowing and all being; that Atman (Mind in
the act of choosing to take the temporal point of view) is
the same as Brahman (Mind in its eternal essence). We
know all this, even though we may never have heard of the
doctrines in which the primordial Fact has been described,
even though, if we happen to be familiar with them, we
may regard these doctrines as so much moonshine. And

we also know their practical corollary, which is that the final end, purpose and point of our existence is to make room in the 'thou' for the 'That,' is to step aside so that the Ground can come to the surface of our consciousness . . . When the phenomenal ego transcends itself, the essential Self is free to realize, in terms of a finite consciousness, the fact of its own eternity, together with the correlative fact that every particular in the world of experience partakes of the timeless and the infinite.

"When the shell of the ego has been cracked and there begins to be a consciousness of the subliminal and physiological othernesses underlying personality, it sometimes happens that we catch a glimpse, fleeting but apocalyptic, of that other Otherness, which is the Ground of all being . . . . Any escape, even by a descending road, out of insulated selfhood makes possible at least a momentary awareness of the not-self on every level, including the highest."

—Aldous Huxley
The Devils of Loudun, pp. 67–69, 323–24
Harper, 1952

Something *New*

"It was said earlier concerning the Mayan astronomers that the connections were what counted. In the archaic universe all things were signs and signatures of each other, inscribed in the hologram, to be divined subtly. This was also the philosophy of the Pythagoreans, and it presides over all of classical language, as distinct from contemporary language. This was pointed out perceptively by a modern critic, Roland Barthes, in *Le degré zero de l'Écriture.*

'The economy of classical language,' he says, 'is rational, which means that in it words are abstracted as much as possible in the interest of relationship . . . No word has a density by itself, it is hardly the sign of a living thing, but rather the means of conveying a connection.' Today, the object of a modern poem is not to define or qualify relations already conventionally agreed; one feels transported, as it were, from the world of classical Newtonian physics to the random world of subatomic particles, ruled by probabilistic theory. The beginning of this was felt in Cézanne, in Rimbaud and Mallarmé. It is 'an explosion of words' and forms, liberated words, independent objects—discontinuous and magical, not controlled, not organized by a sequence of 'neutral signs.' The interrupted flow of the new poetic language, Barthes remarks, 'initiates a discontinuous Nature, which is revealed only piecemeal.' Nature becomes 'a fragmented space, made of objects solitary and terrible, because the links between them are only potential.' More, they are arbitrary. They are supposed to be of the nature of the ancient portentum. The only meaning to be drawn from those links is that they are congenial to the mind that made them. The mind has abdicated, or it shrinks in apocalyptic terror. In the arts we hear of Amorphism, or 'disintegration of form,' of the 'triumph of incoherence' in concrete poetry and contemporary music. The new syntheses, if any are still possible, are beyond the horizon."

                    Giorgio de Santillana and Hertha von Dechend
                                        Hamlet's Mill
                                    Gambit: Boston, 1969

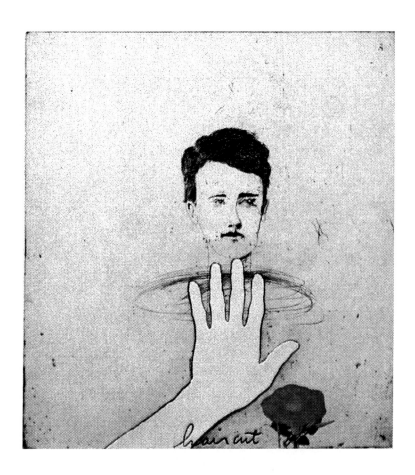

SELECTED FURTHER MEDIA

Books

The Time of the Assassins (a Rimbaud study)
Henry Miller; New Directions, 1956

My Poor Arthur (biography)
Elisabeth Hanson; Henry Holt, 1960

Orpheus in Brooklyn: Orphism, Rimbaud, and Henry Miller
Bertrand Mathieu; Mouton, 1976

Femmes/Hombres: The Erotic Poetry of Paul Verlaine
translation William Packard and John D. Mitchell; illustrated by Michael
Ayrton; Chicago Review Press, 1977

A Night of Serious Drinking (novel as prose-poem)
René Daumal; translation David Coward and E.A. Lovatt; Shambhala,
1979

Splendide-Hôtel (essays, prose-poems)
Gilbert Sorrentino; Dalkey Archive, 1984

The Parisian Prowler (prose-poems of Baudelaire)
translation Edward K. Kaplan; University of Georgia, 1989

The American Night (poems, lyrics)
Jim Morrison; Villard Books, 1990

Rimbaud in Abyssinia (biography-travelogue)
Alain Borer (translation Rosemarie Waldrop); William Morrow & Co., 1991

Rimbaud and Jim Morrison: The Rebel as Poet
Wallace Fowlie; Duke University, 1993

Fear of Dreaming (selected poems); "Rimbaud Scenes" pp. 136–141
Jim Carroll; Penguin, 1993

Delirium: An Interpretation of Arthur Rimbaud
Jeremy Reed; City Lights, 1994

Early Work, 1970–1979 ("Rimbaud" poems, pp. 42 and 102)
Patti Smith; W.W. Norton, 1994

Total Eclipse (screenplay)
Christopher Hampton; Faber & Faber, 1995

Alternative Realities: The Paranormal, the Mystic and the Transcendent in Human Experience
Leonard George, Ph.D.; Facts on File, 1995

The Coral Sea (prose-poems)
Patti Smith; W.W. Norton, 1996

Somebody Else: Rimbaud in Africa (biography)
Charles Nicholl; Jonathan Cape UK, 1997

Passion Rimbaud: l'album d'une vie (pictorial biography, French text)
Claude Jeancolas; Les éditions Textuel, 1998

Arthur Rimbaud (sexuality/biography)
Benjamin Ivry; Absolute Press, 1998

The Poetry of Rimbaud (commentary)
Robert Greer Cohn; University of South Carolina, 1999

Rimbaud: Presence of an Enigma (biography)
Jean-Luc Steinmetz (translation Jon Graham); Welcome Rain, 2001

Selected Poems: Paul Verlaine
("Rimbaud" poems, pp. 69, 71, 77, 133, 135, 199, 217, 219, 259)
Translation Martin Sorrell; Oxford World's Classics, 1999

Film/Video

Total Eclipse (1995, color)
Director: Agnieszka Holland
Screenplay: Christopher Hampton
Music: Jan A.P. Kaczmarek
Leonardo DiCaprio (Rimbaud); David Thewlis (Verlaine)

Une Saison en Enfer (1971, color)
Director and screenplay: Nelo Risi
Music: Maurice Jarre
Terence Stamp (Rimbaud); Jean-Claude Brialy (Verlaine)

Rimbaud (1966, black and white)
Director: Max-Pol Fouchet
Laurent Terzieff (Rimbaud)
French television film

CD-ROM

Beat: The Beat Experience
Voyager CD-ROM, ISBN 1-55940-702-6

Interactive computer software in association with the Whitney Museum of Art exhibit "Beat Culture and the New America, 1950–65." The "Beat Pad" section includes an animated short based on the opening phrases of *Season in Hell,* plus texts and commentary elsewhere. (Click on Book-shelf; click on copy of Illuminations; etc.)

Music

Les Illuminations, Op. 18, by Benjamin Britten (1939)
Nine selected *Illuminations* for tenor or soprano and string orchestra.

Available versions:

· Peter Pears (tenor); Benjamin Britten (conductor); London/Decca
· Heather Harper (soprano); with Charles Groves conductor); IMP/BBC
· Sylvia McNair (soprano); Seiji Ozawa (conductor); Philips
· Martyn Hill (tenor); Richard Hickox (conductor); Virgin
· Barbara Hendricks (soprano); Colin Davis (conductor); EMI

The Girl With Orange Lips (1991), Dawn Upshaw (soprano) with chamber ensemble
Song cycles by Falla, Stravinsky, Ravel, et al., including Earl Kim's *Where Grief Slumbers* (settings of Rimbaud and Mallarmé); Nonesuch 79262

Sahara-Blue, music by Hector Zazou (1992)
Eleven pop/worldbeat settings of Rimbaud's work performed in French and English and Arabic by John Cale, Gérard Depardieu, Anneli Drecker, Lisa Gerrard, Khaled, Bill Laswell, et al.; Tristar Music WK 57779

Easter, by Patti Smith (1978)
Rimbaud appears in the title song, track 11; Arista 18826

Seasons in Hell, opera (1996) by Harold Blumenfeld and Charles Kondek
With Randall Gremillion and Phillip Mark Horst (Rimbaud); Mary Elizabeth Kures (voice), Chad Smith (Verlaine), Elizabeth Sunders (Madame Rimbaud), Gerhard Samuel (conductor); Albany/Troy 262-63; two-CD set with booklet and libretto

Also:

· "Blood on the Tracks," Bob Dylan (1975)
· "Building the Perfect Beast," Don Henley (1984)
· "A Sense of Wonder," Van Morrison (1984)
· "Strange Days," The Doors (1967)
· "I'm Your Man," Leonard Cohen (1988)
· "Odelay," Beck (1996)
· "Catholic Boy," Jim Carroll (1980)
· "Los Angeles," X (1980)

ON TRANSLATION

" ... [A] knowledge of the language is less of the essence than is a sense for the poetry and a knack of doing something about such matters as tone, mood, speed, stress, grace, fire, cadence, and harmony; the ideal situation being, obviously, where the translator makes, in his own language, a twin poem, having the freedom born of a kindred impulse . . .

"Rimbaud is close enough in time and spirit to solicit a more stringent fidelity in both melody and meaning, or rather, the harmony of the two: an affair calling less for 'invention,' let alone intervention, than for simple and complex attention."

—John Theobald
The Lost Wine

"Translation can be a way of finding voices for our own inarticulate obsessions. We are plunged into mysteries we may not have known were haunting us . . . we are forced to confront aspects of ourselves we may not have wanted to acknowledge. Translation, both doing it and reading its results, keeps pushing back the boundaries, moving our lonesome little expedition farther across the frontier, deeper into the interior."

—Stephen Kessler
Poetry Flash no. 286
September–October 2000

TRANSLATOR'S LAST WORD

The several translations of Rimbaud, as Henry Miller has noted in his preface to *The Time of the Assassins*, " . . . reveal a wide and inevitable variety of interpretation. Yet however difficult and unseizable his style and thought may be, Rimbaud is not untranslatable. To do his work justice is another matter . . ."

In attempting to "do justice" to these works, I have consulted previous translations in the following editions:

Oliver Bernard: *Collected Poems* (Penguin 1962)

Wallace Fowlie: *Complete Works, Selected Letters* (University of Chicago, 1966)

Bertrand Mathieu: *A Season in Hell* and *Illuminations* (BOA, 1991)

Paul Schmidt: *Complete Works* (Harper 1976)

Mark Treharne: *A Season in Hell* and *Illuminations* (J. Dent, 1998)

Louise Varèse: *A Season in Hell, Illuminations* (New Directions,1945, 1957)

Translations by Jary, Reed, Schwartz, Sloate, and Theobald proved insightful here and there. I have stood on the shoulders of these poets and scholars to better survey the *voyant*'s domain.

The main French texts from which I worked were those of Gallimard (ed. Forestier) and Flammarion (ed. Steinmetz); *Illuminations* is based on the facsimile of the manuscript printed by Bibliothèque de l'Image.

Le Dictionnaire Rimbaud (ed. Claude Jeancolas) was consulted frequently.

Through the notes as well as the translation, I've attempted to clarify the layered imagery of Rimbaud's work, and express it in an English at once roughly idiomatic and elegantly pitched—to capture something of what he "saw" and heard with such a vivid sensibility. I have tried to pay "simple and complex attention."

ACKNOWLEDGEMENTS

A thousand thanks to Michael Alexander and Robert Phillips of Houston University and Bertrand Mathieu for their perceptive critiques, questions, and corrections on *A Season in Hell*—all of which I took into account. To Professor David Corcos, deep gratitude for the month of days he spent going over every line of *Illuminations* with me; his scrupulous knowledge of the French text was a god-send. Thanks to Marcel Vogely and his family for their hospitality while I visited the Rimbaud sites in Charleville and Brussels; many thanks to M. Gérard Martin of the Bibliothèque Municipale of Charleville-Mézières for giving me access to their extensive Rimbaud collection, as well as for introducing me to Bert Mathieu who had the keys to "the sacred lair of the brat." Thank-yous to Ethan Fischer, Michael Warren, Lawrence A. Jones, Douglas Hansen, Thomas Yotka, Louise Henderson, Lyda Barger Lang, and Maguy Ralbag for moral support and more; kudos to Evelyn Hughes Maslac for typing and formatting the whole thing. And special thanks to Alexia Montibon for her splendid portraits of Rimbaud, her other drawings, and so much more, sweet love.

Further Acknowledgements

To New Directions for permission to quote from Enid Starkie's
  Rimbaud and Henry Miller's *The Time of the Assassins*
To Arlene Phelan of W.W. Norton for permission to quote from
  Allen Tate's introduction to Hart Crane's *White Buildings*.
To Jefferson Humphries for permission to quote his book *Metamorphoses of the Raven* (Louisiana State University Press)
To Bertrand Mathieu for letting me quote from his postscript to his
  translation of *A Season in Hell* and Illuminations
To Alfred A. Knopf for William H. Gass's *Finding A Form*
To the Ralph Vaughan Williams Trust for the quote in the notes to
  EMI's CD 2435 67264-2 (USA) 2435 67240-2 (UK)
To Harper and Row for permission to quote from Aldous Huxley's

The Devils of Loudon and *Rimbaud* by Yves Bonnefoy

To Sean Lennon for his interview quote (*Paper* magazine, June 1998)

To Robert Phillips for permission to use Delmore Schwartz's "Introduction" for *A Season in Hell.*

To the late Dr. Wallace Fowlie for permission to quote his work on Rimbaud.

To Bruce B. Gordon for the first typescript of "The Drunken Boat."

To Mr. Aly Kourouma for the photo-portrait of D JC.

To Michael J. Warren and Martin Kanes for moral and intellectual support.

To Janet Dodson for mailings and salient details.

To Jim Dine for "Haircut" from the *Rimbaud Series:* (Thanks to Barry Douglas)

To Isaac, Taylor, and Zachary Hanson for "This Time Around." Lyrics quoted by permission, © 2000 Jam 'N' Bread Music c/o Heavy Harmony Music (ASCAP).

Thanks to Robert Greer Cohn, whose critical comments made for a "more honest" translation of "Poets At Seven Years Old."

BIBLIOGRAPHY

Absinthe: History in a Bottle
Barnaby Conrad III; Chronicle Books, 1988.

Alchemy: The Art of Knowing (Medieval Wisdom)
Labyrinth Publishing, UK; Chronicle Books, USA, 1994.

Breakfast in the Ruins (Chapter 2, "In the Commune: 1871: A Smile")
Michael Moorcock; Random House, 1971.

Brewer's Dictionary of Phrase and Fable
Harper & Row; revised edition, 1963.

Cassell's New French Dictionary
ed. Boïelle and Payen-Payne; Funk & Wagnalls, 1903.

Le Dictionnaire Rimbaud
Claude Jeancolas; Éditions Balland, 1991.

The Handbook of Classical Literature
Lillian Feder; Da Capo Press, 1998.

The Illustrated Book of Signs and Symbols
Miranda Bruce-Mitford; DK Publishing, 1996.

The Lost Wine (Seven Centuries of French Poetry)
John Theobald; Green Tiger Press, 1980.

Metamorphoses of the Raven
Jefferson Humphries; Louisiana State University Press, 1985.

Arthur Rimbaud
Enid Starkie; New Directions, 1961.

Arthur Rimbaud Oeuvres: Des Ardennes au Désert
ed. Pascaline Mouriere-Casile; Presses Pocket, 1990.

Rimbaud (The Athlone French Poets)
C. Chadwick; University of London, Athlone Press, 1979.

Rimbaud: A Season in Hell
Translation Delmore Schwartz; New Directions, 1940 (second edition)

Rimbaud: Poésies, Une Saison En Enfer, Illuminations
ed. Louis Forestier; Gallimard, 1984.

Rimbaud: Poésies (vol. I), Une Saison En Enfer, Vers Nouveaux (vol. II), Illuminations (vol. III)
ed. Jean-Luc Steinmetz; Flammarion, 1989.

Rimbaud: Illuminations (The Athlone French Poets)
ed. Nick Osmond, Athlone Press, 1976.

Somebody Else: Arthur Rimbaud in Africa
Charles Nicholl; Jonathan Cape, 1997.

Verlaine: Fool of God
Lawrence and Elisabeth Hanson; Random House, 1957.

Verlaine: A Biography
Joanna Richardson; Viking Press, 1971.

INDEX OF FRENCH TITLES